ECOTOURISM

A Guide for Planners and Managers

Volume 2

Edited by

Kreg Lindberg
Research Associate, The Ecotourism Society

Megan Epler Wood
President, The Ecotourism Society

David Engeldrum
Managing Editor, HVS Eco Services

THE ECOTOURISM SOCIETY
NORTH BENNINGTON, VERMONT

THE ECOTOURISM SOCIETY
P.O. Box 755
North Bennington, Vermont 05257

Library of Congress Catalog Card Number 98-071801
ISBN: 0-9636331-3-9

Production Director: Nicole R. Otte
Designers: Lori J. Johnson, Leslie Morris Noyes
Cover Design: Lori J. Johnson
Copy Editor: Lori J. Johnson

Special thanks to International Expeditions for their assistance with the final production of this book.

TABLE OF CONTENTS

Preface

The Ecotourism Society (TES) published *Ecotourism: A Guide for Planners and Managers* in 1993 because there was so little available information focusing on the "how to" aspects of ecotourism planning and management. Though the number of ecotourism books, articles and conferences continues to proliferate, there remain few good resources for planners, managers, students and others in the field. For this reason, The Ecotourism Society is publishing the present book, Volume 2 of *Ecotourism: A Guide for Planners and Managers*.

We should stress that this book is not merely an update of the first volume. Rather, our goal has been to provide coverage of topics not addressed in the first book, such as interpretation. Moreover, our goal has been to enhance the detail and rigor of the presentation. Though there does remain some overlap, there are also important differences, and we believe both volumes will be of interest to students of ecotourism as well as educators in the field. To supplement the information in this volume, the reader may wish to refer to other selected Ecotourism Society publications on such subjects as ecolodge design.

Our intended audience is very broad and includes those enrolled in university courses and training programs, ecotourism industry professionals, planners and managers working in the field of park management, and government agency employees. We intend this book to be of use for countries at varying stages of economic development and across a wide range of ecosystems. We recognize that it is impossible to fully meet the needs of such a broad constituency but feel, nonetheless, that the book will be of value to a wide range of ecotourism professionals.

The definition of ecotourism remains an issue of debate—one which we do not try to resolve in this book. Although the term is used throughout this volume, we recognize that not all activity referred to as "ecotourism" meets The Ecotourism Society, or other, definitions of ecotourism. As David Western noted in the Foreword of the first volume, what matters is tourism's impact, and we publish this book not to certify a specific activity as ecotourism, but in an effort to enhance the positive impacts, and reduce the negative impacts of tourism.

Unless otherwise noted, all monetary figures are in U.S. dollars. An effort has been made to provide exchange rates or U.S. dollar equivalents when other currencies are used, but these should be treated as illustrative, as some exchange rates may have changed substantially since these chapters were written.

As with the first volume, we have selected a group of authors who are experts in the field of ecotourism. They come to us from impressive backgrounds, and from various fields including academia, the ecotourism industry and government agencies. However, the views and opinions expressed by these authors are not necessarily those of The Ecotourism Society.

We owe a special debt of appreciation to the authors and reviewers. The reviewers include:

Jim Birckhead	Deborah McLaren
Rosemary Black	Deborah Meadows Steketee
Elizabeth Boo	Dave Mihalic
Héctor Ceballos-Lascuráin	Gianna Moscardo
Chris Gakahu	Terry Pratt
Troy Hall	Jamie Resor
William Hammit	Isaac Sindiga
Robert Healy	Sheryl Spivack
Herb Hiller	Derek Wade
Edward Inskeep	Geoffrey Wall
Leslie Jarvie	Will Weber
Gail Lash	Rolf Wesche
Michael Lockwood	Sven Wunder

Introduction

Héctor Ceballos-Lascuráin

Five years have passed since the publication of the first volume of *Ecotourism: A Guide for Planners and Managers*. During this time, many developments have taken place in the fields of tourism, ecotourism and conservation throughout the world. Most importantly, ecotourism is no longer a mere concept or a subject of wishful thinking. On the contrary, ecotourism has become a global reality. In some regions its presence is subtle and discreet, and receives little press coverage. In others, ecotourism development receives considerable government attention, widespread commercial publicity and media headlines. Still elsewhere, ecotourism initiatives are not yet clearly identified or defined, and are confused with other activities. Whatever the nuance, there seem to be very few countries in the world in which some type of ecotourism development or discussion is not presently taking place.

Ecotourism is already producing concrete benefits in the fields of conservation and sustainable development. In Costa Rica and Venezuela, a number of cattle ranchers have preserved important stretches of tropical forest, and in doing so have turned these areas into successful ecotourism destinations, helping to conserve natural ecosystems while providing new jobs for local inhabitants. Ecuador uses ecotourism revenue from the Galápagos Islands to help maintain its entire national park network. In the new South Africa, ecotourism is becoming an effective way to raise the standard of living of rural black residents, who are increasingly involving themselves in ecotourism activities. The government of Poland is also actively promoting ecotourism, having recently designated a number of national Nature-and-Tourism Zones to reconcile nature conservation and the development of national tourism. In Australia and New Zealand, a large proportion of tourism activity may be categorized as ecotourism, an industry which ranks high in the economies of both countries.

A lingering problem in any discussion on ecotourism is that the concept of ecotourism is still not well understood and, therefore, is often confused with other types of tourism development. Several institutions have done much to clear up this confusion by promoting the concept of ecotourism as a tool for conservation and sustainable development. The Ecotourism Society's own definition, "responsible travel to natural areas, which conserves the environment and improves the welfare of local people" (Lindberg and Hawkins, 1993), has been widely dispersed. Another prevalent definition, which more specifically links natural and cultural elements, is that expounded by IUCN (The World Conservation Union) which states "ecotourism is environmentally responsible travel and visitation to relatively undisturbed natural areas, in order to enjoy and appreciate nature (and any accompanying cultural features—both past and present) that promotes conservation, has low visitor negative impact and provides for beneficially active socio-economic involvement of local populations" (Ceballos-Lascuráin, 1996).

Though the concept of ecotourism is still often used synonymously with that of sustainable tourism, in reality, ecotourism fits within the larger concept of sustainable tourism. As our millennium draws to a close, it is imperative that all forms of human activity become sustainable—and tourism is no exception. Sustainable tourism denotes all types of tourism (whether based on natural or human-made resources) that contribute to sustainable development (DeKadt, 1990). Ecotourism, then, is to be understood as one of the many sub-categories of sustainable tourism. A big beach or casino resort that conserves energy by not washing guest room towels every day or reduces negative environmental impacts by using biodegradable soap is not an "ecotourism" resort. Having said this, it is by all means encouraging to see traditional modalities of conventional or mass tourism moving towards a more environmentally friendly behavior—in other words, becoming more sustainable.

Ecotourism should also not be equated with "nature-based tourism," since this label may refer to any tourism activity practiced in a natural setting (e.g., snow skiing, mountain biking and rock climbing). Such tourism may or may not be environmentally friendly. Another term that is commonly confused with ecotourism is "adventure tourism," which normally refers to physically exerting sporting activities (frequently involving a certain level of personal risk) also conducted in a natural setting (e.g., hang gliding, whitewater rafting, and mountain biking). These activities also may or may not be environmentally responsible or benefit local people. Therefore, ecotourism should only be used to describe tourism activities in a natural environment when an additional, normative characterization is intended: tourism that actually encourages conservation and helps society achieve sustainable development.

Over these last five years, several countries, including Mexico, Australia, Malaysia and Ecuador, have produced national ecotourism plans or strategies. Unfortunately, not all of these countries have effectively followed up on these documents—lack of government continuity being one of the major obstacles. Also in recent years, many countries (including Ecuador, Brazil, Australia, Kenya,

Estonia, Bolivia, Indonesia and Venezuela) have established national ecotourism associations to promote the appropriate concept and development of ecotourism.

Tourism in general has been increasing sharply over the past four years. Between 1991 and 1995 international tourism grew from 450 million international travelers to 567 million, according to the World Tourism Organization (1996). International tourism receipts (excluding international transport) increased by 7.2% between 1994 and 1995 to $372 billion. International transport receipts are estimated at $60 billion for 1995, a year in which tourism receipts represented more than 8% of the world merchandise exports and one-third of world trade in services. International tourist arrivals are set to double between 1990 and 2010, growing to 1.018 billion in 2010.

While it is clear that international tourism is on the rise, due to the lack of reliable statistics, it is still difficult to measure the impact of ecotourism. Of course, the problem of measuring ecotourism's impact is also linked to the absence of a widespread operational definition of ecotourism. No global initiative presently exists for gathering ecotourism data. Comprehensive and reliable statistics are needed in order to measure the full economic impact of ecotourism worldwide. For the time being, however, there exist some interesting figures which have been compiled in recent years. Filion (1992) estimates in a preliminary study that nature tourism is already contributing as much as $223 billion to the national income of various countries. Part of this income is derived from bird watchers, who constitute a major category of ecotourists. For example, most recent estimates put the total number of North American bird watchers (from the casual to the expert), at 65 million (Miller, 1995). Of these 65 million "birders," more than 24 million make at least one birding trip annually (Gray, 1996).

Besides the difficulty of gathering reliable statistics, another major hindrance for ecotourism has been that active local community participation has not come about as fast and easily as originally envisioned. Greater efforts have to be made at all levels to increase local skills in the field of ecotourism. Training programs are already burgeoning around the globe. Hopefully, in a few years, concrete results will be seen in this domain.

One encouraging indicator is the enormous interest generated over the last three or four years in the field of ecolodge design and development. This growing field reveals a definite trend away from abstract discussion to the concrete realities represented by ecolodges, the adequate and appropriate physical facilities for ecotourism. Important recent documents on the subject of ecolodges include *Guiding Principles of Sustainable Design* (U.S. National Park Service, 1993), *The Ecolodge Sourcebook* (Hawkins et al., 1995), and *Ecolodge Guidelines* (The Ecotourism Society, in press).

Ecotourism has gone through its infancy and adolescence and is now entering its adulthood. Hopefully, the coming years will confirm a productive and propitious maturity.

REFERENCES

Ceballos-Lascuráin, H. 1996. *Tourism, Ecotourism, and Protected Areas*, IUCN, Gland, Switzerland.

DeKadt, E. 1990. *Making the Alternative Sustainable: Lessons from Development for Tourism*, Institute for Development Studies at the University of Sussex, Brighton, United Kingdom.

(The) Ecotourism Society. *Ecolodge Guidelines*, The Ecotourism Society, North Bennington, Vermont. In press.

Filion, F.L., J.P. Foley, A.J. Jacquemot. 1992. "The Economics of Global Ecotourism," paper presented at the IV World Congress on National Parks and Protected Areas, Caracas, Venezuela.

Gray, P. 1996. "The Birdman of America: Roger Tory Peterson, 1908-1996," *Time*. August 12.

Hawkins, D.E., M. Epler Wood, S. Bittman. 1995. *The Ecolodge Sourcebook for Planners and Developers*, The Ecotourism Society, North Bennington, Vermont.

Lindberg, K., D.E. Hawkins. 1993. *Ecotourism: A Guide for Planners and Managers, Volume 1*, The Ecotourism Society, North Bennington, Vermont.

Miller, L. 1995. "Have Binoculars, Will Travel: In Pursuit of Rarities, Bird-Watchers Boost Tourism," *Wall Street Journal*, December 15.

U.S. National Park Service. 1993. *Guiding Principles of Sustainable Design*, United States Department of the Interior.

World Tourism Organization. 1996. *Yearbook of Tourism Statistics*, World Tourism Organization, Madrid, Spain.

Ecotourism Market and Industry Structure

Paul F. J. Eagles and Bryan R. Higgins

DEFINITIONS, FRAMEWORKS AND MARKET STRUCTURE

The term "ecotourism" describes a wide variety of travel phenomena, from a casual, weekend walk in a local nature reserve to an escorted safari in Africa. Although many authors have commented on defining ecotourism (Bandy, 1996; Blamey, 1995; Dann, 1996; McLaren, 1998; Orams, 1995; and Wight, 1993), several definitions and substantial disagreement are found within the literature. This chapter assumes the definition developed by The Ecotourism Society and focuses on international ecotourism.

Trends occur in ecotourism literature. First, most publications on the subject have utilized either a natural or social science framework for analysis. Much less research attention has been focused on the business of ecotourism or on the supply and demand of this travel niche. Little systematic attention was given to the global dimensions of the nature tourism industry or the way in which this emerging business structure is shaping the identity, organization and impacts of ecotourism (Higgins, 1996). The studies examining the demographics and motivations of ecotourists have been limited to particular ecotourism sites or specific national markets. The exception to this is the major market demand study done within large Canadian and American cities (Wight, 1996). Furthermore, although commentators have noted significant differences between ethnic and national markets (Blangy and Hanneberg, 1995; Jepson, 1994), little systematic attention has been given to a global analysis of ecotourism clients or destinations. Because market research is just beginning to explore ecotourism, this chapter first sketches what is known about these emerging trends and then analyzes the significance of this market perspective with case studies of Kenya and Costa Rica.

This chapter investigates market demand and the industry structure of ecotourism. Tourism market demand studies typically probe the character of different kinds of tourists, or potential tourists, by analyzing standard demographic categories (e.g., age, income, gender or place of residence), travel motivations, activity preferences, and landscape preferences. Given the lack of attention by national governments and by traditional sources of tourism information to collecting information which identifies ecotourists, most of the research in this sub-field has been based on surveys, focus group sessions, behavior observation and related methods of primary data collection. Work by Eagles (1992) on ecotourist travel motives has been extensively quoted, but not replicated. One recent study regarding ecotourists is Akama's (1996) comparison of Western environmental values with those of rural peasants in Africa. An insightful exception with ecotourism operators is Sirakaya's (1997) development and testing of a conceptual framework to explain compliance attitudes of ecotour operators with industry guidelines. There is abundant literature on the environmental and travel motives of outdoor recreationists, and it is probable that it is useful for the understanding of ecotourists. Overall, however, insufficient attention has been given to the environmental attitudes of ecotourists and ecotour operators.

The second major topic of this chapter identifies the types of ecotourism businesses, their size, location and character, and connections between separate enterprises as a way to understand the business structure of ecotourism. As with market demand research, few secondary tourism sources contain information regarding such specialty tour operators. Thus, most ecotourism industry studies also involve primary data collection and the related problems of diverse definitions and methodology.

ELEMENTS OF MARKET DEMAND
AN ANALYSIS OF ECOTOURISM MARKET DEMAND

Although several studies present figures on the number and characteristics of ecotourists, a series of issues make it difficult to discuss the global patterns of ecotourism accurately. First, the various national agencies responsible for collecting information about tourist visits give little attention to questions or information concerning specialty travel. Second, many quantitative estimates of ecotourists occur in studies that do not utilize rigorous methodology. Third, the international coverage of well-designed market studies is limited, although analysts suggest significant national differences in tourism behavior (Pisam and Sussman, 1993). Some of the very few studies available include a survey of U.S.-based outbound ecotourism operators (Higgins, 1996), a profile of U.K. outbound operators (Holden, 1996), and a survey of North American-based outbound operators (Crossley and Lee, 1994; Yee, 1992). Fourth, although ecotour operators have administered client surveys and commissioned market demand studies, the results of these proprietary surveys are not publicly available. Many important questions about the character and profile of clients in this sub-sector of the travel industry remain unanswered.

There is an important conceptual distinction between independent ecotourists who arrange their own itineraries and ecotourists who utilize packaged tours. Few studies have examined the independent ecotraveler component. An exception is Zurick's (1995) humanistic inquiry into the subtle impacts of independent travelers visiting remote places untouched by Western culture. Drumm (1995), Wesche (1996) and Epler Wood (1998) developed detailed examinations of the distinct types of nature tourism operations and ecotourism sub-markets. Drumm's study of the Ecuadorean Amazon region identifies and analyzes a five-component typology of nature tourism businesses including backpacker operations, economy lodges, eco-adventure camping, luxury nature lodges and indigenous enterprises. He identifies substantial differences in the economic, ecological and socio-cultural impacts of these distinct operations. Wesche (1996) examines indigenous controlled ecotourism in the Amazon region of Ecuador. He concludes that this unique alternative is the result of an increasingly complex network of links between indigenous groups, private ecotourism operators and non-governmental organizations. Epler Wood's (1998) perceptive study analyzes the planning, market demand and funding of community-based ecotourism in Ecuador. The thoughtful and significant findings of these innovative studies indicate that more systematic attention should be given to studying independent ecotourism clients and the community-based operators they patronize.

Investigations of ecotourism market demand focus on activity preferences, travel motivations, demographic profiles and information sources of clients. Though many studies have an academic focus, one important exception is the market demand assessment performed by HLA Consultants and the ARA Consulting Group (1995) for a consortium of public and private Canadian organizations. This high-quality study utilized a consumer telephone survey, ecotourist mail survey and travel trade survey to analyze the market potential for ecotourism in Alberta and British Columbia. Its attention to methodological issues provides an excellent example of market demand research for the private sector. Recently, the Bureau of Tourism Research in Australia started to publish studies on the size, demographics and travel patterns of the ecotourism market in that country. This work is unique in that it is the first time that a national tourism agency has profiled the national ecotourism industry (Eagles, 1996; Hatch, 1997).

ORIGIN AND LOCATION OF DEMAND

There is a lack of systematic information on the origin and location of the demand for ecotourism. Relatively little is known about the global origin of ecotourists, the international destinations preferred by ecotourists, or comparisons between ecotourists from specific countries. It appears that the international market demand for ecotourism is centered in the western world, concentrated among those cultures in, or developed from, Northern European countries. The English-speaking countries of the world are particularly prominent as sources of, and destinations for, ecotourists. Based upon anecdotal sources, we estimate the most prominent countries supplying ecotourists, in order of market size, to be the United States, the United Kingdom, Germany, Canada, France, Australia, the Netherlands, Sweden, Austria, New Zealand, Norway and Denmark. Japan is a rapidly developing market, so much so that it may soon become a dominant player. However, the Japanese attitude appears to be one of aesthetic appreciation rather than ecological understanding.

The North American market is growing as well. A major 1995 market study in just seven United States and Canadian metropolitan areas identified a market of 13,200,000 people (HLA and ARA Consultants, 1995), much larger than anticipated. Southern European countries and the newly industrialized Asian economies are also growing sources of tourists, and can be expected to provide larger numbers as an ecological attitude spreads through those societies.

Ecotourism is based upon the desires of individuals to learn and experience nature, and all the diversity and richness it provides. How do people gain this desire? The research is incomplete, but enough is known to make a reasonable hypothesis. There are at least three major factors creating this travel motive.

The first factor is a widespread changing environmental attitude (especially in the western world), based upon the recognition of the inter-relationships of species and their environment, the finite character of the earth, and the innate value of all life. This attitude, which developed in the 1960s (Bos et al., 1977) has spread rapidly throughout western society in the last three decades and provides the conceptual base for the development of ecological travel.

The second factor is the development of environmental education in primary and secondary schools. This phenomenon developed over the last four decades, becoming widespread in the 1970s in both regular schools and in specialized environmental education schools, camps and parks. The intensity of these programs varies—some are much more in-depth and effective than others—but sufficient strength has occurred in the movement to create society-wide impacts. In fact, for the first time in world history, we have produced a generation of environmentally literate citizens who regularly seek out environmentally stimulating activities in their leisure time.

The third factor is the development of the environmental mass media. In response to society's emerging ecological attitude, the world's book publishers, film producers and television executives are generating environmentally related products at an unprecedented rate. Nature is now a major focus of the powerful North American and European media. With the power of the mass media, eco-logical attitudes are being reinforced and spread across society.

THE STRUCTURE OF THE ECOTOURISM INDUSTRY
ECOTOURISM BUSINESSES

It is important to identify the types of businesses in the ecotourism industry sector. A key component of this industry is the outbound operator who arranges itineraries and markets tours directly to clients. Though many operators are privately owned, a substantial number are non-profit, environmental organizations providing ecotravel for their members. Some outbound operators act as wholesalers to travel agencies and other outbound operators. Inbound operators are located within destination countries and make all the travel arrangements in their respective countries, often providing at the local level such services as food, lodging and entertainment.

As the size and complexity of ecotourism businesses has grown, so has the variety of ecotourism consulting and supporting businesses. A current snapshot of the scope and character of such ecotourism business consultants is found by examining the international membership directory of The Ecotourism Society (The Ecotourism Society, 1997). It identifies the following business categories: inbound tour operator, outbound tour operator, retail travel agency, hotel/lodging facility or campground, protected area, architect/landscape architect, green product supplies, developer, banking/finance, consultant, guide/interpreter, public relations/marketing, engineer-renewable energy, cruise line, and marketing research.

The diversity in size, location and orientation of ecotourism businesses poses a challenge for the understanding of the business structure supporting ecotourism. Various businesses provide support for the retail sector of ecotourism. These include public relations firms, architecture and landscape architecture firms, investment firms, marketing firms and engineering businesses, to name a few.

OUTBOUND NATURE TOUR OPERATORS

There is a growing number of outbound nature tour operators. Figure 1.1, which uses a non-linear scale on the x-axis, shows the results of a 1994 survey of 83 U.S.-based outbound operators (Higgins, 1996). The youthful status of this tourism sub-sector is made evident by the fact that only nine of these operators were in business in 1970. Despite the growing number and size of outbound operators, few studies have examined the character or organization of these businesses, except for a detailed examination of one adventure travel company by Sorenson (1991), a survey of outbound operators by Rymer (1992), and market surveys of North American tour operators by Higgins (1996) and Yee (1992).

Outbound ecotourism operators are located within source markets (typically developed countries) and provide a crucial link between ecotourists and nature tourism destinations. While an increasing number of airlines and general tour operators have been offering nature tour add-ons with their mass market tours,

FIGURE 1.1
GROWTH IN THE NUMBER OF U.S. NATURE TOUR OPERATORS
(Based on Sample Surveyed)

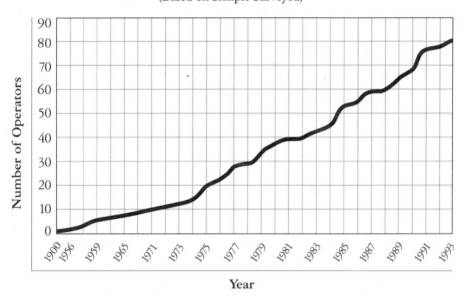

Year

this chapter focuses on nature tours which are organized and marketed by a specialized group of nature tour operators.

Because these outbound U.S. operators collectively guide over 100,000 ecotourists annually, the particular destinations, countries and world regions they utilize have a profound impact on the global structure of ecotourism (Figure 1.2) (Higgins, 1996). The predominant focus of U.S. ecotours is the Western Hemisphere and especially Central America. In addition, while only 9 operators sent more than 25% of their clients outside the Western Hemisphere, only 13 operators offered all their tours within just one world region. Thus, while relatively few operators are global in their offerings, most are organized beyond the scale of individual countries. Finally, this world-regional distribution of ecotours is very different from the global flows of general U.S. tourism, where visits to Europe, Mexico, and the Caribbean constitute much higher percentages of the total.

Research has not identified the number of nature tourists who deal directly with inbound operators or local ecolodges in foreign countries, frequently referred to as free and independent tourists (FITs), nor has it compared this independent market segment with nature tourists who rely upon outbound operators. Thus, the size, profile and behavior of what are likely two distinct market segments are not currently known. Probably, most clients on packaged nature tours make arrangements directly with outbound operators and not through other retail travel operations such as travel agencies. Consequently, outbound ecotour operators play a key role in shaping the choice of destinations and influencing the economic impacts of nature tours. Their professional activities may include: direct marketing of airline connections and tickets, making arrangements with inbound tour operators in foreign countries, developing marketing tools, and managing the sales of the tours.

Non-profit organizations are a major sub-component of the outbound operator industry segment. Higgins (1996) found that 17% of all clients of the surveyed operators travel on trips arranged by non-profit agencies. Thus, these non-profits provide a significant number of ecotours each year. In terms of geographical focus, this study of U.S.-based tour operators indicated that 42% of the non-profit ecotours were conducted within the United States. This domestic focus of ecotours with non-profit agencies is very distinct from the international focus of private-sector operators, where 93% of the ecotours take place outside the United States (Higgins, 1996). Because over a dozen non-profit organizations served more than 20,000 ecotourists (Higgins, 1996), it is clear that this sub-sector warrants more research attention.

The client size of surveyed U.S. operators ranged from a low of 25 to a high of 15,000 with an average of 1,674 per year (Higgins, 1996). While this study shows many small operators have under 1,000 clients per year, importantly, a small

FIGURE 1.2
PERCENTAGES OF CLIENTS TRAVELING
FROM THE U.S. TO SELECT WORLD REGIONS
(Based on Surveyed Operators)

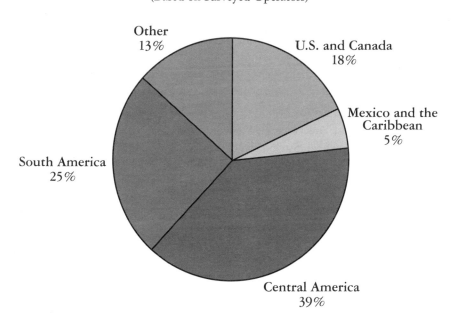

Other 13%

U.S. and Canada 18%

Mexico and the Caribbean 5%

South America 25%

Central America 39%

number of large operators have over 10,000 clients per year, indicating a substantial market share held by a small number of firms. In fact, the five largest operations in this study served a total of nearly 50,000 clients, or 40% of the market; the top 35 firms each had 1,000 or more clients and captured 90% of this total market. This very uneven distribution of market share among outbound operators presents a serious challenge for new operators. It also serves to concentrate ecotourists and their environmental and economic impacts.

INBOUND NATURE TOUR OPERATORS

Inbound nature tour operators are based within the host countries, usually in the largest cities. They specialize primarily in providing services within one country, but may operate in several. Inbound operators prepare itineraries, arrange ground transportation, negotiate accommodation rates, and provide guides and interpreters for nature trips. They market their services to a combination of travel agents, outbound nature tour operators and nature tourists (the latter to whom they market directly). There has been little research to examine this component of the ecotourism industry. Two exceptions are the dated assessment of the nature tourism industry structure and development needs within Ecuador (Wilson, 1987) and the recent examination of product, market and business potential in Canada (Tourism Canada, 1995).

One of the key attributes of inbound operators is their form of ownership, including: transnational branch offices, transnational franchises, subsidiaries of outbound nature tour operators, foreign corporations owned by expatriates, joint ventures, subsidiaries of large national corporations, nationally owned independents, and cooperatives. Each of these distinct forms of ownership entails a particular set of relations with other stakeholders in the industry. For example, franchises and branches of transnational corporations have special marketing connections to the upstream flow of nature tourism clients in industrialized countries and concentrate on properties they own in a host country. Likewise, large inbound nature tour operators often have their own lodges and concentrate their clients at these destinations. Even though the control, benefits and impact of these distinct ownership forms are very different, little systematic attention has been given to these distinct forms of business organization or to their impact on the character of ecotourism.

LOCAL NATURE TOUR BUSINESSES

Local nature tour businesses may include ecolodges, private nature reserves, hotels, restaurants, bars, transportation services, souvenir vendors, guides and providers of entertainment. Detailed examinations of ecolodges include: a survey of planning, sustainable design, financing, and standards and guidelines (Hawkins et al., 1995); and a comprehensive evaluation of eight registered lodges in the Brazilian Amazon (Wallace and Pierce, 1996). The broadest study of private nature reserves surveyed 93 privately owned reserves within Latin America and Africa (Alderman, 1990). Another major study critically evaluated 23 examples of a new approach called integrated conservation-development projects (Wells and Brandon, 1993). With respect to local economic development, this report concluded that most visitor spending on transportation, food, lodging and park entry fees went directly to the central treasury or to private corporate interests that had concessions. The study concluded that it was extremely rare for a revenue share to go to local peoples (Wells and Brandon, 1993).

A number of case studies examined the business impacts of nature tourism on particular localities, including: an assessment of tourism and local business development following the formation of a national park in Tortuguero, Costa Rica (Place, 1991; 1995); an analysis of business development with nature tourism in the Galápagos and Monteverde (Honey, 1994); and a look at the impact of gray whale tourism on local businesses in Baja California, (Dedina and Young, 1995). As with other nature tour businesses, these local operators also display diversity in their form of ownership. For example, an ecolodge may be owned by a transnational corporation, an outbound ecotour operator, a large inbound ecotour operator or a local family. Little systematic research has empirically examined either the extent or influence of these ownership connections.

CASE STUDIES IN ECOTOURISM MARKET ANALYSIS
ANALYZING THE ECOTOURISM MARKET

Kenya and Costa Rica have mature tourism industries—their countries' most important and high-profile foreign exchange earners. In both countries, tourism is the result of successful cooperation between the private and public tourism sectors. The experiences of these countries can be useful guides to the development and operation of national ecotourism markets (Eagles et al., 1992).

FIGURE 1.3
MARKET EVALUATION MODEL

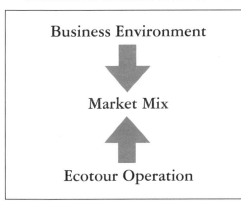

Business Environment

Market Mix

Ecotour Operation

Figure 1.3 shows a model for the evaluation of a tourism market. The central element in this model is the market mix of price, promotion, product and place, which provides the base for the tourism product. The price of the product is always an important decision point for consumers. The level of promotion influences consumer expectation. The product—the trip—is influenced by many factors, including the philosophy of the businesses and government agencies involved. The place is very important in ecotourism because the experience is so heavily influenced by the characteristics of the site visited. Two components, the external business environment and the actual operation of the ecotours, influence this market mix.

The first component, the business environment, includes factors that are, to some degree, external to the tourism operator, such as market demand (the larger players in the market can influence demand through advertising), existing services already in place, or external political and economic conditions. Many agencies provide services to the traveler—some fall under the control of the ecotour operator, though many services are provided by other agencies—such as transport companies. External conditions include the time and information available, the money needed, the political situation in the country, and an important external condition, the level of competition for the tourism product. A country has a certain level of capability, such as its managerial experience, that is dependent upon the capital and human resources available nationally.

The second component is the ecotour operation. The provision of ecotour services to the consumer falls under the control of the tourism operators and is the element of ecotourism most influenced by standard business management principles. Usually, after delivery of the program, evaluation data is analyzed for the purpose of improving the overall product. This market analysis framework is used to describe both Kenya's and Costa Rica's ecotourism industries.

THE ECOTOURISM MARKET IN KENYA

In 1994, tourism was the single biggest export earner for Kenya, contributing 35% of the country's foreign exchange and 11% of the GDP (KK Consulting, 1996). This nature-based tourism was centered primarily around Kenya's wildlife parks and Indian Ocean coast. In 1996, the national parks and game reserves, (an area of 35,037 km^2), constituted 6% of the country (World Conservation Monitoring Centre, 1997). In addition, Kenya had 50 private game reserves totaling 12,211 km^2, and constituting 2.1% of the country's land area (Watkins et al., 1996). In 1994, 55% of Kenya's foreign tourists came from Europe, 8% from North America, 6% from Asia and 29% from Africa (KK Consulting, 1996).

Western (1997) notes that Kenya portrays both the best and worst of nature tourism. The positive elements include the protection of a wide range of spectacular natural phenomenon, a well-developed international market profile, park budgets being covered by tourism income, and substantial levels of benefits flowing into local communities. The negative elements include environmental impacts due to congestion and unregulated park use, degenerating park infrastructure due to a lack of capital reinvestment, lax lodge and operator supervision due to political corruption, and too much emphasis on the viewing of just a few large mammals. Western (1997) suggests that these negative elements arose because of a lack of vision, planning and regulation—issues now being addressed through government action.

MARKET DEMAND—What are ecotourists looking for in Kenya? Surprisingly, few studies of travel motives have taken place. However, Ballantine (1991) studied Canadians who had traveled to Kenya in the previous three years with the African Safari Club, one of Kenya's largest tourism companies. Table 1.1 presents the most important social motives for these visitors.

TABLE 1.1
IMPORTANT SOCIAL MOTIVES FOR SURVEYED TOURISTS VISITING KENYA

Photograph Landscape and Wildlife
Learn About Nature
Experience New and Different Lifestyles
See as Much as Possible
Visit Historically Important Places

Ballantine (1991) found that these visitors showed interest in viewing, learning and photographing. They also wanted to experience the local lifestyles since Kenya was viewed as being historically important. They wanted to do all of this efficiently, seeing as much as possible in the time available. The most important attraction motives for their visits to Kenya were centered on nature (Table 1.2). Visiting the parks and reserves allowed for viewing of Africa's spectacular mammals and birds. There was a broad appreciation of nature, with forests given high priority along with wildlife.

TABLE 1.2
IMPORTANT ATTRACTION MOTIVES FOR SURVEYED TOURISTS VISITING KENYA

National Parks and Reserves
Wilderness
Mammals
Birds
Tropical Forests

These ecotourists had a high education level, with 46.6% having at least one university degree. This was compared to the general Canadian population in which 11.4% of those more than 15 years of age had a university degree in 1991 (Colombo, 1994). The mean age of the tourists was 49 and the group was 55% female.

The social profile of learning, photography, and searching for new experience, combined with the attraction motives of wild nature, is typically associated with high education levels. The reasons for the correlation are not known, making this a fertile area for tourism research.

AGENCIES, SERVICES AND EXTERNAL CONDITIONS—The government authority responsible for tourism in Kenya is the Ministry of Tourism and Wildlife. The Kenya Wildlife Service (KWS) is responsible for management of the national parks and game reserves. Its parastatal designation allows the KWS to function as a corporation, with retention of monies earned by the parks. International fundraising is an important source of revenue. The KWS has recently established a tourism department that is expected to take an active role in tourism marketing and promotion (Sindiga, 1995).

The key factors in ecotourism to Kenya are the internationally known national parks and wildlife reserves. Names such as Amboseli, Nakuru, Tsavo and Maasai Mara are well recognized. Because the Kenyan Wildlife Service is parastatal, it is financially independent from government. Therefore, the KWS can assume the role of a private ecotourist company, which is administratively substantially different from most national park agencies that function as government departments. Most private tourist operations in Kenya are critically dependent upon the public sector's protection and management of the natural resources on which safari tourism depends.

The Kenya Tourist Development Corporation (KTDC) is a public corporation with the objectives of developing the tourism industry, promoting domestic interests in the tourism industry, and promoting domestic tourism. Since its formation through an Act of Parliament in 1965, the KTDC has discharged its responsibilities through equity investments, commercial loans and extension services. If current plans are implemented, it will be transformed into a tourism development bank (Sindiga, 1997).

In 1996 the Kenya Tourist Board was established by the national government for promotion and marketing, coordinated resource management and capacity building (Redfern, 1996; Western, 1997). The private sector is expected to play a leading role, through a majority of the membership and possibly through financing. The initial board has a strong government presence including the KWS director and three permanent secretaries. However, since this Board was announced in 1996 its status has not been formalized through Regulation or an Act of Parliament; it is not clear how it will be funded (Sindiga, 1997).

The tourism industry grew on the merits of its own natural attractions and the efforts of many private-sector organizations (Economist Intelligence Unit, 1991).

The African Safari Club (ASC), one of Kenya's largest hotel and tourist organizations, is one such organization. The ASC owns 15 club hotels on the Indian Ocean coast, a safari lodge in Nairobi and a safari camp at the Maasai Mara Game Reserve. It provides transportation, meals and accommodation services to slightly more than 50,000 tourists annually (Bell, 1990). By offering both beach and safari tours, the ASC has provided programs to meet the diverse needs of their clients. This company is an example of the vertically integrated private tourism sector in Kenya and was chosen for a detailed study of its clients by Ballantine (1991).

In 1996 the Ecotourism Society of Kenya was formed to promote and assist community ecotourism projects, publish ecotourism codes of conduct, and develop auditing procedures to confirm the industry's commitment to environmental conservation (Opala, 1996). Such groups can act as honest brokers within government and private industry. The group can also develop, implement and monitor standards of environmental behavior in tourism.

Kenya's tourism industry developed within the context of a stable government and functioning public administration. Foreign visitation numbers increased from 346,000 in 1977, peaking at 870,000 visitors in 1994, and dropping considerably to 688,000 in 1995 (KK Consulting, 1996). The visitation drop after 1995 was due to the media's extensive coverage of Kenya's political unrest and violence. While Kenya's numbers dropped, Tanzania's visitation rose, suggesting a market shift from Kenya to its neighbor to the south.

Many Kenyan tourism operations are integrated companies that offer clients a wide range of services including accommodations in various parts of the country, domestic transport by van, truck and aircraft, safaris throughout the country, and a range of entertainment programs. These companies provide for all tourist needs during their stay in Kenya, an approach that leads to higher gross incomes for the tourist companies, but concentrates that income into only a few hands.

The Kenya Wildlife Service manages Kenya's parks, provides security, and makes its natural features available to tourists by maintaining the road system and a few primitive campgrounds within the park boundaries. The service does not provide interpretive or other basic visitor services, as do parks agencies in many other countries. In general, the service and its staff have little contact with the tourists. However, the recent creation of a tourism section within the KWS signals a possible move into the provision of tourism services (Sindiga, 1997).

MARKET MIX: PRODUCT, PRICE, PROMOTION AND PLACE—More than 95% of ASC clients are from European countries. About 63% of these tourists take wildlife safaris, with the remainder keeping to the beach hotels on the Indian Ocean coast (Bell, 1990). Although Canadians account for only a small portion of ASC's total visitors, 100% of them participate in at least one safari. A significant amount of their time (35%) is also spent at the beach resorts. A good combination of low cost and trip value was one of the primary reasons that Canadians chose to travel with the ASC for their trip to Kenya (Ballantine, 1991).

The average length of stay for tourists to Kenya varies between 11 and 17 days, depending upon the time of year and nationality of the tourists (KK Consulting, 1996). There are no national statistics on the age distribution or the average expenditures of tourists to Kenya (KK Consulting, 1996). However, Ballantine (1991) found the average family income for the Canadian visitors to be C$72,523 ($61,460*), well above the Canadian average for 1989 of C$53,131 ($41,519) (Colombo, 1994). On average, each person spent C$9,391 ($7,959) on travel the previous year (Ballantine, 1991) and spent an average of C$7,042 ($5,968) on their trip to Kenya. Given the average trip length of 21.4 days, this allows for an expenditure of C$329 ($279) per day. While this seems expensive, Ballantine found that the population she studied frequently spent this amount of money on travel. It is important to recognize that a substantial amount of this expenditure would have occurred outside Kenya, (e.g., for international airfare). The issue of economic leakage in ecotourism is important, and needs more study.

For ecotourists, the product's quality (defined to include significant natural features, high levels of learning opportunity and efficient visitor service) is as important as the cost of the product.

In the early years, parks and game reserves in Kenya were funded from central government coffers, often leading to weak budgets and insufficient site management. Starting in 1993, park entrance fees were raised from $5 to $20 a day for foreign tourists. This money was retained by the Kenya Wildlife Service for site management and to provide funding to local communities around the parks (Christ, 1994), resulting in a much healthier budget.

Historically, Kenya has been promoted through word-of-mouth by tourists and through various activities of the private sector (KK Consulting, 1996). (Government promotion has been almost nonexistent.) Kenya has also received much free publicity from the world's mainstream and environmental media (Redfern, 1996). Books, art and films on Kenyan wildlife are widespread, and provide a fertile bed of background information for the potential ecotourist. Ballantine (1991) found that surveyed tourists indicated that the most common sources of pre-trip information included travel brochures, travel agents and magazine articles (Table 1.3).

However, the most important sources of information had a different rank from that of most utilized. Both travel brochures and travel agents were frequently consulted, but were near the bottom of the list in importance to the consumers. The more important influencing factors were word of mouth and media information (including film-making)—sources difficult for a tourism supplier to influence.

It was found that these ecotourists frequently belonged to wildlife and outdoors-oriented organizations and that 43% of respondents had membership in at least

---

*Unless otherwise indicated, all monetary references are in U.S. dollars.

TABLE 1.3
SOURCES OF INFORMATION ABOUT KENYA

SOURCE	PERCENT*	IMPORTANCE**
Travel Brochures	83	0.79
Travel Agents	79	0.62
Magazine Articles	67	0.84
Books	57	1.02
Newspapers	56	0.97
Films	55	1.06
Friends and Family	55	1.75
Journal Articles	42	0.12
Other	35	1.67

* Percent of respondents using information source
** Average ranking given by respondents on a scale of 0 to 3 (3 being highest in importance)

one conservation association (Ballantine, 1991). Thus, it was determined that travel agencies could target these specific groups by advertising through outdoors associations.

ECOTOUR OPERATION—Kenya has an ecotourism delivery infrastructure dependent upon both the public and private sector. The public sector provides the parks, wildlife protection, landscape management and most of the facilities, such as roads. The private sector provides the accommodations, guide services, food and advertising.

Western (1997) documented the recent development of private and community-run ecolodges and wildlife sanctuaries throughout Kenya. It was noted that some of the new sites are located well away from national parks, on private ranches and community lands, and are typically locally operated, providing for a high level of personal service to the tourist. Such local initiatives are encouraged by government policy so as to provide a diversified set of ecotourist destinations for the benefit of both wildlife conservation and local communities.

KENYA ECOTOURISM MARKET EVALUATION—How many tourists surveyed are ecotourists? Ballantine and Eagles (1994) found that 84% of respondents fulfilled the criteria of having a social motive (to learn about nature), a site attraction motive (to visit wilderness or undisturbed areas) and a time commitment (to spend an average of 33% of their trip on safari), and were therefore classified as ecotourists. The utilization of a social motive, an attraction motive and a time commitment in defining "ecotourists" has attracted interest among those wishing to differentiate ecotourists from the general travel population.

These Kenyan ecotourists were also involved in activities and destinations extending beyond ecotourism. Some visited the beach, some viewed cultural events, and some went shopping. Although this interweaving of travel motives and activities adds to the complexity of the definition and management of ecotourism, the information, overall, can be used for market discrimination.

Tourists who traveled to Kenya with the ASC were pleased with most aspects of their experience. They indicated a very high level of satisfaction with both the pre-trip information and the trip services. They were most satisfied with the information provided on the trip, the weather and the accommodations. They were least satisfied with the coverage of conservation issues, the food, the level of organization and the guiding services. Clearly, this group was looking for higher levels of conservation messages and interpretive services than were provided by their tour company. Such a desire for emphasis on environmental education is not surprising given the ecological travel motives of these ecotourists. However, the ASC provided both safari and beach tourism experiences, possibly leading to weakening of focus on the environmental side (Ballantine, 1991).

Many tour companies in Kenya use driver-guides, most with more training in mechanics than in interpretation or ecology. The use of trained tour guides would cost more, potentially reducing profits (Sindiga, 1997). Clearly, there is a market opportunity for tour companies that use accredited guides, and advertise this fact to potential consumers.

International aid, lending and conservation institutions play important roles in the management of parks and their ecotourism industries in many countries, with Kenya being a prime example. In recent years a shift has occurred in emphasis from strict conservation to sustainable development. Since ecotourism is a prime vehicle for long-term sustainable economic development, considerable activity has started to take place in capacity building for tourism management. This is leading to conservation with an immediate economic focus.

Kenya is a leader in the provision of African wildlife tourism. Western (1997) maintains that visitor satisfaction in Kenya ranks higher than for any other African country when it comes to natural spectacles and sheer scenic diversity. However, other countries, such as Tanzania, Botswana and South Africa, are increasingly providing effective competition. It is important to note that systematic studies of tourist satisfaction with the ecotourism product in Kenya, or elsewhere in Africa, are very rare and those that do occur are geographically quite limited.

Within Africa those countries providing the best combination of wildlife experience, trip cost and service quality will gain the largest market share. All organizations, public and private, could use program evaluations to monitor their services in an effort to better meet the needs of their clients. At the present time the level of program evaluation of the ecotourist industry is very low in Kenya, specifically, and throughout Africa generally. Interestingly, the aggressive private game reserve operators in South Africa are becoming prominent, and are competing well with many national parks, due to their effective service quality management.

THE ECOTOURISM MARKET IN COSTA RICA

During the 9-year period 1986 to 1995, the number of foreign tourists entering Costa Rica increased from 260,840 to 792,287, the latter generating $661.3 million in direct revenues. In 1992, tourism surpassed banana exports to become the most important economic activity in the country in terms of foreign exchange earnings and creation of employment. Tourism represented 19.4% of the nation's export earnings in 1995, 8.9% of the country's GDP in 1994, and accounted for 12% of the labor pool. In 1995, arrivals at the main international airport showed 56% of the visitors to be from North America, 20% from Europe, 9% from Central America, 9% from South America and 2% from Asia (Budowski, 1996; Monet, 1996).

Costa Rica's tourism market is based on a mixture of soft adventure, nature and ecotourism. An important facet of the ecotourism situation there is the inter-relation between ecotourism and mass tourism. Because "ecotourism" comes in many shades of green in Costa Rica, the scope and distribution of tour alternatives between mass tourism and more explicit environmental tourism is important, but difficult to define. Unlike most other countries, though, independent green evaluations have been completed for many different ecotourism operations within the country, such as the high quality and innovative evaluation by Blake and Becher (1997).

For some time now, the success of tourism and ecotourism in Costa Rica has placed increasing tension on both natural and human resources (Hill, 1990). For example, the popularity and increasing development of Monteverde, Manuel Antonio, Tortuguero and other sites has put a strain on both the environment and the employees. Honey (1994) and Morrison (1994) have documented the tensions surrounding the increasing popularity and subsequent impacts of the ecotourism in Monteverde. For a detailed look at the challenges facing Tortuguero see Place's (1995) examination of the role of the national park in the local economy. Also of interest is a recently organized association of home tourism sites called TUR-CASA, which offers a creative attempt at increasing the share of tourism revenue for women in Costa Rica (Shumaker, 1995).

The development of tourism in Costa Rica has been rapid. Much of the more recent development has been centered around mainstream beach tourism along the Pacific and Caribbean coasts. Large amounts of foreign investment, escalating land costs and intensive development have characterized this trend. Many involved in ecotourism feel this is an unfortunate direction and wonder if the movement from ecotourism to other forms of tourism is a trend that could be repeated elsewhere (Epler Wood, 1997).

MARKET DEMAND—What are ecotourists looking for in Costa Rica? Fennell (1990) studied Canadians who had traveled to Costa Rica in the previous five years with nine tour companies. All tours were guided. Table 1.4 lists the five most important social motives for these visitors.

TABLE 1.4
IMPORTANT SOCIAL MOTIVES FOR
SURVEYED TOURISTS VISITING COSTA RICA

Learning About Nature
Photographing Landscapes and Wildlife
Seeing as Much as Possible
Being Physically Active
Meeting People with Similar Interests

For these visitors, learning about nature was the most important motivation and aspects of the trip that aided in such learning experiences were appreciated. Photography is a method of preserving a valuable experience and was seen as a form of learning. The desire to see as much as possible in the time available suggested an active approach to a vacation. These people wanted to keep on the move and gain new experiences. The data also suggested that they appreciated the presence of other active, interested, nature-loving travelers with similar interests.

Table 1.5 lists the most important attraction motives for these visitors. Tropical forests were the number one attraction. These ecotourists were very interested in trees, flowers and birdlife. Being in forested wilderness areas was of primary importance, especially in protected parks. Fennell (1990) found that 65% of the people had at least one university degree, as compared to about 11.5% of Canadians more than 15 years of age who had a university degree in 1991 (Colombo, 1994). Obviously, these ecotourists were a highly educated group. The mean age of the ecotourists was 54 and the group was 55% male.

TABLE 1.5
IMPORTANT ATTRACTION MOTIVES FOR
SURVEYED TOURISTS VISITING COSTA RICA

Tropical Forests
Wilderness Areas
Trees and Flowers
National Parks and Reserves
Birds

The combination of social motives (characterized by learning, photography and high activity levels), and attraction motives (based on nature and advanced levels of formal education), is typical of ecotourists who are attracted early to a developing destination. In 1990, Costa Rica began to attract visitors from a broader sector of the market. These people were interested in nature, but showed more interest in creature comforts, wanted more relaxation time in their itineraries, had higher expectations of service, were less tolerant of the local culture, and were less prepared for the ecotourist experience (Horizontes Nature Tours, 1996). This movement from the hard-core ecotourist to the soft-experience ecotourist is to be expected as the market moves from the early adventurers into a broadly-based mass ecotourism market.

AGENCIES, SERVICES AND EXTERNAL CONDITIONS—The Costa Rican Tourist Board, Costa Rica's national tourist agency, has the major role of providing advertising and infrastructure services for the industry. The National Parks Service is responsible for the maintenance of the national parks and wildlife reserves. Its primary goal is land protection, with tourism a tangential benefit.

The private sector shoulders much of the responsibility for tourism. It handles visitor needs for transportation, food, accommodations and information (Fennell and Eagles, 1990). Rovinski (1991) described the unique private reserves serviced by ecotourism companies in Costa Rica. The largest, the complex containing the Monteverde Cloud Forest Reserve, the Children's Rainforest and the Santa Elena Reserve, contains 29,000 hectares of valuable mountain forests (Budowski, 1996) and caters to slightly more than 15,000 visitors per year.

Costa Rica has long been a stable democracy in a regional sea of political upheaval. This fact is well recognized by potential tourists and helps create a positive travel image. The Costa Rican National Report on Tourism (Anonymous, 1987) recognized that special-interest tourism should be a major factor in the country's tourism industry. Activities such as bird watching, river rafting, nature photography and deep-sea fishing are especially suited to this country. However, Rovinski (1991) reported that the ecotourism phenomenon was not a priority in the budget of the national tourism agency.

The adequacy of conservation protection is an issue in Costa Rica. User conflicts and environmental degradation in the high-intensity use areas have become controversial. Market pressure has increased, as demonstrated by the fact that in 1993, 3,000 new hotel rooms were constructed, many of them located immediately outside protected areas. The negative environmental impacts at such heavily used sites as Manuel Antonio National Park became a serious issue (Norris, 1994), and one yet to be resolved.

Budowski (1996) documented several concerns about the development of tourism in Costa Rica: 1) The rapid increase in tourism was not well planned. For example, the hotel industry over built, creating more supply than demand. 2) The national parks and wildlife reserves were poorly designed for visitor use. Better trail systems, interpretive centers, assistance with the training of local guides, extension of visitor hours, and better access to the parks were all needed. 3) The money to develop these services was wanting. 4) Inappropriate marketing was a problem. Many brochures showed pictures of the large cats, such as jaguars, which are seldom seen in the rainforest. Promotions often mentioned that the country has 250 species of mammals, but 105 of these are bats and many more are rodents—species not high on most visitors' want list. Many of the wildflowers, such as orchids, are arboreal and are not accessible to ground-bound tourists. These promotional excesses created unrealistic expectations by many tourists. 5) Some international and local tour operators used the ecotourism label inappropriately, creating confusion in the market and frustration with some tourists looking for a high-quality experience. 6) And, finally, good security for tourists and their belongings has recently became more of an issue.

Costa Rica has competition from nearby nations with similar resources; Belize, Ecuador and Venezuela are prime examples. However, none of these countries has the sophisticated mix of national parks, specialized ecotourist lodges, experienced nature guides, scientific research establishments, nature media attention, and international tourist operations, as does Costa Rica.

MARKET MIX: PRODUCT, PRICE, PROMOTION, PLACE—The key reason for Costa Rica's successful ecotourism is the country's outstanding natural sites. The national parks and wildlife reserves are unique and contain interesting and spectacular tropical ecosystems (Boza, 1988). In 1991, half of Costa Rica's foreign tourists visited a park or natural site (Epler Wood, 1993). The National Parks Service is responsible for establishing and managing the national parks and wildlife refuges. Its primary role is one of protection; it provides very few visitor services. Many private ecotourist lodges have sprung up in areas near the parks to provide the food, accommodation, and information services not available in the parks.

A very diverse set of private companies provides basic services to ecotourists. There are many bus and tour companies. Dozens of independent tour guides provide services to tour companies and to independent travelers (Rovinski, 1991). Nearly 90% of the hotels are small lodges and inns with fewer than 60 rooms. These are scattered throughout the country, and many are owned by nationals. Furthermore, in some regions, there is a well-developed private service industry of locals who own small boats, taxis, horses, restaurants, variety stores and cottage craft enterprises. These locally owned businesses, their small size of operation, and the fact that they are widespread, result in a good distribution of jobs as well as a positive economic impact throughout the country (Budowski, 1996).

Little has been published about the number, size or structure of ecotourism businesses within Costa Rica. However, one of the few studies of this specialty sector was Baez' (1993) survey of operators. This limited survey identified a range of different size ecotourism businesses including seven operators who indicated they had 1 to 5 employees, four who had 6 to 10, four who had 11 to 20, and two who said they had 21 to 30 (Baez, 1993). The largest 6 businesses, all with more than 11 employees, employed more than two-thirds of this sample's labor market.

Fennell (1990) found the average family income for the surveyed Canadian visitors was C$69,295 ($58,725), well above the Canadian average for 1991 of C$53,131 ($41,519) (Colombo, 1994). The ecotourists stayed an average of 14.4 days. Over this period, they spent an average of C$2,140 ($1814), or C$152 ($129) per day. This was similar to the $148 reported for clients of Costa Rica Expeditions (Rovinski, 1991) and much more than the $85 per day identified by the Costa Rican Institute of Tourism (Monet, 1996). Depending upon the type of tour offered, prices typically included air travel, accommodations, some meals, a multilingual guide, local transportation and access to parks. Monet (1996) reported that the average length of stay of foreign tourists varies from 3 to 15 days, with Europeans staying longer than North Americans.

Many ecotourists expressed a desire to see the maximum conservation benefit come from their expenditures. Many voluntarily contributed to local conservation organizations in order to further conservation and education efforts in-country even more (Fennell, 1990).

Management of national parks and wildlife refuges takes money. The Costa Rican park system has been traditionally funded by small and insufficient government grants. With rapid increases in park visitation, (up to 250,000 in 1991), environmental degradation due to a lack of protection and management became obvious. There was worry that the quality of the natural environment could not be maintained in the future with such increased visitor use and limited management capability (Rovinski, 1991). Tourist expenditures were not being captured in any significant way by the park agency and, as a result, the agency could not respond sufficiently to the pressures of tourism. For example, basic sanitary facilities, such as toilets, were either nonexistent or in very poor shape. An international effort, spearheaded by The Ecotourism Society, to increase entrance fees for foreign tourists (Epler Wood, 1993) resulted in a 10-fold increase in entry fees, to $15 a day, to pay for tourism management within the parks (Anonymous, 1994). A backlash against this large increase resulted in a drop back to $6 a day (Budowski, 1996). The issue of creating sufficient cash flow through the parks to adequately fund protection and management remains important.

Costa Rica has recently divided the entire country into nine major conservation zones, each with a mixture of private and public protected areas. The management plans for these areas include public and private lands and operations. Tourism entrance fees are no longer applied to a central government fund, but are, instead, remaining locally-based to fund the needs identified. This is a major initiative to develop institutions for tourism-based sustainable development (Budowski, 1996).

The Costa Rican Institute of Tourism is financed by tourist taxes as well as by the private sector, but infrequently utilizes the funds to undertake international promotion efforts (Monet, 1996). Fennell (1990) asked surveyed Canadian visitors to list the promotional sources that brought Costa Rica to their attention. Most people consulted magazine articles, books, friends and family (Table 1.6). When asked to rank the sources in order of importance, nature clubs, friends and films were indicated as the most influential. Clearly, the most important sources of information fell outside the authority of government or national tourism organizations. Significantly, these tourists had a very high conservation group affiliation, with each person having an average of 2.7 memberships. Combining this affiliation with the importance given to nature clubs in finding out about Costa Rica provides important insight into the roles that environmental groups play in ecotourism promotion.

Costa Rica receives a substantial amount of free publicity in environmental magazines and journals. A special feature of the Costa Rican ecotourism market is the large number of natural scientists who visit, and arrange for students to visit, this country. In particular, the Organization for Tropical Studies, a consortium of United States universities, organizes a significant number of the ecology students and faculty who visit Costa Rica. A survey of past participants found a mean of 3.2 return visits for each initial participant (Laarman and Perdue, 1989). This very high return-visitation rate and high rates of word-of-mouth communication noted by these natural science travelers identify one of the major sub-currents of ecotourism within Costa Rica.

TABLE 1.6
SOURCES OF INFORMATION ABOUT COSTA RICA

SOURCE	PERCENT*	IMPORTANCE**
Magazine Articles	70	1.4
Books	69	0.8
Friends and Family	54	2.1
Journal Articles	50	0.7
Travel Brochures	46	0.5
Travel Agents	40	0.5
Newspapers	29	0.7
Other	28	2.6
Films	24	1.6

* Percent of respondents using information source
** Average ranking given by respondents on a scale of 0 to 3 (3 being highest in importance)

The conservation community frequently publishes articles on the various natural features of Costa Rica. Fennell (1990) found that journals are a more important source of information than either tourist brochures or travel agents. The country is also used extensively by the nature film industry. Since journals and films are seen as separate from tourism promotions, they are considered independent sources of information. All of this publicity, therefore, occurs with little or no promotional expenditure by the Costa Rican government or its agencies.

Since about 1980, ecotour companies in Canada promoted Costa Rica as a great destination for the naturalist. Since 1990, large international operators, such as Fiesta Tours and Air Canada, have become involved. This combination of small, specialized firms and larger mass-oriented firms provided a unique set of experiences ranging from specialized tours, such as bird watching, to general tours for nature appreciation. However, large tourism providers can overwhelm a destination, culturally and environmentally, unless local operations are very carefully handled.

ECOTOUR OPERATION—Costa Rica's national tourist slogan has changed many times, from "Costa Rica: It Is Only Natural," to "Tan Your Soul," to "Costa Rica: No Artificial Ingredients." Each of the slogans became well known, but the frequency of changes led to confusion.

Costa Rica's ecotourism market is heavily based upon parks and protected areas. In recent years private ecolodges have become a factor in the market. Private reserves, both large and small, provide a combination of high-quality natural environments and good quality service. The parks and the private reserves both receive self-guided visitors, as well as individuals who utilize ecotour operators.

If ecotourism is to be sustained in Costa Rica, the management policies for parks, private reserves and national tourism must ensure that the country's natural attractiveness remains intact. The task, then, for Costa Rica is to maintain its natural odyssey within an appropriate level of social and recreational impact.

COSTA RICA ECOTOURISM EVALUATION—Fennell (1990) found that the visitors reported highest satisfaction levels with the information provided on their trip, the weather and the guide service. Clearly, the interpretive services on Costa Rican ecotours were considered to be of high quality. However, ecotourists reported the lowest satisfaction levels with sanitary conditions, indicating the level of infrastructure available in national parks at that time.

The foreign visitation goals for Costa Rica were exceeded in the early 1990s. Tourism growth was, and continues to be, massive. If these numbers are to be sustained within sensitive ecosystems, visitor services in the parks must be improved. The basic infrastructure must be upgraded to handle increased numbers. Many sensitive environmental features, such as steep mountain paths, must be better protected. Interpretive centers are badly needed to give visitors a better idea of the unique features available, and the best ways to safely experience the natural environment. The facilities at Volcan Poas National Park, with hard trail surfaces, paved roads, a modern visitor center and well-planned information facilities, are a good example of what needs to be done elsewhere.

The private ecolodge and inbound ecotour operators in Costa Rica are, for the most part, advanced, providing quality tourism programs, as well as being active in environmental conservation. Despite this success, a significant debate exists concerning tourism impacts at heavily used sites and the uneven distribution of economic benefits.

CONCLUSIONS FROM THE CASE STUDIES

The case studies of the ecotourism markets in Kenya and Costa Rica reveal principles that can be useful elsewhere. The development of a solid, sustainable ecotourism industry is dependent upon several key factors. Important ecological sites must be protected within a set of national parks and reserves that are well managed and available for tourism use. Most ecotourists visit public reserves, but private reserves can play a role through the provision of specialized programs and services.

The long-term success of park tourism requires cooperation between the public and private sectors. An ecotourism industry can not survive if the quality of the natural environment is degraded. Protected sites best survive when a mobilized constituency, including the tourism industry, argues for their existence.

The public sector typically has the unique role, based on a societal mandate, of resource protection (Table 1.7). This also involves determination of acceptable uses and use levels. Security of the environment and the public is a government responsibility. In wealthier countries, basic tourism infrastructure is funded by public monies, but in poorer countries foreign aid and tourism fees pay for tourism infrastructure. In wealthier countries, information is provided by both the public and private sectors. In poorer countries, the private sector is dominant in information provision. This puts the park agencies at a severe disadvantage because the information provided on park management, infrastructure, allowable activities and destinations is usually not screened by the agency, and possibly not even known to these authorities. The public sector is responsible for setting environmental goals, for monitoring the impact of tourism on environmental quality, for allocation of access and enforcement of management decisions. These functions can be invalidated when, as was observed in Kenya, politically powerful groups, such as lodge owners or tour agencies, use bribery to allow their activities to be relieved of general rules and regulations.

Government agencies play important roles in the ecotourism market by encouraging scientific research in their parks, providing transportation infrastructure and security for tourists, and developing a financial system for capturing tourist expenditures which are sufficient to pay for necessary environmental management.

TABLE 1.7
PUBLIC SECTOR ROLE IN PARK TOURISM

ROLE
1. Environmental Protection
2. Infrastructure (*Roads, Airports, Rail Lines, Electricity, Sanitation*)
3. Security and Enforcement
4. Monitoring of Impacts; Evaluation of Quality
5. Allocation of Access
6. Limits of Acceptable Change
7. Information (*Interpretation, Visitor Centers*)
8. Conflict Resolution

Typically, the private sector provides most of the consumer services and products (Table 1.8). Private operators provide accommodation, food, transport, media, and advertising. The private sector has the ability to respond quickly to consumer demands and to develop specialized products. In poorer countries, such as Africa, private operators provide most tourism information. The private sector relies heavily on the public sector for resource protection, infrastructure and security services. The public sector relies heavily on the private sector for handling the day-by-day activities of the visitors.

The private sector provides accommodations, ensures that various forms of transportation are available, develops information and interpretive services, makes

TABLE 1.8
PRIVATE SECTOR ROLE IN PARK TOURISM

ROLE
1. Accommodations and Food
2. Transportation (*Buses, Automobiles, Airplanes*)
3. Information (*Guides, Advertising*)
4. Media (*Films, Books, Videos*)
5. Site Promotion and Advertising
6. Consumer Products (*Clothes, Souvenirs, Equipment*)
7. Personal Services (*Entertainment*)

food available, and assists in the job of promotion and advertising. The ability of the private sector to respond to market niches results in a wide variety of tour offerings, ranging from mass tourism to species-specific trips.

The dissemination of travel information about nature is achieved through a diverse set of independent organizations—many outside land management agencies. The scientific community in the industrialized world provides an information and intellectual base that attracts the interest of ecotourists who are highly educated and widely read. The film industry provides key exposure through the development of films showing the intricacies of nature in a positive and non-threatening fashion. The films of Alan Root in Kenya and the Hughes in Costa Rica are classic examples. The environmental movement in developed countries is important in providing provocative portraits of conflicts and resource exploitation—through the role of conservation educators and lobbyists, environmental groups spread messages widely. These three factors—science publications, films and conservation actions—set a receptive mood for the naturalist traveler.

Public and private cooperation is evident in the provision of information databases on the internet. Information becoming available in this fashion includes that which is typically available in visitor centers, park publications, and guide books. It is expected that all major ecotourist destinations will have this type of information available in the future. The ecotourist industry is well positioned to take advantage of this new technology as the socio-demographic profiles of ecotourists suggest that they are well-educated and, therefore, likely to be computer literate (Eagles and Cascagnette, 1995). However, almost none of the internet information now available on Kenya and Costa Rica comes from the agencies responsible for park management, or from national tourism organizations. Most comes from the private sector, both ecotour companies and non-governmental environmental groups.

Kenya and Costa Rica prove that countries geographically removed from potential customers can tap into the international ecotourism market. Distance is not as important as market profile and information availability. The slow and thoughtful development of a country's ecotourism industry can lead to policies that are suitable to a broader sector of society. Rapid development and entrenched tourism businesses can lead to individual priorities overwhelming the larger societal objectives of environmental protection and community development.

The number of people desiring to experience nature through travel is increasing. Ecotourists are primarily interested in learning about nature firsthand. They want to see, feel and experience wildness. While it is the job of the ecotourist industry to provide the services, programs and sites to fulfill this need, it is also important to understand the social, environmental and business implications of this growing sub-sector. It is surprising how few detailed studies are publicly available on the market structures of emerging ecotourism industries in many countries.

Early ecotourism is represented by a few, hardy individuals traveling alone or in small tour groups. These people use the accommodations, food and information found locally. Once visitor patterns are established, larger-scale operations evolve. Specialized accommodations, usually rustic and environmentally sensitive, and well-trained guides, who can explain the features of the environment, develop. Transportation carriers begin to offer specialized services. These sectors of the market utilize the existing image of the area and exploit it by providing a way for the tourist to experience the natural features.

The larger ecotourist organizations now utilizing Kenya and Costa Rica advertise in specialized publications, such as nature and outdoor recreation magazines, and in newspapers. However, the latter is often not successful (Bell, 1990) since the ads consist primarily of making a link between the resource, about which the tourist has already heard, and the tour agency providing the means for the tourist to experience that resource.

Alderman (1990) and Langholz (1996) documented the rapidly growing private nature reserve and ecolodge developments worldwide. These innovative approaches involve private individuals and corporations who are developing "mini" national parks, complete with the protection of a valuable ecological resource and quality visitor services. Their market niche appears to be dependent upon the provision of high-quality personal services to the ecotourist. Examples include highly trained guides, well-stocked libraries, small laboratories, specialized viewing opportunities, environmentally appropriate site operations, cultural sensitivity, and personal service. Both Kenya and Costa Rica have interesting private nature reserves and ecolodges. However, Costa Rica is much further developed in this regard.

Over time, the industry has expanded from servicing the hard-core ecotourist, who is very interested in nature study and is willing to accept local conditions, to the soft-experience ecotourist who wants more creature comforts and shows a less intense level of nature interest. The hard-core ecotourists who first visit a site have realistic expectations of environmental features, the local culture and the available services. Those who visit later are not as well informed, and require more personal service, better trained guides and higher levels of comfort. It is possible that in some countries ecotourism could lead to the development of high-volume mass tourism.

The ecotourism industry requires close cooperation between the government sector (which provides the natural resources), the private sector (which provides capital and travel arrangements), and the local residents (who provide labor and cultural diversity of local communities). In a well-planned and managed system, the visitor relies upon, and benefits from, all of these sectors.

ACKNOWLEDGEMENTS

Thanks to David Fennell at the University of Regina for his research on the Costa Rican tourism market. Thanks to Jennifer Ballantine of Agriculture Canada for her research on the Kenyan tourism market. Special thanks to Dr. Isaac Sindiga, Head of the Department of Tourism at Moi University in Kenya, for personal conversations on the subject and for comments on the paper. Terry Pratt, an ecotourism consultant in San Jose, Costa Rica, provided extensive and valuable comments. Derek Wade, a specialist in park tourism business planning, contributed many comments as well. Thanks, also, to the editors and reviewers for their comments.

REFERENCES

Akama, J. S. 1996. "Western Environmental Values and Nature-Based Tourism in Kenya," *Tourism Management*, vol. 17, no. 8, pp. 567-574.

Alderman, C.L. 1990. *A Study of the Role of Privately Owned Lands Used for Nature Tourism, Education and Conservation*, Conservation International, Washington, D.C.

Anonymous. 1987. "National Report on Tourism," *International Tourism Reports*, pp. 66-69, 71, 73.

Anonymous. 1994. "Foreign Tourists to Costa Rica's National Parks," *The Ecotourism Society Newsletter*, vol. 4, no. 4.

Baez, A. 1993. "Binomio Turismo-Conservacion: Una Alternativa Desarrollo," *Technitur*, Professional Tourism Association of Costa Rica, June, no. 46, pp. 48-53.

Ballantine, J.L. 1991. "An Analysis of the Characteristics of a Population of Canadian Tourists to Kenya," master's thesis, Department of Recreation and Leisure Studies, University of Waterloo, Waterloo, Ontario, Canada.

Ballantine, J.L., P.F.J. Eagles. 1994. "Defining Canadian Ecotourists," *Journal of Sustainable Tourism*, vol. 2, no. 1, pp.1-5.

Bandy, J. 1996. "Managing the Other of Nature: Sustainability, Spectacle, and Global Regimes of Capital in Ecotourism," *Public Culture*, vol. 8, no. 3, pp. 539-566.

Bell, W. 1990. Personal communication, general manager, African Safari Club of Canada, Toronto, Ontario, Canada.

Blake, B., A. Becher. 1997. *The New Key to Costa Rica*. Ulysses Press, Berkeley, California.

Blamey, R. 1995."The Elusive Market Profile: Operationalising Ecotourism," paper presented at the Geography of Tourism Conference, Canberra, Australia.

Blangy, S., P. Hanneberg. 1995. "Ecotourism in Europe: Two Views," *The Ecotourism Society Newsletter*, vol. 5, no. 2, pp. 1-3.

Bos, W., L. Brisson, P. Eagles. 1977. "A Study of Attitudinal Orientations of Central Canadian Cultures Towards Wildlife," *Environment Canada*, Canadian Wildlife Service.

Boza, M. A. 1988. "Costa Rica National Parks," *Editorial Heliconia*, Fundacion Neotropica, San Jose, Costa Rica.

Budowski, T. 1996. Personal communication, e-mail, May 15, 1997.

Burak Jacobson, Inc. 1985. "Segmentation Analysis for the Canadian Tourism Attitude and Motivation Study," Department of Regional and Industrial Expansion, Tourism Canada, Ottawa, Ontario, Canada.

Christ, C. 1994. "Kenya Makes Revenue Sharing Top Priority," *The Ecotourism Society Newsletter*, vol. 4, no. 1, pp.1-5.

Colombo, J. R. 1994. *The Canadian Global Almanac*, MacMillan, Toronto, Ontario, Canada.

Crossley, J., B. Lee. 1994. "Ecotourists and Mass Tourists: A Difference in Benefits Sought," proceedings of the Travel and Tourism Research Association Conference, Bal Harbour, Florida.

Dann, G. 1996. "Greenspeak: An Analysis of the Language of Eco-tourism," *Progress in Tourism and Hospitality Research*, vol. 2, nos. 3 and 4, pp. 247-259.

Dedina, S., E. Young. 1995. "Conservation as Communication," *Whalewatcher*, vol. 29, no. 2, pp. 8-13.

Drumm, A. 1995. "Integrated Impact Assessment of Nature Tourism in Ecuador's Amazon Region," FEPROTUR, Quito, Ecuador.

Eagles, P.F.J. 1992. "The Travel Motivations of Canadian Ecotourists," *Journal of Travel Research*, vol. 31, no. 2, pp. 3-7.

Eagles, P.F.J. 1996. "Issues in Tourism Management in Parks: The Experience in Australia," *Australian Leisure*, vol. 7, no. 2, pp. 29-37.

Eagles, Paul F.J., J.L. Ballantine, D. A. Fennell. 1992. "Marketing to the Ecotourist: Case Studies from Kenya and Costa Rica," unpublished paper presented at the IVth World Congress on National Parks and Protected Areas, Caracas, Venezuela.

Eagles, P.F.J., J.W. Cascagnette. 1995. "Canadian Ecotourists: Who Are They?" *Tourism Recreation Research*, vol. 20, no. 1, pp. 22-28.

Eagles, P.F.J., E. Wind. 1994. "The Advertising of Canadian Ecotours in 1992," *Journal of Applied Recreation Research*, vol. 19, no. 1, pp. 67-87.

Economist Intelligence Unit. 1991. Kenya. *International Tourism Reports #2,"* Business International Ltd., London, pp. 48-66.

(The) Ecotourism Society. 1997. *International Membership Directory*, North Bennington, Vermont.

Epler Wood, M. 1993. "Costa Rican Parks Threatened by Tourism Boom," *The Ecotourism Society Newsletter*, vol. 3, no. 1, pp.1-2.

Epler Wood, M. 1997. Personal communication, August 29, 1997.

Epler Wood, M. 1998. "Meeting the Global Challenge of Community Participation in Ecotourism: Case Studies and Lessons from Ecuador," *America Verde* series, Latin America and Caribbean Division, The Nature Conservancy.

Fennell, D.A. 1990. "A Profile of Ecotourists and the Benefits Derived from their Experience: A Costa Rican Case Study," master's thesis, Department of Recreation and Leisure Studies, University of Waterloo, Waterloo, Ontario, Canada.

Fennell, D.A., P.F.J. Eagles. 1990. "Ecotourism in Costa Rica: A Conceptual Framework," *Journal of Parks and Recreation Administration*, vol. 8, no. 1, pp. 23-34.

Hatch, D. 1997. "Understanding the Ecotourism Market," unpublished paper presented at the Ecotourism Association of Australia Conference, Port Stephens, Australia.

Hawkins, D., M. Epler Wood, S. Bittman. 1995. *The Ecolodge Sourcebook for Planners and Developers*, The Ecotourism Society, North Bennington, Vermont.

Higgins, B.R. 1996. "The Global Structure of the Nature Tourism Industry: Ecotourists, Tour Operators and Local Business," *Journal of Travel Research*, vol. 35, no. 2, pp. 11-18.

Hill, C. 1990. "The Paradox of Tourism in Costa Rica," *Cultural Survival Quarterly*, vol. 14, no. 1, pp. 14-19.

HLA Consultants, ARA Consulting Group. 1995. "Ecotourism—Nature/ Adventure/ Culture," Alberta and British Columbia Market Demand Assessment, Main Report, Canadian Heritage, Calgary, Alberta, Canada.

Holden, A. 1996. "A Profile of U.K. Outbound 'Environmentally Friendly' Tour Operators," *Tourism Management*, vol. 17, no. 1, pp. 60-64.

Honey, M. 1994. "Paying the Price of Ecotourism," *AmÉricas* vol. 46, no. 6, pp. 40-47.

Horizontes Nature Tours. 1996. "A Brief History of Tourism to Costa Rica," unpublished document, San Jose, Costa Rica.

Jepson, E. 1994. "Ethnic Variation in Leisure and Recreational Interests," *Bibliography 311,* Council of Planning Librarians, Chicago, Illinois.

KK Consulting. 1996. Kenya. *International Tourism Reports*, vol. 4, pp. 45-69.

Laarman, J., R. Perdue. 1989. "Science Tourism in Costa Rica," *Annals of Tourism Research*, vol. 16, pp. 205-215.

Langholz, J. 1996. "Economics, Objectives, and Success of Private Nature Reserves in Sub-Saharan Africa and Latin America," *Conservation Biology*, vol. 10, no. 1, pp. 271-280.

McLaren, D. 1998. *Rethinking Tourism and Ecotravel*, Kumarin Press, West Hartford, Connecticut.

Monet, R. L. 1996. Costa Rica. *International Tourism Reports*, vol. 4, pp. 5-24.

Morrison, P. 1994. "The Monteverde Area of Costa Rica: A Case Study of Ecotourism Development," master's thesis, Latin American Studies and Community and Regional Planning, University of Texas at Austin.

Norris, R. 1994. "Ecotourism in the National Parks of Latin America," *National Parks*, pp. 33-37.

Opala, K. 1996. "Body Set Up to Boost Tourism," *Daily Nation*, September 13, Nairobi, Kenya.

Orams, M. 1995. "Towards a More Desirable Form of Ecotourism," *Tourism Management*, vol. 16, no. 1, pp. 3-8.

Pisam, A., S. Sussmann. 1993. "Does Nationality Affect Tourist Behavior?" *Annals of Tourism Research*, vol. 22, no. 4, pp. 901-917.

Place, S. 1991. "Nature Tourism and Rural Development in Tortuguero," *Annals of Tourism Research*, vol. 18, no. 2, pp. 186-201.

Place, S. 1995. "Ecotourism for Sustainable Development: Oxymoron or Plausible Strategy?" *GeoJournal*, vol. 35, no. 2, pp. 161-173.

Redfern, P. 1996. "Tourism Board Maps Out Strategy," *Daily Nation*, November 19, Nairobi, Kenya.

Rovinski, Y. 1991. "Private Reserves, Parks and Ecotourism in Costa Rica," Chapter 3 in T. Whelan's, *Nature Tourism*, Island Press, Covelo, California.

Rymer, T. 1992. "Growth of U.S. Ecotourism and Its Future in the 1990s," *Florida International University Hospitality Review*, vol. 10, no. 1, pp. 1-10.

Salant, P., D. Dillman. 1994. *How To Conduct Your Own Survey*, John Wiley and Sons, Inc., New York.

Shumaker, N. 1995. "Democratizing the Tourist Dollar in Costa Rica," *Annals of Tourism Research*, vol. 22, no. 2, pp. 479-489.

Sindiga, I. 1995. "Wildlife-based Tourism in Kenya," *The Journal of Tourism Studies*, vol. 6, no. 2, pp. 45-55.

Sindiga, I. 1997. Personal communication, May 27, 1997.

Sirakaya, E. 1997. "Attitudinal Compliance with Ecotourism Guidelines," *Annals of Tourism Research*, vol. 24, no. 4, pp. 919-950.

Sorenson, R. 1991. Overseas Adventure Travel, Inc., case study 9-391-068, Harvard Business School, Boston, Massachusetts.

Tourism Canada. 1995. *Adventure Travel in Canada: An Overview of Product, Market and Business Potential*, Canadian Tourism Commission, Ottawa, Ontario, Canada.

Wallace, G., S. Pierce. 1996. "An Evaluation of Ecotourism in Amazonas, Brazil," *Annals of Tourism Research*, vol. 23, no. 4, pp. 843-873.

Watkins C.W., A.M. Barrett, R. Smith, J.R. Paine. 1996. "Private Protected Areas: A Preliminary Study of Private Initiatives to Conserve Biodiversity in Selected African Countries," World Conservation Monitoring Centre. ftp:ftp.wcmc.org.uk/products/wcmc.publications/reports/private_protected areas/text.htm

Wells, M.P., K.E. Brandon. 1993. "The Principles and Practice of Buffer Zones and Local Participation in Biodiversity Conservation," *Ambio*, vol. 22, nos. 2 and 3, pp. 157-62.

Wesche, R. 1996. "Developed Country Environmentalism and Indigenous Community Controlled Ecotourism in the Ecuadorian Amazon," *Geographische Zeitschrift*, vol. 84, nos. 3 and 4.

Western, D. 1997. "Ecotourism at the Crossroads in Kenya," *The Ecotourism Society Newsletter*, Third Quarter, pp. 1-4.

Wight, P. 1993. "Sustainable Ecotourism: Balancing Economic, Environmental, and Social Goals Within an Ethical Framework," *The Journal of Tourism Studies*, vol. 4, no. 2, pp. 54-65.

Wight, P. 1996. "North American Ecotourists: Market Profile and Trip Characteristics," *Journal of Travel Research*, vol. 34, no. 4, pp. 2-10.

Wilson, M.A. 1987. "Nature Oriented Tourism in Ecuador: Assessment of Industry Structure and Development Needs," Southeastern Center for Forest Economics Research, Research Triangle Park, North Carolina.

World Conservation Monitoring Centre. 1997. "Protected Areas Summary: 1996," Global Protected Areas Summary. http://www.wcmc.org.uk.

Yee, J.G. 1992. *Ecotourism Market Survey: A Survey of North American Ecotourism Tour Operators*, The Intelligence Centre, Pacific Asia Travel Association, San Francisco, California.

Zurick, D. 1995. *Errant Journeys—Adventure in a Modern Age*, University of Texas Press, Austin, Texas.

New Directions in the Ecotourism Industry

Megan Epler Wood

Since ecotourism was identified as a travel phenomenon in the mid-1980s, the industry has quickly broadened from an emphasis on raw encounters with the outdoors to include highly structured, guided programs that provide travelers with an in-depth understanding of the natural environment and local cultures.

This chapter presents trends identified through observations made by the author, and informal interviews conducted with various industry leaders selected for their insights and successes in the business. Those interviewed do not represent a random sample. Nonetheless, because the interviews were conducted with opinion leaders in the North American ecotourism industry and with highly respected business owners in several destinations throughout the world, the trends noted are likely to be quite representative of how the industry is evolving. However, trends can be ephemeral. One reviewer commented that this is a dynamic and shifting industry, and it is important to separate established from advancing practice (Weber, 1997). This chapter gives a brief overview of industry structure and a brief introduction to standard ecotourism industry practice. The remaining text documents how the business of ecotourism is advancing as of 1997. Readers seeking to come to a basic understanding of how ecotourism businesses operate may wish to consult additional reference materials. (Patterson, 1997; McKercher, 1998).

There has always been a market for nature and culture tourism. Many ecotourism industry players cut their teeth on handling the first wave of naturalist-explorers who were only concerned with seeing the next bird on their life list or the most remote village in Tibet. But the clientele for ecotourism is both deepening and broadening simultaneously. Interviews with a range of North American tour operators show that the market is attracting inexperienced travelers who have, for example, seen National Geographic television programs and want a quick introduction to the natural world. At the same time, ecotour companies must appeal to experienced ecotourists who are finding that basic naturalist programs are no longer satisfactory.

Not surprisingly, the ecotourism industry is responding by offering more general interest ecotourism programs, while also developing a wide range of special interest educational programs with topics as diverse as jungle pharmacology, Incan archaeology and savannah ecology. But the specialization of ecotourism goes well beyond educational forums. Operators are developing programs in cooperation with local communities by working with indigenous organizations and local non-governmental groups. They are adding new types of transport, such as live-aboard boats that can cruise the most remote regions of the Amazon with low impact. And they are developing an increasing array of ecolodges that meet high environmental standards, operate out of the most remote destinations without access to city infrastructure, and devote profits and staff time to community development issues.

INDUSTRY STRUCTURE

A discussion of the direction of ecotourism cannot be instructive without a brief description of the industry's structure. The ecotourism industry has evolved its own set of names for the contractual players who deliver the ecotourism product. While, for the most part, the titles of these players, shown in Table 2.1, are not really different than those in the travel industry as a whole, each segment of the ecotourism industry has defined itself somewhat differently than the mainstream travel industry. And, each must be analyzed separately when considering who will have the most influence on the ecotourism product of the future.

TABLE 2.1
BASIC ECOTOURISM INDUSTRY STRUCTURE

Travel Agents/Retailers
Outbound Tour Operators
Inbound/Ground Operators
Ecolodges/Accommodations
Local Vendors

Travel agents operate for the most part as store-front, retail operations, historically selling both land and air travel products for a 10% commission (though this rate has been changing). Outbound tour operators are the primary sales and marketing organizations within the ecotourism industry. They are sometimes called wholesalers, as they sell tours in packages. But, in fact, almost all outbound tour operators in the ecotourism industry work at the retail level via direct mail, advertising, catalogues and other consumer marketing mechanisms. Outbound tour operators create the brand names that sell ecotourism. They provide all pre-departure information to the customer, but the majority do not handle the details of the tour operation once the client lands in the destination country or countries. Outbound operators generally charge a 30-40% mark-up on the travel products they represent plus additional mark-ups on the wholesale prices they receive on airline tickets.

Inbound operators are the companies that carry out all the day-to-day details of tour operations in destination countries. They contract all in-country services necessary to operate the tour, including tour guides, vans, hotels, restaurants and local air transportation. The inbound tour operator creates the local itinerary, either on a standardized or customized basis, working hand-in-hand with outbound operators to meet the needs of the clientele. They charge a 30-40% mark-up on the in-country services they contract.

Ecolodges are an emerging sector of the larger accommodations industry. (Efforts to create a new paradigm within the lodge industry will be discussed later in this chapter.) Lodge owners identified by research (Russell et al., 1995) as running "nature dependent" lodges offer pricing that includes meals, local guides and nature interpretation activities. Many depend on outbound tour operators to provide a steady, predictable client base. Others are also adept at marketing directly to independent travelers via guidebooks, local publications, local hotels and national tourism boards.

Local vendors, contracted by the ecotourism industry, provide a wide variety of services including ground transportation services, specialized recreation services (e.g., horses, boats, rafts, bikes and skis), and the heart and soul of the ecotourism industry—guides. These businesses are often village-based micro-businesses with a small amount of capital and low overhead. Most highly trained ecotourism guides work at the national level, on a freelance basis, moving between the best ecotourism companies, operating as entrepreneurs in their own right, and marketing their services to the highest bidders. Each inbound operator tries to keep a "stable" of the best guides working steadily, to be on hand as their core guiding staff. Some companies rate their guides according to ability, for example as "master naturalists, naturalists, service guides, river guides, platform-certified guides, and guides that specialize in specific destinations such as Tortuguero, Monteverde, or Corcovado" (Costa Rica Expeditions, 1997). Local ecotourism guides working at the community level, who can meet the standards of the international ecotourism industry, are still few and far between (Jenks, 1997).

TRAVEL AGENTS IN THE ECOTOURISM INDUSTRY

Travel agencies have never played a big role in the nature travel or adventure travel industry, and are not having much luck moving into the ecotourism market either. According to Jan Cooper, Vice President of Special Expeditions, "95-98% of travel agents can't even get their hands around it" (Kalosh, 1997). The primary reasons travel agents do not sell ecotours are that they lack the time to educate themselves about these highly specialized products, and they lack the motivation to do so since many ecotour operators have not worked with retail travel agencies in the marketing of their products.

The travel agency world is coping with reduced commission structures on air tickets and the ballooning of direct travel booking on the Internet. Some ecotourism agencies have begun to charge clients a per-ticket transaction fee to make up for their loss of commission, and are stressing their expertise in providing information on the best ecotours (Kietzke, 1998). Whether agents can attract new business by getting involved in the ecotourism industry is still an open question. One way for agents to play a more significant role in ecotourism is by working with "preferred suppliers," whereby agents can team up with the tour operators they feature to offer the best rates and high-quality itineraries (Kutay, 1997). This can put the agent into a better position to play an informed role, without paying for in-house expertise (Kalosh, 1997).

OUTBOUND TOUR OPERATORS AND THE CHANGING FACE OF THE ECOTOURISM MARKET INDUSTRY

Many U.S.-based outbound tour operators were delivering a nature tourism product long before the word "ecotourism" was coined. In the early 1980s, longer trips (2-4 weeks) were more likely to sell, even if some hardship and uncomfortable conditions were involved. However, "there has been a market shift to softer and shorter trips," says one tour operator (Abbott, 1997). Another tour operator comments: "In the past five years, we have been offering shorter journeys. One week is quite common now." (Lindblad, 1997). This change parallels changes throughout the tourism industry in general.

The best statistics indicate that the average age for an ecotourist is about 50 (Wight, 1997), which indicates that the baby boom generation is the target market. These ecotravelers are in the midst of the most work intensive years of their lives. It is therefore not surprising that customized, short trips for the busy professional couple, often with children, are in demand. As this generation ages and retires, a shift back to longer trips may once again take place.

The industry has never been more able to respond to the current demand for short ecotourism journeys. For example, local infrastructure in high-demand destinations such as Peru, Argentina and Kenya, is now much better organized. Clients can be easily shuttled to a remote destination from a capital city gateway on a regularly scheduled in-country flight, instead of an expensive charter. Vans are now available to transport passengers to local properties. And local guides understand how to deliver high-quality, short courses on their destinations, making the novice more comfortable (Kutay, 1997).

For the consumer seeking a quick trip to multiple remote locations, "a consistent level of service across many destinations can be offered, and operators often assist with lots of arcane plane connections" (Weber, 1997).

Despite the hurried behavior of the typical baby boom ecotraveler, there is also a greater demand for more in-depth travel experiences. Operators all comment that travelers are looking for genuine experiences, a sense of discovery, better cross-cultural communication, and more sophisticated learning opportunities.

Improving the educational content of existing tours is a prime opportunity for most ecotour operators. Archeology programs are just one example of specialty tours that are attracting new people, "...people whose avocation may be archeology and may have found this type of academic program only through universities in the past" (Rodney, 1997). A whole new audience for a tried-and-true destination, Machu Picchu in Peru, can be created by offering an in-depth education program, such as Wilderness Travel's "Incas in Peru." In this program, tour group members met for two-and-a-half days in Cuzco, Peru, to hear lectures from experts on Inca culture. They then had the choice to participate in a variety of special treks and tours with these experts to the key sites discussed in their lectures.

Some of the first ecotourism workshops to successfully use nature as a classroom were International Expeditions' successful Rainforest Workshops in Peru. Today, this program continues to expand to meet the demands of specific fields, including the medical and pharmacological disciplines. "Ecotourism is practically becoming a branch of formal education, with close linkages to continuing education programs. This is opening up significant new opportunities for more crossover between the education community and the ecotourism industry of the future" (Ryel, 1997).

ITINERARY DEVELOPMENT AND CONSERVATION ISSUES

Ecotourism is a "responsible travel" paradigm that has helped to transform the nature and adventure tourism industry. The Ecotourism Society published "Ecotourism Guidelines for Nature Tour Operators" (1993) to make clear ecotourism operators' responsibilities to the environment and local communities. Developing successful itineraries that meet ecotourism standards is becoming part of the "modus operandi" of the industry. Ecotourism companies focus on creating itineraries, "with a view to exploring new areas, providing opportunity to local businesses, and giving the visitor the best possible ecotourism experience, while minimizing the impact on natural and cultural resources" (Horizontes, 1996). While there are still many token gestures made by ecotourism companies, travelers increasingly expect educational content and environmental sensitivity.

As the field becomes more crowded, the impacts of ecotourism on vulnerable flagship species and highly popular destinations are becoming a growing concern. More ecotour operators are using private reserves to avoid the crowds and the mismanagement associated with national parks. Companies in Kenya are increasingly seeking buffer zones, outside of national parks and reserves, for their safari camps, due to the well-known crowding in destinations such as Maasai Mara and Amboseli. "This has created new partnerships with local Maasai communities who lease their campsites directly to safari camp operators, and thus receive direct benefits from ecotourism development" (Cheli and Peacock Safaris, 1996). Because 70% of Kenya's wildlife lives outside the parks and protected areas (Western, 1997), these community partnerships are a crucial avenue to the survival of the majority of wildlife in Kenya.

However, the use of private reserves funnels funds away from the public protected area system. Well-to-do landowners with the resources to put aside land for conservation are benefiting by working with tour operators in a system of partnerships that is expanding throughout East and Southern Africa. "There are land operators in Kenya who no longer use public reserves, preferring to contain an entire itinerary within their own network of private ranches" (Weber, 1997). This leads to questions about how the public land system will be supported and whether such private systems allow for local community benefits. Some private landowners in Kenya and Southern Africa have responded by working with local communities on development projects (Christ, 1997) and by assisting with the establishment of community lodges in the buffer zones of private reserves (Epler Wood, 1998a).

Ecotourism companies can be caught in complicated circumstances relating to government policy regarding the conservation of flagship species and famous destinations. In Baja, Mexico, regulators shut down all grey whale watching on weekends in an effort protect the species. According to tour operators, this encouraged corruption and a general atmosphere of lack of respect for regulations (O'Brien, 1997). Similar situations have been well documented in such destinations as the Galápagos Islands, where well-intended, strict regulations limiting tourism resulted in more under-the-table business for unscrupulous operators (Miller, 1991). In these cases, ecotour operators have formed coalitions, such as the Galápagos Tour Operators Association (The Ecotourism Society, 1991) and the Asociación de Kayakismo y Ecoturismo in Baja (The Ecotourism Society, 1997a), to work with local non-governmental organizations and government to: bring sensible regulations to the region that protect tourism-targeted species and the ecosystem, help provide for better monitoring of tourism impacts by working with local communities, and encourage fair visitor management policies that respond to industry needs and the need for local development.

CRITICAL ROLE OF THE INBOUND OPERATOR

The inbound operator takes primary responsibility for the client during the trip, ensuring that the traveler receives a high-quality, educational experience meeting ecotourism standards. If inbound operators employ superior guides, they can market this valuable commodity to their outbound clients. The inbound operator also needs a network of lodges that are comfortable but rustic, offering a good backcountry experience with excellent wildlife viewing, while meeting standards of environmental sustainability. There is still a shortage of lodging in this category in many ecotourism destinations.

Hotel development seems to be one area that many inbound tour operators are entering out of necessity. Oswaldo Muñoz, President of Nuevo Mundo Expeditions in Ecuador, recalls that the need for good remote jungle lodging forced Metropolitan Touring into the hotel business back in 1974. Muñoz now owns two of his own hotels. He built the Cuyabeno River Lodge in 1990 because of the need to: collaborate with officials to monitor and control the region; diversify his company's investments; to secure good accommodations with healthy, sanitary food for his guests; and provide job opportunities for local settlers and indigenous people (Muñoz, 1997).

Albert C.K. Teo, Managing Director of Borneo Ecotours in Malaysia, began promoting wildlife tours to Sabah, Malaysia, in 1988. He offered overnight trips, using basic accommodations owned by another tour operator, but began to hear complaints that his clients were receiving sub-standard food, services and accommodations during the overnight segment. Teo decided to build his own lodge in 1993 and was determined to deliver consistent, high-quality service with a strong respect for the environment. He now distinguishes his tours from his competitors' by highlighting a stay at his company's own Sukau Lodge, which uses solar energy, has an active conservation program, and hires local people.

Many inbound tour operators concentrate almost entirely on working with outbound operator partners. For example, group itineraries that are custom-designed for outbound clients constitute 75% of the business for Costa Rican tour operator, Horizontes (Horizontes, 1996). However, there is an indication in the marketplace that inbound tour operators may become increasingly involved in marketing directly to the consumer. This is particularly true because of the Internet. The World Wide Web provides low-cost marketing power to companies that are located in remote destinations. Although it will have a major impact on how the ecotourism business is transacted in the future, it is still too early to document what changes will take place. "Trustworthiness is still what sells an ecotourism product, not an undocumented name on the Internet" (Ryel, 1997). Outbound tour operators have an advantage currently, because they have already succeeded at establishing a brand name with the general public. But inbound operators are seeing increasing success by bringing their products directly to the consumer via the World Wide Web.

ECOLODGE TRENDS

Ecolodges were once a scarce commodity. But the demand for environmentally friendly accommodations has developers working busily behind the scenes to create a whole new generation of hotels and lodges for the ecotourism customer. One of the most interesting experiments in this field is being launched by a non-profit organization, the Conservation Lodge Foundation (CLF), whose capital investment is provided by one non-profit source, the Pew Foundation. After completion of a five-year feasibility study, development is now underway in Florida, with other lodges on the drawing boards for Hawaii, the Yucatan Peninsula and the Bahamas. The organization's primary goals, according to a CLF report (1997), are "to produce an ongoing source of revenue that helps finance conservation, to provide alternative sources of employment and income for residents of ecologically sensitive areas, to develop models of low-impact architecture, and to educate people about terrestrial and marine systems."

Florida is the site of the first lodge because of the state's progressive land acquisition policy. "The state has acquired thousands of acres of important land for conservation," says John Yost, Executive Director of CLF, "but they have no funds for management. This is where our policy of support can make a difference."

Another development company looking to create a new brand name in ecotourism resorts is Footprints International. This company is angling to build as many as 12 four-star ecoresorts in three years. It is focusing on easy-to-reach destinations for the U.S. consumer, including the U.S., Bahamas, Mexico, and the Caribbean. A brand name for safe, all-inclusive ecotourism destinations, driven by an educational approach, and appropriate for families, could garner a new market for ecotourism. Footprints has associated itself with such environmental non-profit organizations as The Nature Conservancy and the National Audubon Society. These organizations have agreed to co-market the resort chain in return for a guaranteed percentage on resort bed-nights. In addition, Footprints customers will be given the option of making a donation to partner conservation organizations when paying the bill for their stay. Along with the Footprints specialist advisory committee (of which the author was a member), the environmental organizations are being asked to provide guidance to the resort on site selection, environmental standards and community relations. These partnerships are likely to provide the resort with an environmentally sound image while substantially broadening its marketing capability.

The South Africa-based Conservation Corporation of Africa (CCA) is the most successful ecolodge chain in the world, and the only existing hotel chain that is working hard to meet the full range of ecotourism standards. Founded by two brothers who inherited Londolozi Farm in South Africa, the company presently manages twenty-two properties in East and Southern Africa (Christ, 1997). Approximately ten of these hotels were built by CCA; the remainder are properties purchased for renovation and refurbishing. In 1990, the brothers met a financier willing to put his expertise in international investment to work for conservation. This financier attracted investor Gordon Getty, who put up about one-third of the $26 million investment that launched CCA (Ginsberg, 1997). The properties are relatively small—eighty percent have no more than twenty rooms—but all charge rates of at least $200 per person, per night (including game drives and food). This elite formula has turned impressive profits, $200,000 of which was invested annually in a separate non-profit organization for community development called the Rural Investment Fund (RIF). The RIF has leveraged more than $1 million for community development projects associated with the rural communities surrounding the CCA lodges. It has assisted with primary school expansions, a community center and a health clinic serving some 30,000 people. It has also worked with local people to establish micro-enterprises, such as a brick making cooperative, and a sustainable charcoal and a bush-clearing project (Christ, 1997). Up to now, CCA has concentrated on Africa's premiere safari destinations, such as South Africa, Botswana, Tanzania and Kenya. However, they are branching out to new countries, such as heavily-poached Zambia, where ecotourism is almost nil. Zambia will be a stiff test for CCA's philosophy. If ecotourism can cut poaching, it will have reduced a problem that has resisted the efforts of the richest environmental organizations in the world and Africa's best governments (Ginsberg, 1997). (See more on CCA in Chapter 8—editor.)

While ecoresort chains are clearly becoming a reality, small, home-grown ecolodges are still the heart of the ecotourism lodging market. A new generation of small-scale lodges in remote destinations is seeking to meet high environmental standards, and to sustain long-term, very personal relationships with local communities. These lodges are constructed with little disturbance to the natural landscapes. They are minimizing all use of non-renewable resources; reducing, reusing and recycling their waste products; and working to ensure that their clientele have a harmonious stay within a pristine environment that they are striving to protect through proactive environmental policies. Tortillis Camp in Kenya was built with local materials, "not from stripping local resources, but by carefully sourcing the best materials from different areas of Kenya" (Cheli and Peacock Safaris, 1996). Lapa Rios in Costa Rica consists of 14 bungalows on a 1000-acre private forest reserve composed of more than 80% virgin rainforest. The owners plan to "dedicate the private reserve as a wildlife refuge under the 'La Vida Silvestre' law and to develop a rainforest products program, etc." (Lapa Rios, 1996). Kapawi in Amazonian Ecuador has set out to replace destructive environmental activities, such as cattle ranching, and to provide monthly economic means of support to the indigenous Achuar community. "In 15 years the owners of Kapawi will recover their investment, turning over the lodge and its marketing network in entirety to the Achuar" (Kapawi, 1996).

NGOs and Their Impact on the Industry

The ecotourism industry has seen the influence of non-governmental organizations (NGOs) as: purveyors of standards within the ecotourism field; marketers of non-profit, outbound travel programs; specialists in the field of sustainable development (often with funding from major international donor institutions such as the World Bank); and developers of ecotourism projects in destination countries. One of the most compatible working relationships can be found between the staff of the travel departments of the major environmental NGOs and ecotourism outbound operators. Travel/development professionals hired by the NGOs work to develop customized trips for their membership in close partnership with the commercial outbound tour operator sector. This symbiotic relationship has built strong, productive ties between the ecotourism industry and the conservation sector.

The private sector also has played a growing role of support, not only for international NGOs, but also for a variety of local NGOs. Collaborative relationships can be established to produce conservation results. Special Expeditions looks for individual projects where the company can creatively use their resources. In Baja, Mexico, "there was a need for a community-based guide training program. Special Expeditions worked with the NGO, RARE, to deliver it" (O'Brien, 1997).

While NGOs are increasingly entering the tourism business, their development of ecotourism projects is "at an awkward stage, because there is inadequate experience in business, and a refusal to acknowledge business needs. This is leading to discouragement and territoriality" (Ryel, 1997).

Patricia Leon encounters a pressing need for business planning expertise on a daily basis as part of her work as Enterprise Development Specialist for the Latin America Division of The Nature Conservancy (TNC). TNC has 60 non-governmental partners in Latin America, 36 of which are requesting assistance with feasibility studies for ecotourism development. Nine of these partners presently have some kind of tourism infrastructure. Leon does much of the pre-feasibility and feasibility work for these local NGOs. Her mission is to provide local NGO leaders with a knowledge base that will allow them to conserve their land, while generating income at the same time. She has, however, found it extremely difficult to locate appropriate personnel with which to work in these areas, as there seems to be a deep-seated mistrust of business approaches and business planning when applied to the work of conservation. Leon says, "It takes time to establish trust, and sometimes we need an intermediary to work on a long-term basis with the NGO."

There is no question that most of these NGOs need the assistance of the private sector in order to succeed. But evidence is mounting throughout the developing world that NGOs are picking their projects based on criteria incompatible with travel industry needs. Millions of dollars of funding may be going to projects that are not commercially viable. Often projects are supported for a two-to-five year time period and then left to be managed locally. NGO project leaders often lack the experience or expertise to make a travel enterprise tick. In the end this can create a harmful scenario in which local communities' hopes are greatly raised and then dashed by project failure (Epler Wood, 1998c).

The goal is clearly for NGOs and private enterprise to work in closer harmony, particularly during the project development phase. Some of the most creative new ecotourism projects result from this kind of collaboration. Kurt Kutay is one entrepreneur that has worked with both international and local NGOs to market projects such as the Scarlet Macaw Trail in Guatemala and the Tambopata region of Peru. Customers, however, are still not rushing to visit these exciting new projects, since, as Kutay comments, "It is not easy to convert places that do not have word of mouth." The ability of the NGO to draw attention to its own project site through the media is critical. "What will help to sell new places," says Kutay, "is the attention received outside of the operator's own promotions."

Another symbiotic relationship between NGOs and tour operators that has not truly blossomed is the opportunity for local NGOs and tour operators to work together to raise funds for conservation and development projects by arranging presentations for visiting tour groups. In the Green Evaluations study in Ecuador undertaken by The Ecotourism Society it was found that less than 50% of the tourists were asked for contributions to local conservation initiatives during the trip (Norman et al., 1997). Tom O'Brien comments that local NGOs are often unprepared to make presentations, even when a company such as "Special Expeditions is ready to match all visitor contributions dollar for dollar."

GROWING ENTREPRENEURSHIP IN COMMUNITIES

Community-based ecotourism projects are growing in number throughout the world (Wesche, 1996; Sproule, 1996), and communities are becoming increasingly adept at providing services to tour operators, from craft production to recreation services. The issue of building better relationships between local communities and tour operators is still one of the biggest challenges in the industry (Epler Wood, 1998c). Tour operators are faced with a growing set of expectations from communities, and are in the process of learning how to manage community relationships appropriately.

"The attitude of tour operators who are forced to give to locals can become resentful when local communities are not accepting their responsibility to protect resources" (Muñoz, 1997). Muñoz is one of the few to voice his concerns on this subject openly, but many other tour operators in Africa and Asia have privately mentioned similar concerns. A sense of betrayal is often quietly expressed among private-sector entrepreneurs after they make elaborate plans to assist communities and then find that the locals are in no way meeting their obligation.

According to Tom O'Brien, there are "unreasonable expectations for payments to communities. Prices can escalate too rapidly, resulting in the entire community losing a steady stream of visitors" (O'Brien, 1997).

But model long-term relationships with local communities do exist. Wilderness Travel has been working successfully with the Cofan of Amazonian Ecuador for nineteen years. The entire business relationship is handled through Randy Borman (Abbott, 1997), an Ecuadorean-born missionary's son. Borman married a Cofan woman and led a group of four Cofan families away from the oil boomtown of Lago Agrio to the rainforest village of Zabalo, where they still reside. He has acted as an ideal intermediary for the Cofan in many regards, working, for example, with Wilderness Travel to determine pricing by first establishing the economic needs of his community. His goal is not to interrupt their culture but to provide economic incentives that will give it value. In the beginning, Borman acted as a tour guide, but now many other Cofan provide these services. Groups take long day hikes into the rainforest with these guides, often finding peccaries, and visiting a small lake to look for salt licks. Borman joins the group at the beginning and the end of the tour to fully interpret the experience of being within this complex ecosystem in the company of indigenous people. (See more on the Cofan in Chapter 9—editor.)

Other operators comment about the unique, local intermediaries who provide close ties to local communities. Profits are going to conservation causes in many instances, and local communities are able to maintain their traditional livelihoods. In Kenya, Maasai leaders are becoming extremely adept at working with safari companies. In certain instances, Maasai leaders educated in the Western traditions of accounting and legal agreements return to their communities to act as intermediaries with outside donors and businesses. In the buffer zone of Amboseli National Park, the group ranches are forming a confederation with the encouragement of a unique, Western-educated Maasai man, Kokoi Olitiptip. Their goal is to better coordinate tourism and other business ventures for the group ranches. Each group ranch already accounts for funds earned for the community by donor funds, tourism and other businesses, and each is publishing annual financial reports. Lease agreements for safari camps with tour operators are providing significant revenue to the Maasai in park buffer zones, and the Maasai are well aware that safari camp lease compensation exists for the protection of the wildlife which exists on their lands.

SETTING STANDARDS

One of the biggest challenges for the ecotourism industry is coming to a consensus on whether a set of standards can be established allowing for the certification and monitoring of legitimate ecotourism businesses (Epler Wood, 1998b). The Ecotourism Society published Guidelines for Nature Tour Operators in 1993 and is also in the process of researching guidelines for ecolodges, marine ecotourism, and community participation in ecotourism. Because the industry is so new, there is still a great deal of practical work and research needed on what can be achieved by responsible businesses and what cannot. The Ecotourism Society carried out a national Green Evaluation Program with the Ecuadorean Ecotourism Association in 1996 and 1997 to begin to answer these questions (Norman et al., 1997). Australia is the first country to achieve national ecotourism accreditation. This program, launched in 1996, is managed by The Ecotourism Association of Australia (Chester, 1997). Costa Rica is in the process of creating its own green seal program for hotel properties (Instituto Constarricense de Turismo, 1997).

It is unreasonable to expect that the small-business ecotourism sector will be able to fully support its own accreditation programs. In fact, funding for such programs is lacking in most parts of the world. Ecotourism Society research indicates that tour operators and lodges are willing to pay for evaluation or accreditation (The Ecotourism Society, 1993), but the fees will never cover a full-fledged program that includes independent assessment of performance. On-site monitoring would be tremendously expensive to undertake locally, nationally or internationally. Several private companies and some international trade groups are entering the certification game by offering green seals for a straight fee, or green seals tied to a consulting program that can help ecotourism accommodations green their hotel property. While these programs vary in their usefulness, they do not solve the problem of setting genuine, nationally or internationally accepted standards of accountability.

All destinations in large demand are now aware of ecotourism standards (Ryel, 1997), and the industry knows of the need for legitimate accreditation programs. In fact, in countries such as Kenya, the industry is beginning to demand assistance from the government at the national level to establish legitimate accreditation programs for ecotourism. Given the costs of launching a program with proper monitoring and assessment design, it is critical that the private sector work with government to achieve the goal of national accreditation. Using the guidelines established by The Ecotourism Society or the Ecotourism Association of Australia will make the process of launching a program less research intensive, and increase the likelihood of a system that meets international standards.

FINDING NEW MODELS OF SUSTAINABILITY

The ecotourism industry has entered into many innovative projects in the last five years, leading to conservation and sustainability. An association of private reserve managers in Costa Rica is working directly with the Costa Rican Park Service to assist ecotourism business owners who now manage significant biological resources (The Ecotourism Society, 1997b). The ACEER foundation in Peru is conserving over 100,000 hectares of pristine rainforest, because of the success of International Expeditions' Rainforest Workshops. This innovative foundation is deeply involved in local education and development issues and is now a leading conservation player in the country of Peru. Big conservation organizations—such as World Wildlife Fund and IUCN—that once shunned ecotourism because of its perceived unreliability as a conservation tool are now establishing ecotourism projects throughout the world. Even the development banks have tried to enter the field. However, they have found that, more often than not, small-scale ecotourism is difficult to fund since banks typically back projects in the $5-10 million category and above (Hawkins, 1996).

Ecotourism can be an important part of the larger formula for sustainable development. It already supports a thriving set of businesses that do not need financial assistance from the NGO or development communities. But despite the NGO and development community's will to design the ecotourism industry within the prospectuses of their conservation and sustainability annual reports, ecotourism sustainability models must first and foremost be generated by the private sector itself. Finding new models of sustainability is a process that must have all the stakeholders involved at the initiation of the project. While the local community is certainly a vital stakeholder, so is the private sector.

Many questions still remain about how tourism revenues can be attracted to important biological regions that lack basic infrastructure, guide and hospitality worker training, business management and finance expertise, and marketing savvy. Managers of non-governmental organization programs who are seeking sustainable development alternatives for their constituents are encountering hundreds of sites that need such assistance throughout the biologically important zones of the world. Development aid would best be focused on helping the local people hone their tourism-related business skills, while at the same time addressing their urgent education and development needs. The private sector should likewise receive support to concentrate on what it does best—develop, implement and market successful, responsible ecotourism products. If this is done in designated "ecotourism development zones" that have been targeted by the NGO community, government, and the private sector, the chances for success will be greatly improved.

CONCLUSION

Ecotourism is a creative, entrepreneur-driven industry in its first generation of development. There are no publicly owned ecotourism companies to date. Even the largest ecotourism lodge development chains are still launched with no more than $25 million, and most lodges are built for well under $1 million. Nearly all ecotourism company owners founded their businesses and remain today as owners.

Efforts to create franchises and brand names for ecotourism are still in the early phases of development. And, so, for the time being, it remains a very personal business of individual owners, not large corporations. For many communities and local vendors, it is an opportunity for development that introduces them to the business world for the first time.

Few ecotourism businesses apparently engage in strategic planning. They are managed by good instincts and gut reactions. Partnerships between local destination-based companies and international marketing companies are the fundamental relationships in the industry—relationships often based on personal contacts and friendships as much as strategic business alliances.

The growth of interest in ecotourism within the baby boom generation indicates that the industry will be handling an increasing market demand for at least the next twenty-five years. The industry will, therefore, have to grow and mature during this time, and deftly handle the transition to the next generation of owners. However, it is unlikely that the ecotourism industry will ever be patterned after multi-national business, wherein shareholders become the primary beneficiaries of corporate profits. The demands of working within rural, remote destinations seem to attract owners who enjoy a business not entirely oriented to the bottom line and one that is very personalized and innovative. This augurs well for an industry that should continue to attempt to meet high standards of conservation and sustainable development world wide.

REFERENCES

Abbott, B. 1997. Personal communication, Wilderness Travel, Berkeley, California.

Cheli and Peacock Safaris. 1996. "Tortilis Camp Statement on Ecotourism," Nairobi, Kenya.

Chester, G. 1997. "Australia Ecotourism Accreditation Off and Running," *The Ecotourism Society Newsletter*, Second Quarter.

Christ, C. 1997. Personal communication, Atlanta, Georgia.

Conservation Lodge Foundation. 1997. Annual report, Pew Foundation, Philadelphia, Pennsylvania.

Costa Rica Expeditions. 1997. Promotional catalogue, San Jose, Costa Rica.

Eagles, P., B. Higgins. 1998. "Ecotourism Market and Industry Structure," *Ecotourism: A Guide for Planners and Managers*, vol. 2, The Ecotourism Society, North Bennington, Vermont.

(The) Ecotourism Society. 1991. International Galápagos Tour Operators Association, *The Ecotourism Society Newsletter*, First Quarter, The Ecotourism Society, North Bennington, Vermont.

(The) Ecotourism Society. 1993. "Ecotourism Guidelines for Nature Tour Operators," The Ecotourism Society, North Bennington, Vermont.

(The) Ecotourism Society. 1997a. International Update, *The Ecotourism Society Newsletter*, Third Quarter, The Ecotourism Society, North Bennington, Vermont.

(The) Ecotourism Society. 1997b. "Costa Rican Network of Natural Reserves," *The Ecotourism Society Newsletter*, Fourth Quarter, The Ecotourism Society, North Bennington, Vermont.

Epler Wood, M. 1998a. "Ecotourism at a Crossroads: Charting the Way Forward," Nairobi, Kenya, The Ecotourism Society, North Bennington, Vermont.

Epler Wood, M. 1998b. "Ecotourism Accreditation: Progress and Prospects," The Ecotourism Society, North Bennington, Vermont. Forthcoming.

Epler Wood, M. 1998c. "Meeting the Global Challenge of Community Participation in Ecotourism: Case Studies and Lessons from Ecuador," *America Verde* series, The Nature Conservancy, Arlington, Virginia.

Ginsberg, S. 1997. "Millionaire Getty Takes Aim at Wealthy Ecotourists in New African Big Game Hunt," *Business and Environment*, San Francisco, California.

Hawkins, D.E. 1996. "Ecolodge Finance and Investment Strategies," *The Ecolodge Sourcebook*, The Ecotourism Society, North Bennington, Vermont.

Horizontes. 1996. "A Brief History of Horizontes," San Jose, Costa Rica.

Instituto Constarricense de Turismo (ICT). 1997. "Certification for Sustainable Tourism: Establishing a Competitive Advantage," Department of Sustainable Tourism, Ministry of Tourism, San Jose, Costa Rica.

Jenks, B. 1997. "The Question of Local Guides in Latin America," *The Ecotourism Society Newsletter*, Second Quarter, The Ecotourism Society, North Bennington, Vermont.

Kalosh, A. 1997. "With the Aging of the Baby Boomers, It's a Huge Market!" *ASTA Industry and Environment*, Alexandria, Virginia.

Kapawi. 1996. *Kapawi Newsletter*, Guayaquil, Ecuador.

Kietzke, M.J. 1998. *The Travel Specialists*, Winter 1997-1998, vol. 11, no. 7.

Kutay, K. 1997. Personal communication, Wildland Journeys, Seattle, Washington.

Lapa Rios. 1996. Brochure, Puerto Jimenez, Costa Rica.

Lindblad, S. 1997. Personal communication, Special Expeditions, New York City, New York.

McKercher, R.D. 1998. *The Business of Nature-based Tourism*, Hospitality Press, Melbourne, Australia.

Miller, A.C. 1991. "Galápagos at the Crossroads," *The Ecotourism Society Newsletter*, Spring, The Ecotourism Society, North Bennington, Vermont.

Muñoz, O. 1997. Personal communication, Nuevo Mundo Expeditions, Quito, Ecuador.

Norman, W.C., E. Frauman, L. Toepper, E. Sirakaya. 1997. "Evaluation Program and Compliance of Nature Tour Operators," The Ecotourism Society, North Bennington, Vermont.

O'Brien, T. 1997. Personal communication, Special Expeditions, Seattle, Washington.

Patterson, C. 1997. "The Business of Ecotourism," Explorer's Guide Publishing, Rhinelander, Wisconsin.

Rodney, R. 1997. Personal communication, Wilderness Travel, Berkeley, California.

Russell, D., C. Bottrill, G. Meredith. 1995. "International Ecolodge Survey," *The Ecolodge Sourcebook*, The Ecotourism Society, North Bennington, Vermont.

Ryel, R. 1997. Personal communication, International Expeditions, Birmingham, Alabama.

Sproule, K. 1996. "Community-based Ecotourism Development: Identifying Partners in the Process," *The Ecotourism Equation, Measuring the Impacts*, Yale University, New Haven, Connecticut.

Weber, W. 1997. Personal communication, Journeys, Ann Arbor, Michigan.

Wesche, R. 1996. "Developed Country Environmentalism and Indigenous Community Controlled Ecotourism in the Ecuadorian Amazon," *Geographische Zeitschrift*, vols. 3 and 4, no. 84, pp. 157-168.

Western, D. 1997. "Ecotourism at a Crossroads in Kenya," *The Ecotourism Society Newsletter*, Fourth Quarter.

Wight, P. 1997. "North American Ecotourists: Market Profile and Trip Characteristics," *Journal of Travel Research*, Spring, vol.. 24, no. 4, pp. 2-10.

Introducing the Undercapitalized World of Interpretation

Simon McArthur

Interpretation is not information. It's not a visitor center, a sign, a brochure or the pointing out of attractions as they pop into view. It's not a slide show or a role play. These are merely techniques by which interpretation can be delivered. Interpretation goes beyond focusing on the oldest, the largest or the rarest. It goes beyond telling people the name of a plant species or the age of a building. Interpretation is a coordinated, creative and inspiring form of learning. It provides a means of discovering the many complexities of the world and our role within it. It leaves people moved, their assumptions challenged and their interest in learning stimulated. Good interpretation is still thought about at breakfast the next morning, or over the dinner table the following week. If properly delivered, interpretation not only enriches an ecotourism experience, it provides the foundation for remembering and reliving it. In this way, interpretation should be the nexus of an ecotourism experience.

However, interpretation remains at the periphery of ecotourism. Like other components of the ecotourism equation, interpretation has taken a back seat to environmental components such as minimizing visitor impact and maximizing the application of ecologically sustainable development. While this chapter offers no criticism on the worth of these initiatives, it notes with some irony their ultimate requirement for clients to be sufficiently environmentally aware as to be supportive and prepared to pay for such initiatives. High-quality interpretation reinforces this by interpreting the ecotourism operation, clients, behavior, and the values and assumptions of both client and operator. Therefore, high-quality interpretation is fundamental to making ecotourism sustainable.

DEFINING INTERPRETATION

There is no single definition of interpretation that has been adopted by most practitioners. Nonetheless, the definitions noted in Table 3.1 collectively reflect most of the elements which interpreters have considered when developing interpretive experiences. The most widely quoted definition has been that of Freeman Tilden (Tilden, 1977), but different organizations use different definitions to reflect their cultural and organizational value base. For example, some tourism operators use interpretation as a value-adding exercise to attract higher-yield markets. Heritage management organizations utilizing interpretation emphasize communicating conservation values and a conservation ethic. Cultural tourism operators stress cultural sensitivity and accuracy. Ecotourism operators typically attempt to position themselves in the middle of all of these perspectives—many ecotourism operations dabble in interpretation to:

- value add and better position their product;
- attract high-yield markets;
- reflect personal or organizational ethics; or
- appease the heritage management organization responsible for the property on which they operate.

TABLE 3.1
DEFINITIONS OF INTERPRETATION

DEFINITION	SOURCE
An educational activity which aims to reveal meaning and relationships through the use of original objects, by first hand experience, and by illustrative media, rather than simply to communicate factual information	Freeman Tilden (Tilden, 1977)
The communication process which aims at helping people to discover the significance of things, places, people and events...helping people change the way they perceive themselves and their world through a greater understanding of the world and themselves	Colonial Williamsburg, USA (MacFarlane, 1994)
The process of stimulating and encouraging an appreciation of our natural and cultural heritage and of communicating nature conservation ideals and practices	Queensland National Parks and Wildlife Service (Davie, 1993)
Creating an experience or situation in which individuals are challenged to think about and possibly make decisions concerning natural resources	Vermont Department of Forests, Parks and Recreation (MacFarlane, 1994)
A means of communicating ideas and feelings which helps people enrich their understanding and appreciation of their world, and their role within it	Interpretation Australia Association (1995)

Like the term "ecotourism," interpretation has been plagued by a great deal of emphasis on definition at the expense of getting on with establishing authenticity, quality and accountability. To deliver these elements it is useful to briefly explore how interpretation evolved, how it has been used, and why it has generally not been given the chance to meet its potential.

THE DEVELOPMENT OF INTERPRETATION

Tourism operators added interpretation to their product long before the terms interpretation or ecotourism were generated. Many tours integrated it as a core part of the travel experience without realizing it—calling it guiding, rather than interpretation.

Until the 1980s the most influential developments in interpretation occurred in the United States (Machlis and Field, 1992; Regnier et al., 1992). The initial flourish was largely stimulated by Ernos Mills, who worked as a nature guide in Colorado's Rocky Mountains between 1889 and 1922. Mills was a keen advocate of monitoring his visitors' behavior and responding accordingly. He prompted guides to concentrate on inspiring visitors by communicating big ideas rather than masses of unrelated information. Mills developed principles and techniques which laid the foundation for interpretation. In the early 1970s, the evolving ideas and principles were assembled into a publication specifically about interpretation. *Interpreting our Heritage* by Freeman Tilden was the first book written solely to define the profession of interpretation, and contained two concepts central to the philosophy of interpretation: that "Interpretation is the revelation of a larger truth that lies behind any statement of fact;" and that "Interpretation should capitalize on mere curiosity for the enrichment of the human mind and spirit" (Tilden, 1977).

In the 1970s and '80s, the prominence of interpretation in Australia was boosted as elements of North American national park-based interpretation were somewhat blindly imported and replicated across the country (O'Brien, 1985). One of the consequences of this blind importation has been a focus on developing non-verbal interpretation (McArthur, 1995) which has typically involved self-guiding brochures and infrastructure such as visitor centers and interpretation signs. These techniques have tended to be untargeted to any market segment and have lacked the continual feedback that is a natural part of verbal interpretation. Most have quickly aged and now require upgrading to remain relevant and stimulating to a more discerning audience (McArthur, 1996). Thus, while the 1970s and '80s may have increased the provision and profile of interpretation, the investment failed to pay the dividends it could have.

As visitor interest in the environment grew in the mid- to late-1980s, a small part of the market became interested in doing more than looking at natural areas—it wanted to understand more about them. In response, some tourism operators began to elevate the role of interpretation, contributing to the creation of the niche market experience known as ecotourism. Ecotourism operators utilized interpretation as a value-adding or niche-marketing exercise which, in turn, provided access to high-yield markets (Commonwealth Department of Tourism, 1994). A select few ecotourism operators and most protected area managers today use interpretation to achieve a number of other objectives, such as to:

- differentiate their tourism product from more mainstream products;
- attract higher yield clientele;
- enrich the visitor's experience and increase client satisfaction;
- assist the visitor in developing a keener awareness, appreciation and understanding of the area being visited;
- contribute to an ethical position held by the operation;
- encourage thoughtful visitor behavior to ensure the experience is a sustainable one;
- increase guide satisfaction;
- promote public understanding of protected area management; and
- gain more favorable treatment from heritage managers (Sharpe, 1982; O'Brien, 1985; Beckmann, 1988, 1992; Saunders, 1992; Forestry Tasmania, 1994).

Interestingly, the comparative degree of emphasis that each organization places on these objectives is rarely discussed or debated.

PLANNING INTERPRETATION

There are some very clever, innovative interpretation techniques used by ecotourism operators. Unfortunately, the effectiveness of these techniques has generally been limited by poor planning (Trapp et al., 1991; Veverka, 1992; Hall and McArthur, 1993). Without adequate planning, most interpretation programs eventually become ineffective and ultimately redundant. Evidence of poor planning is easy to spot. For example, touring programs that are not thematically linked will appear disjointed, while untargeted commentaries will fail to stimulate anyone in particular. Planning binds the three essential ingredients of ecotourism-based interpretation together— the audience, the message and the technique. These three components define the three key planning stages required for successful interpretation.

STEP 1: DEFINING A TARGET AUDIENCE

The first step is to define a target audience. Every client is different. Each one has different values, different interests, and different mental and physical characteristics. Operators using interpretation must recognize client differences—as well as commonalities—and tailor the interpretation to those predicted traits. This tailoring works under the same principles as target marketing. Identifying a target audience ensures that the interpretation is relevant to each client's needs.

The most typical criteria for identifying the characteristics of the operation's key clientele are demographic characteristics—particularly age, education level and origin. This information is useful in suggesting familiarity with the heritage site, likely participation in certain recreational activities and comprehension level. However, demographics alone are rarely sufficient to develop effective interpretation. For example, people access information and understanding from many other sources outside of their formal education, and may not necessarily be any more familiar with a heritage site just because they live within the region. Psychographic characteristics reflect more personal traits about people, such as their motivations and expectations for undertaking an activity, or their attitude, level of interest and understanding about a topic.

Ecotourism operators can define their own profile of a target audience, or they can adopt one from existing market segmentation studies. The most relevant segmentation systems for interpretation are those developed for state or national tourism organizations. Tapping into market segmentation systems already used by the tourism marketing sector permits interpreters to 'share the same language' and design programs accordingly. This means that each part of the ecotourism product, such as the marketing, the infrastructure or transport, the interpretation and the monitoring of performance, can be tailored to a definable audience. An example of a target audience derived largely from psychographic characteristics is shown in Table 3.2.

STEP 2: DETERMINING CONTENT AND ITS STRUCTURE

The second step is to determine and structure the content of the interpretation. The content of ecotourism-driven interpretation typically needs to reflect an amalgam of four components:

- the natural area being visited;
- the characteristics of the target audience;
- the expectations of the natural-area manager; and
- the interests of the interpreter (Hall and McArthur, in press).

The natural area provides the baseline source of interpretive content, but typically there are limits to how much can be accessed in the time available and how much can be presented to clients because of their varied interests and capabilities. If the client has no interest, the interpretation will fail to gain their attention or provide enjoyment. In addition, there may be a need to incorporate information and perspectives from relevant natural-area managers. These managers may well expect a discussion of issues which they face in managing the site. Incorporating these expectations helps ensure that the managers see merit in the operation, which is likely to result in a more favorable and constructive relationship.

TABLE 3.2
EXAMPLES OF PSYCHOGRAPHIC CHARACTERISTICS
OF A TARGET AUDIENCE FOR INTERPRETATION

CHARACTERISTIC	EXAMPLES
Group Size	• Prefers small group of 10-15 clients per tour
Demographics	• Tertiary education and professional employment • Annual income of $35,000-$55,000
Experiential Interests	• Be fully briefed along the way to the destination • Participate in a variety of related short walks of up to one hour • Sit down in a relevant area and have a detailed discussion
Content Interests	Most clients have a strong interest in: • The reason native vegetation grows so slowly • The relationship between the plants and indigenous peoples • Uses of plants for medicinal purposes
Experiential Dislikes	• Being rushed or having no choice in the way they experience the area
Mental Capabilities	• In comfortable conditions clients lose interest after about 20 minutes • In uncomfortable conditions, clients need more briefing before and after the experience to minimize exposure • Clients struggle to understand interpretation without a map
Bonuses Well Received	• Special guest interpreters who offer highly specialized expertise or local perspective

The clearest way to develop and refine the content is through a structure which, at its most basic level, defines the key messages to be communicated. A structure featuring a theme, a group of messages, and an overall concept is recommended. The use of a theme ensures that the interpretation is relevant to the site and is comparatively easy to create since it reflects the characteristics of the site being interpreted (Hall et al., 1993). A theme might be the rainforest, geology, indigenous culture. Themes do not on their own specify the content to be presented: this is done by a group of messages which add definition and clarity, and present a statement of meaning. Concepts group the messages together (like a topic sentence) to provide a framework that leads to greater visitor understanding. Examples of interpretive theme, concept and message are shown in Table 3.3.

STEP 3: SELECTING A TECHNIQUE

The third and final step is to select and refine the technique. Selecting the technique is typically—and incorrectly—undertaken before the first two stages. Many interpreters who attempt to define their audience and content usually try to make

TABLE 3.3
EXAMPLES OF THEME, CONCEPT AND MESSAGE

INTERPRETIVE THEME	INTERPRETIVE CONCEPT	INTERPRETIVE MESSAGE
Mixed, wet and gallery rainforests	Forests are naturally dynamic systems because they can incorporate change into those systems	Forests are complex natural systems
Mixed forests that have received natural impacts	Forests are naturally dynamic systems because they can incorporate change into those systems	Forests have changed their diversity, structure and complexity in response to fire

them fit their preferred technique. Most interpreters spend their planning effort on developing a technique at the expense of audience identification and content development. This is tantamount to producing a television advertisement with no notion of who it should reach, or designing a lodge without visiting the site where it is to be built. For this reason, a description of techniques has been held back until this point in the chapter.

DIFFERENT FORMS OF INTERPRETATION

There are countless ways in which to interpret, yet in essence they all strive to utilize either verbal or non-verbal techniques, or a combination of both. Verbal techniques revolve around face-to-face communication and include: commentary, discussion, performance-based entertainment, creative activities, theme parks (the living/breathing re-creation of a setting), and television and radio programs. Non-verbal techniques include: publications, self-guiding signs, audio/visual presentations, visitor centers, museums, paintings, sculptures, and the location, design and construction of buildings.

Different techniques have different strengths and weaknesses. Verbal interpretation is generally considered to be far more powerful than non-verbal because the interpreter can respond to changing conditions, particularly the diverse needs of individual clients. Verbal interpretation is also more effective at delivering complex and abstract ideas and is generally considered by most audiences to be of greater interest and thus greater value. Most interpretation provided by ecotourism operations is verbal.

Choosing the type of verbal technique is more difficult and should reflect an amalgam of content, audience needs, site opportunities and restraints, and the individual(s) responsible for delivering it. For detailed coverage of interpretive techniques, the reader is referred to Ham (1992). Four techniques have been highlighted for their relevance and use in ecotourism: organized talks and discussions, guided tours and walks, theatrical productions and the location and design of buildings.

ORGANIZED TALKS AND DISCUSSIONS

A talk is designed to be conversational so that it sounds spontaneous and informal. Talks typically introduce an audience to a subject. For example, talks often present basic orientation and introductory information about a site, object or experience. Discussions tend to assume a greater level of audience interest and awareness about the subject. They therefore use communication techniques which are more intellectually challenging, such as question and answer formats, debates and audience participation in demonstrating a relationship or process. The most frequently used settings for talks and discussions are amphitheaters, visitor centers, museums and campfires. The most frequently used props are the interpreter's own character and enthusiasm, slides and heritage objects (the favorite being a cute, small animal). Talks can be almost instantly modified to reflect the feelings of the interpreter, the characteristics of the site and, of course, the attitude of the audience. The interpreter may be feeling happy, highly charged or reflective. The site may be influenced by the time of day, the weather or the presence of additional stimuli. The audience may be influenced by group size, age and level of interest. Therefore, one of the greatest strengths of organized talks and discussions is that they are very personal and responsive to changing circumstances.

GUIDED TOURS AND WALKS

Guided tours and walks are a specialized form of organized talks and discussions. The principle difference is that they are more mobile, linking various attractions together and thus maintaining a more stimulating environment for learning. Tours are typically more visually rewarding in their presentation of heritage (offering the opportunity to stop and photograph), but require more commitment from the audience, since traveling from place to place can be exhausting. The most popular tour form is vehicle based (usually a bus or four-wheel-drive auto), allowing the group to travel conveniently to a series of attractions within a given region. These attractions, typically distinctive and accessible, are introduced by the guide, with general commentary on their significance. The next most popular tour form is the guided walk. People choose this over a vehicle when they wish to gain a more intimate experience with heritage. Because walkers have greater access to the guide, the character of the guide is critical, and the interpretation must be more adaptable and comprehensive. Tours typically last from one hour to a week, although some continue for months. The majority of guided tours are undertaken commercially by tourism operators rather than heritage managers. Unfortunately for interpretation, this has largely resulted in most tours being dominated by sightseeing. The learning component has been relegated to unusual tidbits of information rather than an interlinked learning and discovery experience (the exception in the past five years has been the emergent ecotourism industry, which has improved the quality of commentaries to the extent that some now offer genuine interpretation).

THEATRICAL PERFORMANCE

Theatrical performance is one of the more creative and artistic forms of learning. The performance may be delivered at the heritage site or it may be a traveling show, delivered in places such as shopping centers, libraries and local parks. If the performance is part of a broader educational initiative then it is usually delivered at a school as the centerpiece to a combination of educational activities that lead up to, and then build on, the performance. The most frequently targeted audience is children and the most popular form of performance is the play or pantomime.

The play or pantomime may be undertaken by a drama group, school group or additional staff from the heritage management organization. The interpreter usually writes the storyline, and produces sets and costumes with help from an artist. In the case of educationally orientated plays, the costumes and sets are made by the children acting in the production.

A second form of theatrical performance for children is the puppet show. While musical performance may not be as direct a communicator of heritage values and issues, it can transcend the age of the audience to maximize audience reach. The strength of musical performance may therefore lie in its simplicity and opportunity for each individual to shape their own interpretation.

Another form of theatrical performance is storytelling. More than just the reading of a book to a group of children, storytelling is a very personal recollection of a story as told by an individual with substantial imagination and acting skill.

Most theatrical performances ensure that messages are kept simple and positive. A narrator is often used to ensure that the events are simplified and the message communicated directly through narration as well as indirectly through the acting. Animals, plants and buildings are anthropomorphized so that children can relate to them as individuals with feelings. Performances are usually repeated many times over for new audiences and may attract interest from other stakeholders such as organizers of special events, or a restaurant or guest house owner operating close to the heritage site. A more subtle advantage of theatrical performance is that even though it is pitched at children, adults are also usually exposed as part of their parental role of accompanying and supporting their children.

BUILDING LOCATION, DESIGN, CONSTRUCTION AND OPERATION

Demonstration can be an equally powerful form of interpretation to conventional communication. Perhaps one of the most frequently used non-verbal interpretive techniques by the ecotourism sector is demonstration of messages through clever location, design, construction and operation. In the case of developments, buildings are a kind of sculpture, reflecting local characteristics and demonstrating ecologically sustainable principles. The positioning of buildings can help highlight particular views, which in turn emphasize a certain aspect about the surrounding landscape. The construction can draw upon local timber, rock, even natural color dyes to demonstrate that ecotourism is about fitting into the local environment. The design can utilize light, space and even sound to help guests interact with the environment or each other. The operation and its interaction with guests can serve as a highly interactive interpretive experience. The case study of Maho Bay in the Virgin Islands (page 79) helps demonstrate this interpretive technique.

STRUCTURING AND TUNING A GUIDED TOUR

Guided tours are typically structured around the direction in which the vehicle or path takes the group. However, this random order creates a random story. Imagine ripping the pages out of a book, throwing them up in the air, then beginning the story with whatever page you find first; that's what it's like to experience unstructured tours. A logically structured guided tour typically has four key components: staging, introduction, body and conclusion. Table 3.4 outlines the purpose of these four components and the likely response from the client.

Structured, guided tours deliver a sequential, logically flowing story. For example, a geographically based structure might start at a national level, go regional, then local, and, finally, site-specific. A land management-based structure might start with basic biological components, then go into ecological systems, followed by environmental issues, and finally, possible solutions. Structured tours link places and messages in as logical and entertaining a fashion as possible. This helps build ideas into frameworks, and builds emotions from cursory interest into a major focus that leads to a highlight.

Therefore, structuring involves looking at a variety of ways of visiting and experiencing a site or combination of sites. Sometimes several sites can offer the same story, sometimes a site can offer only one. So it's a good idea to start with the sites offering only one message, then identify sites that have generic messages. Some interpreters sit down with the operator and create a table with the sites in one column and the messages they could offer in another. They then cut out each site and its messages, and place them on a map with the existing route marked. They then look at how the structure would ideally fall out, and how this would effect the order of stops. The aim, then, is to try and re-order the sequence of stops, or try out a different direction, different focal points and varying durations at each stop.

Another dimension to structuring a guided tour is deciding what to say at each stop. It often helps to begin with a sentence which focuses the group on an

TABLE 3.4

PURPOSE AND LIKELY CLIENT RESPONSE FROM VARIOUS PARTS OF A GUIDED INTERPRETIVE EXPERIENCE

PART OF TOUR	PURPOSE	CLIENT RESPONSE
Staging	• Greet and welcome clients, establish rapport • Provide strategic information about the experience to follow	• Feel accepted and more comfortable • Feel more confident that needs will be taken care of
Introduction	• Create interest in interpretive theme and introduce conceptual framework by linking the key parts of the tour with the key interpretive messages • Update the most pertinent strategic information	• Realize that the tour is coordinated and may be mentally stimulating • Feel more confident that all needs will be taken care of
Body	• Link the interpretive messages to pertinent sites and objects of interest • Open discussions up for questions • Update the most pertinent strategic information	• Feel that each part of the tour is related and has a purpose • Feel intellectually stimulated • Feel confident and comfortable that focus can remain on enjoyment
Conclusion	• Reinforce the conceptual framework by linking the various attractions with interpretive messages • Seek feedback on the experience • Leave follow-up questions for further thought by clients • Thank clients for their involvement	• Feel awakened and enlightened • Feel that operator cares • Feel that ideas can be taken away and further built on • Feel that operator cares

object, scene or idea. Asking a question of the group is an excellent way to focus attention since clients are usually curious about each other's behavior, and thus the responses of other group members. The main part of the interpretation can then follow, in which key features are described according to the message about to be delivered. Another popular idea is to determine the answer to the question by integrating a participatory activity into the discussion, such as counting the growth rings on a tree stump. The next stage involves linking the description just outlined to an interpretive message. This reveals a meaning for the outline and at least part of the reason for stopping. The next stage, the transition, brings the current discussion to an end, signals the group to move on and foreshadows the next stop. It will ideally link to an earlier experience or discussion to increase client expectations and help them mentally or even physically prepare for the experience to come.

Fine tuning a guided tour goes beyond the tour structure to acknowledge and work with the characteristics of each individual guide. The first step is, therefore, to identify the guide's unique characteristics in order to help him/her create a personal style of interpretation, which will result in client responses specific to that experience. Table 3.5 outlines some of the types of guides often practicing interpretation. A guide who understands his/her personal characteristics can then use them to advantage to further color the interpretation. For more detail on both guiding and guiding techniques, the reader is referred to Lingle Pond (1993).

TABLE 3.5
TYPES OF GUIDES IN ECOTOURISM

TYPES OF GUIDES	TRAITS
Cops	• Perceive visitor activity as threatening to local environment • Tolerate audience by issuing many rules for visitor behavior
Machines	• Regurgitate the same performance without modification • No spontaneity, personal input or adaptation to audience variation • Disapprove of client questioning or requests to change format
Know-it-Alls	• Focus on imparting information to suggest superiority • Cannot admit lack of knowledge, prefer to pretend
Hosts	• Perceive audiences as guests • Offer all clients the opportunity to speak and contribute to discussions • Happily take questions, chat and joke • Respond to audience needs, even if it means deviating from planned interpretation (Adapted from Ham, 1992)

ISSUES FACING INTERPRETATION

Unfortunately, interpretation in the ecotourism sector has yet to reach its full potential. Some of the reasons for this unfulfilled potential include:

- a lack of understanding of what interpretation is and can be;
- poor information about the market;
- a narrow scope of content;
- unimaginative and generic communication techniques;
- a lack of feedback and evaluation culture; and
- limited training opportunities that reflect operator needs (adapted from Hall and McArthur, in press).

Table 3.6 identifies a number of hints to maximize the effectiveness of interpretation.

LACK OF UNDERSTANDING OF WHAT INTERPRETATION IS AND CAN BE

While most ecotourism operators are keen to offer brochures, displays, guides and resource material, they have a limited understanding of how interpretation is different from information. The attention applied to interpretation has been focused largely on interpretive content, as various interest groups lobby for particular value systems and supporting insights to be included. What has been most conspicuous in its absence is how to stimulate and move clients—what some call the spiritual dimension.

Compounding this problem is the lack of attention that interpretation receives in marketing material. Promotional material tends to acknowledge the interpretive

Table 3.6
Hints for Interpretation

Hint	Explanation
Expect to increase time proportionally to group size	The larger the group, the more complex their movements and responses—allow more time for preparation and presentation.
Set the theme and concept early in the experience	Interpretation and clients need warming up; an introduction using maps, figures and artifacts helps establish realistic expectations.
Carry communication helpers	Visual aids and objects help explain complex ideas. They can also help with interpretation in a vehicle or building when the weather doesn't permit the group to be outdoors.
Involve the client	Getting clients to do something makes them feel more involved and, thus, more useful and interested.
Ensure that sentences are short, positive and active	Client satisfaction can easily diminish if they feel they are being lectured to or are hearing repeated information.
Avoid jargon and technical terms	Most interpretive language should be able to be understood at a sixth or seventh grade reading level (11 or 12 years old).
Be relevant to the heritage being interpreted	Try to keep on-site interpretation centered around a real object on which clients can focus and with which they can, ideally, interact.
Read body language and respond accordingly	Signs of disinterest during interpretation include straying from the group, engaging in individual conversations, and playing with objects.
Give equal attention to clients	Involve all clients at some stage, if something is raised in a small group discussion that could be useful for all, reintroduce it later on.
Continually seek feedback	Ask people what they thought of the interpretation and the experience and keep probing until something concrete is gained which can be used to further tailor the service.
Be accurate in your knowledge; get to know your subject	Some clients will ask questions that demand a thorough explanation of the subject being discussed. Acknowledge your limits, and, if necessary, consult other resources. Then, come back to your client.
Ensure neutrality and cover a range of views	Ecotourism clients are often exposed to management issues—avoid making individual value judgements. If clients request an opinion, make sure you acknowledge it as such.
Continually involve clients	Interpretation needs mental, and—ideally—physical, involvement of the audience. Ask for contributions via client recollections, the handling of artifacts or assistance with activities.

medium rather than the interpretive experience. For example, many ecotourism product brochures promote the use of guides, naturalists and rangers, and acknowledge their scientific qualifications or experience with the site. However, few brochures explain the nature of the interpretive experience, such as what clients will be confronted with and how they will feel during and after the event. Operators are unlikely to improve basic interpretation until those who already provide sophisticated interpretation acknowledge it in their promotions and thus gain a marketing advantage.

POOR INFORMATION ABOUT THE MARKET

Interpreters are communicators. Therefore, the more an interpreter knows about his/her audience, the more tailored the communication should be. Demographic information typically collected by the tourism industry is useful but it is the psychographic characteristics that are of most use. Unfortunately, psychographic characteristics are rarely collected and made available to interpreters (Hall and McArthur, in press), who literally dream of being able to access information on awareness, interest and attitude towards the environment and the way it is managed, as well as the preferred communication and learning styles of their audiences. Most monitoring by the tourism industry tends to be economically oriented and most market research is oriented around choice of tourist product rather than experience. The solution is obvious: integrate more psychographic and experiential aspects into monitoring and research, and feed this information directly to those providing the experience, which of course includes the interpreters.

NARROW SCOPE OF CONTENT

Interpretation should be thorough and balanced in its presentation and discussion of content. Unfortunately, most interpretive content remains unnecessarily narrow in its scope. An examination of the content of interpretation within many ecotourism experiences suggests that this issue has manifested itself in several guises, including:

- a preference to address natural rather than cultural values;
- a reluctance to present cultural heritage as a living entity;
- a general reluctance to recognize and respond to relevant issues confronting heritage managers; and
- a preoccupation with interesting facts and figures, rather than concepts that build frameworks with which to understand complicated processes (Hall and McArthur, 1996).

Given limitations of space, this chapter will address the last of these issues—preoccupation—with interesting facts and figures, but refers the reader to Hall and McArthur (1996) for coverage of the previous three.

Imagine visiting a gallery, stopping in front of a painting, and being told only that it was painted on a 16 x 12 canvas, covered with 12 acrylic paints, framed in oak and hung with cable wire and two locking bolts. Now, imagine two people acting out the moment captured in the painting with so much passion and conviction that you felt emotionally moved by their very actions towards each other, then inspired by the revelation that you felt to be unfolding before you. At the end of this performance, imagine applauding, even before you recognized your decision to do so.

Interpretation within a narrow scope, and involving only facts and figures, does nothing for the experience, and, thus, adds little value to the product— here, ecotourism. While the presentation of building ages, species names and tree heights are interesting and in demand, they do not promote "understanding," a term frequently quoted in interpretation objectives. As indicated earlier, interpretation goes beyond the presentation of facts and figures; regardless of how enjoyable the technique makes them. At the cognitive level, interpretation is about building conceptual frameworks from which people can assimilate information and give it meaning. At the emotional level, interpretation is about creating interest in the world, and feelings that give color to cognitive dimension. The problem is deeply rooted among those interpreting natural heritage, which is generally dominated by ecological paradigms, and is conservative in its adoption and integration of other perspectives (Griffiths, 1990). Interpretation within ecotourism is highly susceptible to this issue. Guides tend to narrow their focus to a specific site and its geographic, geological and biological elements. Furthermore, the sources of interpretive content are highly internalized with very little contribution coming from external stakeholders, let alone the community (Masberg and Savige, 1996).

Nonetheless, some interpreters have made genuine and substantial attempts to broaden their focus. Many can draw upon their diverse backgrounds (e.g. education, sociology, cultural studies and the arts) to quickly detect and respond to alternative perspectives. There are several ways for interpretation to broaden its content focus. These include:

- structuring interpretation around a story, selectively communicating only what is needed to tell the story;
- presenting a range of perspectives;
- sharing with the audience the perspective of the interpreter, then asking the audience for their perspective; and
- tackling issues and conflict over how to resolve them.

The first technique has been covered in interpretive planning. To achieve it requires the interpreter to play a key role in the creation of the experience, as opposed to logistics such as where the toilets are located or where morning tea will be served. The interpreter can then create a story and select stops that demonstrate each key part of the story. The second way is to present a range of perspectives other than the central one typically told. This means the interpreter must let go of his/her own value systems and perspectives, and communicate those of others. This is done to some extent when contrasting indigenous and non-indigenous perspectives, but could easily be further broken down to include different indigenous tribes, city and rural populations, industry and government. This technique can be easily expanded when the interpreter briefly covers his/her own perspective, then asks for that of each of the audience members. This technique can help differentiate and bond the audience, and also provides the interpreter with more useful information about the market for further adaptation of the interpretation. The fourth technique to widen scope and attract audience interest is to tackle issues. By presenting relevant political and social aspects of heritage and how it is managed, visitors can start to become aware of the role that the community has in heritage management. This awareness allows them to develop a more informed opinion, and, ultimately, an opportunity to become more effectively involved in the decision making. The case study on the Belize Zoo (page 82) demonstrates how content can be successfully broadened.

UNIMAGINATIVE AND GENERIC COMMUNICATION TECHNIQUES

Surrounding the creative world of interpretation are many heritage managers and ecotourism operators who either don't have the time, understanding or commitment to generate new interpretive experiences. The tendency has been to duplicate techniques generated elsewhere and blindly import them into a new product. Good examples are the prevalence of visitor centers, self-guided walks that use brochures or interpretation signs, and of course the "look to your left then look to your right," guided tour. While the setting may be different, the technique is remarkably similar to other places the visitor has been. These techniques have thus become so copied and generic that they can actually reduce the quality of other elements of the ecotourism experience. Generic techniques are more likely to be selected when interpretive planning is avoided or neglected. Planning helps shape who the target audience is and what needs to be communicated. Armed with this information, it is difficult to justify generic techniques.

LACK OF FEEDBACK AND EVALUATION CULTURE

Most research suggests that the considerable effort made to ensure enjoyable interpretive experiences for visitors has been worthwhile (McArthur, 1995). However, there has been little research or evaluation undertaken in these countries to determine whether interpretation helps to develop visitor understanding and modify attitude and behavior. This objective often forms the crux of why many heritage managers fund, develop and maintain interpretive programs. Without the benefit of feedback, it is difficult to determine the current value and ongoing potential of interpretation. This scenario reduces the likelihood of ecotourism operators elevating the role and corresponding support for interpretation.

Limited Training Opportunities That Reflect Operator Needs

One of the reasons for these issues not being adequately addressed is that people are not being adequately trained to recognize them, let alone deal with them. Training in interpretation is generally limited to developed countries yet even here there are significant problems. A recent survey of ecotourism operators in Australia revealed limited opportunity for training in interpretation and some alarming attitudes towards education and training (Crabtree and McArthur, 1997). In terms of supply, training was found to be dominated by two ends of the spectrum: complex and time consuming courses, or extremely basic courses of limited long-term application. In terms of demand, ecotourism operators were not found to be helping the situation. Operators surveyed downgraded the importance of training in "soft" skills, such as interpretation, for "hard" skills such as duty of care and workplace safety. In addition, there were limited incentives to entice people to undertake training and those that had were not gaining professional recognition. Until training is improved and made accessible to most ecotourism operations, the quality of interpretation will be dependent upon the personal communication skills and commitment of the individual.

CASE STUDIES

HARMONY RESORT, MAHO BAY, VIRGIN ISLANDS—The Harmony Resort was designed and built using ecologically sustainable development principles. Many people have read about the extensive use of recycled materials, the minimal use of products and water, and the highly efficient waste management system. Each guest room has been carefully located to maximize the interaction that each guest feels with the external environment. Formal interpretation includes signs identifying locally indigenous vegetation, signs suggesting ways for guests to minimize water use, an evening slide presentation and discussion, and tours of the facility to learn about its construction, self-sufficiency and conservation practices. Guests are also offered a training program called the "Four Hour Worker Program," where they can work and learn about "responsible tourism." The operation of the resort is itself a continual interpretive activity. For example:

> ➤ vegetarian entrées are offered so that guests can experience eating lower down the food chain;

↩ cookies are baked in a solar oven and sold in the store with accompanying background information on the oven itself;

↩ guests are asked to clear their plates and separate their food scraps for composting; and

↩ water is carried from centrally located spigots to the tent cottages so that guests are totally aware of their consumption.

The delivery of interpretive messages is much stronger when guests are asked to change their behavior first, and are then offered the rationale. Placing responsibility with the client is a far more interactive and empowering interpretive approach than doing something for them and, maybe, telling them a little about it. Perhaps the most empowering interpretive practice of all is getting guests to manage their own consumption of energy. Each guest room has a computer to establish and monitor the energy use within the room. Guests can then decide how they will meet their budget in terms of which facilities they will use and for how long.

However, it should be stressed that Maho Bay sometimes suffers from the same issue in interpretive delivery as most operators—consistency. Many of the interpretive initiatives just outlined lack staff training and conviction. Reports from visiting ecotourism specialists suggest poor staff familiarity with their surrounding environment, poor introduction to the computer monitoring system and a management culture that sometimes suggests guests should not have their island escape impinged upon by interpretation. While ecological sustainability can be delivered with smart technology, interpretation requires an operator to instill in his/her staff a cultural commitment for continual creativity and self-improvement.

RARA AVIS, COSTA RICA—Rara Avis is an ecotourism operation in the heart of Costa Rica. Only a small proportion of the 1,335 hectares is utilized with the majority being principally managed for preservation. The ownership and use of private property stimulates a wide range of initiatives to be undertaken which may not have been permitted or encouraged within lands managed by the government. Both the areas managed by Rara Avis and Selvatica back onto the Braulio Carrillo National Park, which provides a guaranteed backdrop for tourism marketing and a backup habitat for plants and animals.

Though it takes less than an hour to drive from San Jose to within 15 kilometers of Rara Avis, it's a further four hour crawl by tractor along a muddy corduroy trail to the rainforest lodge. The difficult access creates a significant operating cost and tends to reduce the attractiveness of a visit to all but the adventurous. Nonetheless, in an effort to turn the trip to a marketing advantage, promotional brochures are written to read "come prepared to get wet, muddy, tired and enchanted."

Tourism is the bread and butter of the Rara Avis operation. The Waterfall Lodge was developed to provide comfortable accommodation for ecotourists with a strong desire to learn about the rainforest and its ongoing management. The eight rooms each have their own bathroom and balcony overlooking the rainforest. Tilley lamps create an ambient atmosphere for sumptuous homestyle Costa Rican meals and relaxed conversation. Typical capacity is just 16 people and demand in the peak season (December to July) outstrips supply, with two out of three booking requests unfulfilled.

During the day, clients are given the opportunity to undertake a variety of guided walks led by a guide with a thorough understanding of the rainforest, as well as the political, social and cultural issues facing its ongoing management. The other components of the Rara Avis initiative typically become the main discussion points and many visitors leave inspired to take some form of action that will contribute to its ongoing success. A large range of natural history publications are also available for those with a keen interest in learning more for themselves.

In addition, clients can explore the rainforest canopy via a motorized flying fox known as 'The Webb.' The transportation system was originally designed to carry scientists through the canopy and is suspended 150 feet above the ground between two large trees 700 meters apart. Researchers staying at Rara Avis act as operators and guides for clients to travel across the valley. This typically results in the clients gaining a firsthand experience of both the work and the mindset of researchers, which in turn contributes towards a change in understanding and attitude that may not have been achieved through more conventional guiding methods. The $25 per-person fee is returned to fund ongoing scientific monitoring and research programs.

The reason for presenting Rara Avis as best practice interpretation is because the entire experience is interpretive. While the guided tours are stimulating and demonstrate excellent communication skills, it is the integration of every aspect of the operation that keeps clients totally stimulated and absorbed. Instead of having neat packages of learning and relaxation, the Rara Avis approach breaks down the boundaries and allows the client to explore what and how they would like to discover.

OZ TOURS, AUSTRALIA—A Daintree Tour in far north Queensland run by Oz Tours melds a sense of adventure to attract client attention, then holds attention through the use of confronting perspectives and controversial issues. Part of the tour involves a stop at the treetop home of marine biologist Walter Stark. Walter takes the group on a walk through a mangrove swamp, then boats them up the Daintree River a short distance. He purposely stops the boat to drift in shallow water in the middle of the river, creating a sense of adventure, and stimulating client attention so they are ready for the interpretation. He then squats at the front of the boat and delves into the role of disturbance in maintaining species diversity within the two systems, before challenging various notions of environmental sensitivity. Clients are captivated, moved and enlightened. They leave discussing some of the ideas generated in the interpretation.

BELIZE ZOO, BELIZE—The Belize Zoo is located an hour north of Belize City. It contains a rich collection of over 100 animals native to Belize, some of which are endangered. The interpretation is structured and delivered at several levels. The first level is a part information, part interpretive sign. It is built from the slab of a tree and its text is painted on with a sense of randomness characteristic of the Caribbean. The text sounds like it was written by a local resident, but from the perspective of an animal. This style is not only low key but contains jokes and slang that makes it highly amusing and perfectly placed to appeal to its target audience. By combining the character of the animal with the pitch of a Creole a unique relationship is introduced that suggests the local animals and people share the land in a sustainable way through understanding and appreciation. Each sign nonetheless features a comment on human threats to the animals' existence. These threats are deliberately oriented around day-to-day pressures associated with urban living, rather than the conventional easy target of forestry.

The second level of interpretation is a larger set of two signs located at the main viewing area of each exhibit. At the top is a basic information sign designed to introduce the name, visual image and key characteristic of the animal. The text has again been written using the local Creole accent and roughly painted onto a slab of timber. Each animal is given a common name, scientific name, local name and colorful painting. Below this is a more sophisticated metal sign featuring an outline of the animal for children to draw from, a detailed line drawing and text about the distribution and characteristics of the animal. A column alongside is specifically devoted to the conservation status of the animal, identifying major threats, status and initiatives being undertaken to address the threats.

The third level is the running of guided tours by local volunteers with a passion for the animals and their conservation. These tours offer deeper interpretation into the animal and its habitat. A sign towards the end of the trails seeks to remotivate and inspire, and reads:

> *Throughout the world tropical forests are being destroyed, and animals, dependent on these forests, are disappearing. Much of Belize remains forested, and healthy populations of its wildlife live on. Belize stands proud—as a nation, this richness of your flora and fauna will be an everlasting enhancement to your natural heritage.*

(Interpretation Sign at Belize Zoo, 1994)

The interpretation is therefore deliberately pitched at locals. Nonetheless, international visitors find the Creole characterization equally stimulating and entertaining because it sounds so authentic. The success of the interpretation has stimulated a series of outreach programs that tour Belize's schools and teach children about their country's wildlife.

CONCLUSION

Interpretation is the art of helping people to learn. It is a complex activity that goes beyond making the communication of information enjoyable. Best practice interpretation requires a thorough understanding and integration of audience, message and technique. Most interpreters require training to achieve this degree of performance. However, most courses have focused more on interpretive content, resulting in participants increasing their knowledge about the environment, but not having the skill to adequately interpret their knowledge to their clients. Consequently, there are significant limitations to the quality of most interpretation practiced in the ecotourism industry. Two actions must occur to address this situation: first, a greater portion of the ecotourism industry must sufficiently value interpretation in order to improve its delivery; and second, those responsible for ecotourism training must link up with those delivering best practice interpretation to increase understanding and proficiency.

REFERENCES

Beckmann, E. 1988. "Interpretation in Australia—Current Status and Future Prospects," *Australian Parks and Recreation*, vol. 23, no. 6, pp. 6-14.

Beckmann, E. 1992. "Educating the Community in Australia," *Australian Parks and Recreation*, vol. 28, no. 2, page 5.

Commonwealth Department of Tourism. 1994. *National Ecotourism Strategy*, Australian Government Service, Canberra, Australia.

Commonwealth Department of Tourism. 1995. *National Ecotourism Training Manual*, Australian Government Service, Canberra, Australia.

Crabtree, A., S. McArthur. 1997. "Education and Training Opportunities in Ecotourism," *Australian Ecotourism Guide 1997/98*, Ecotourism Association of Australia, Brisbane, Australia.

Davie, F. 1992. "Regional Interpretive Planning: From Chaos to Creative Connective," *Open to Interpretation 1993*, proceedings from the 1993 National Conference of the Interpretation Australia Association, University of Newcastle, Newcastle, Australia.

Forestry Tasmania. 1994. "Guided Nature-based Tourism in Tasmania's Forests: Trends, Constraints and Implications," *Forestry Tasmania*, Hobart.

Gabor, M.T. "A Millenium Vision for Tourism—A Government Perspective," 1997 Australian Tourism Conference, Tourism Council Australia. In press.

Griffiths, T. 1990. "History and Natural History: Conservation Movements in Conflict," The Humanities and the Australian Environment, papers from the Australian Academy of the Humanities Symposium.

Hall, C.M., S. McArthur. 1993. "Visitor Management, Interpretation and Marketing," Heritage Management in New Zealand and Australia, Oxford University Press, Auckland, New Zealand.

Hall, C.M., S. McArthur. 1996. "The Human Dimension," Heritage Management in Australia and New Zealand, Oxford University Press, Melbourne, Australia.

Hall, C.M., S. McArthur. Integrated Heritage Management. In press.

Hall, C.M., D. Springett, B. Springett. 1993. "The Development of an Environmental Education Tourist Product: A Case Study of the New Zealand Natural Heritage Foundation's Nature of New Zealand Programme," Journal of Sustainable Tourism, vol. 1, no. 2, pp. 130-136.

Ham, S. 1992. Environmental Interpretation: A Practical Guide for People With Big Ideas and Small Budgets, North American Press, Colorado.

Interpretation Australia Association. 1995. Welcome to the IAA, Interpretation Australia Association, Collingwood, Australia.

Knapman, B. 1991. "Tourists in Kakadu National Park," results from a 1990 Visitor Survey, University of Technology, Sydney, Australia.

Lingle Pond, K. 1993. The Professional Guide: Dynamics of Tour Guiding, Van Nostrand Reinhold, New York.

MacFarlane, J. 1994. "Some Definitions of Interpretation," HII News, July.

Machlis, G., D. Field. 1992. On Interpretation: Sociology for Interpreters of Natural and Cultural History, Oregon State University Press, Corvallis, Oregon.

Masberg, B.A., M. Savige. 1996. "Incorporating Ecotourist Needs Data Into the Interpretive Planning Process," The Journal of Environmental Education, vol. 27, no. 3, pp. 34-40.

McArthur, S. 1995. "Evaluating Interpretation—What's Been Done and Where to From Here: Interpretation Attached to Heritage," papers presented at the Third Annual Conference of Interpretation Australia Association, Interpretation Australia Association, Collingwood, Australia.

McArthur, S. 1996. "Interpretation in Australia—Is It Running on Borrowed Time?" Australian Parks and Recreation, vol. 32, no. 22.

O'Brien, C. 1985. "Current Status of Interpretation in Australia," paper presented to the First World Congress on Heritage Interpretation and Presentation, Banff, Australia.

Regnier, K., M. Gross, R. Zimmerman. 1992. *The Interpreters Guidebook: Techniques for Programs and Presentations*, University of Wisconsin, Wisconsin.

Saunders, R. 1992. "Voices in the Wilderness—Interpreting Tasmania's World Heritage Area," *Australian Parks and Recreation*, vol. 28, no. 1.

Sharpe, G.W. 1982, *Interpreting the Environment*, John Wiley, New York.

Tilden, J. 1977. *Interpreting Our Heritage*, 3rd Edition, University of North Carolina Press, Chapel Hill.

Trapp, S., M. Gross, R. Zimmerman. 1991. *Signs, Trails, and Wayside Exhibits: Connecting People and Places*, UW-SP Foundation Press, University of Wisconsin, Stephens Point, Wisconsin.

Veverka, J. 1992. "Developing Interpretation Master Plans: Joining Hands for Quality Tourism," proceedings from the Heritage Interpretation International Third Global Conference, University of Hawaii, Honolulu, Hawaii.

Economic Aspects of Ecotourism

Kreg Lindberg

There are various stakeholders in the field of ecotourism, including operators, natural-area managers and local communities. One thing they have in common is that they often seek economic benefits from ecotourism, whether it be sales and profits for operators, user fee revenues or increased political support for natural-area management, or jobs and income for local communities. However, many observers feel that desired economic benefits from ecotourism have not been fully achieved. This chapter outlines three economic aspects of ecotourism:

- tourism's share in the benefits and costs of natural areas;
- user fees and revenue generation to support natural-area protection; and
- ecotourism and economic development.

The last area is discussed relatively briefly because it is treated in other chapters of this book. This chapter focuses on general principles and provides examples of strategies and tools for increasing economic benefits and park revenues. There is wide variation across locations not only with respect to the ecotourism attractions themselves, but also with respect to socio-economic and political conditions. Therefore, the appropriateness and effectiveness of the tools and strategies will vary from site to site. There is a large and expanding literature on the various economic aspects of ecotourism, and several references are provided in this chapter. Wells (1997) also provides a good overview of issues and a list of references.

TOURISM'S SHARE IN THE BENEFITS AND COSTS OF NATURAL AREAS

Natural areas provide many benefits to society, and several of these can be incorporated into an economic benefit-cost analysis framework. One of the benefits is that they provide opportunities for tourism. However, they also provide watershed protection, conservation of biodiversity and ecological processes, education and research opportunities, existence and option values, and, in some cases, a variety of consumptive benefits (further detail in Dixon and Sherman, 1990). Of course, they also generate costs, including direct costs such as construction and maintenance, indirect costs such as damage to adjacent agricultural activities by protected animals, and opportunity costs due to the inability to use the land for other (non-compatible) purposes.

In some cases, the ecotourism benefits may be very large and, indeed, critical in the decision to protect a natural area. However, these benefits will not always be apparent, especially when no fee is charged to visit an area. In economic benefit-cost analyses, ecotourism benefits are measured in terms of economic value and are typically represented by "willingness-to-pay" (WTP) to visit a site. An important point is that WTP may be substantial even if ecotourists do not actually pay for the visit.

Ideally, the demand curve, and thus WTP, will be estimated by varying the price of the good (in this case a visit to the natural area) and observing how many people visit at each price. This demand curve can then be used to calculate an estimate of economic value. However, not all areas charge fees, and those that do rarely adjust their fees sufficiently to estimate a demand curve. Economists have developed alternative techniques, including the "travel cost method" (TCM) and the "contingent valuation method" (CVM), for estimating the demand curve and/or WTP for "non-market" goods like visits to natural areas. TCM uses expenditure on various trip costs, such as transportation, to infer the value visitors place on the destination visit itself. CVM uses visitor responses to hypothetical fee scenarios to infer the value they place on their visit. Though both methods involve strong assumptions and have been criticized, they allow analysts to estimate the value of such non-market goods (see Mitchell and Carson, 1989, and Walsh, 1986, for more information on these methods).

Example
LAKE NAKURU NATIONAL PARK
KENYA

Navrud and Mungatana (1994) used both TCM and CVM to estimate the ecotourism (recreation) value of wildlife viewing in Lake Nakuru National Park in Kenya. The travel cost analysis generated value estimates of $114-$120 per visit for foreigners and $68-$85 per visit for residents. Applying these estimates to all visitors in 1991 generated ecotourism value for that year of $13.7-$15.1 million. The contingent valuation analysis generated lower value estimates of $73 for foreigners and $20 for residents, which yields an annual estimate of $7.5 million in value. TCM and CVM also have been applied at numerous other sites around the world (e.g., Bennett, 1995; Kramer et al., 1995; Maille and Mendelsohn, 1993; Walsh, 1986).

This example illustrates the substantial economic value that ecotourism can generate. However, economic value is a measure of human welfare used in benefit-cost analyses. Though it may include visitor spending, which may lead to the tangible benefits of financial return and jobs, part or all of the economic value may be retained by the visitor and thus not provide tangible benefit. Moreover, at some sites, most of this value will accrue to foreigners because they outnumber resident visitors and/or because on average their WTP is greater. A resident and a foreigner may enjoy the visit in equal amounts, but due to higher income the foreigner may be willing to pay more for the visit; in economic terms, this means the foreigner values it more. As a result, there can be a discrepancy between those who receive most of the benefit (foreign visitors) and those who bear most of the cost (residents who pay taxes that fund the natural area, as well as local residents in particular who may suffer damage to their agricultural activities or loss of access to traditional resources).

To some degree, economic value can be converted to financial return by charging fees—and not charging what areas are worth may undermine the economic justification for keeping them (because without a fee the value is "lost" to foreigners, or because even with domestic visitation WTP is less apparent than fee revenue, and thus often is ignored or undervalued). In fact, Lake Nakuru National Park does charge fees. However, at the time of the study, entrance and royalty fees amounted to only $800,000, which constituted only 5-10% of the observed ecotourism value. Though, in practice, it is impossible to convert all economic value to financial return, opportunities often exist for capturing a larger percentage of this value through higher fees. This is the focus of the next section.

In addition, part of the economic value that visitors receive from their visit, or their trip as a whole, ultimately benefits residents, to varying degrees, as a result of visitor spending. To use a simplified example, a British tourist might decide to fly to Kenya to spend a week at Lake Nakuru. She might value the whole trip at $4,000, so this would be her WTP for the trip. But perhaps her total expenses for the trip were only $3,000, so she received benefit over and above her expenditure. Of the $3,000, perhaps $1,000 was spent on food, accommodations, and souvenirs in the Lake Nakuru region. This leads to benefits for residents, and is the focus of the third section.

Due to the popularity and accessibility of its wildlife, certain parts of Africa have particularly strong potential for generating financial and economic returns. For example, Price Waterhouse (1994) evaluated the financial and economic desirability of cattle ranching versus wildlife and tourism for conservancies in Zimbabwe. For the Devure Ranch, they estimate that cattle had the potential to generate gross revenue of Z$22 per hectare per year using a realistic stocking rate, and Z$37/ha/yr using a high stocking rate (Z$6.5=U.S.$1 at the time of the estimates). On the other hand, a small wildlife operation with tourism, hunting and culling was estimated to generate Z$67/ha/yr. Of course, tourism will not always be more financially attractive than alternative land uses, so one must also rely on non-tourism benefits to justify conservation.

Example
CATTLE RANCHING VERSUS WILDLIFE TOURISM
SOUTH AFRICA

Price Waterhouse (1994) also provides figures from a comparison in Madikwe, South Africa, as follows (all figures, except jobs, in rand; R4.4 = U.S.$1 as of April 1997).

INCOME/EXPENDITURES	CATTLE RANCHING	WILDLIFE TOURISM
Gross Income	2,500,000	27,430,000
Net Income	1,300,000	14,130,000
Government Income	80,000	4,840,000
Capital Expenditure	12,050,000	35,400,000
Wages Earned per Year	480,000	7,300,000
Number of Jobs	80	1,214

USER FEES AND REVENUE GENERATION
SHOULD FEES BE CHARGED?

The issue of user fees has been controversial in many countries and has generated a substantial literature (e.g., Harris and Driver, 1987; Laarman and Gregersen, 1996; Lindberg et al., 1996; Mak and Moncur, 1995; McCarville et al., 1996; Tisdell, 1996). Many members of the general public and the tourism industry oppose fees at public natural areas. Citizens may feel that visitation to these areas is part of their national heritage and is a "public good," like defense, that should be provided by the government to all citizens, with funding ultimately being based on taxes or other government revenue sources. Particularly in certain developed countries, some feel that fees for residents represent a double charge in that they already have paid through taxes.

In addition, there is concern that fees will change the nature of the visitor experience by making it more structured and commercialized. Similarly, it may increase visitor expectations to be "entertained," which may diverge from management agency efforts to use visits as opportunities for interpretation and education. Communities dependent upon industry and tourism may feel that fees would reduce the number of visitors, and thus their business opportunities and jobs.

Fee supporters note that visitation imposes costs on natural areas, including environmental, financial (e.g., construction and management of facilities), and experiential (e.g., congestion) costs. They feel that these costs should be paid by those who impose them—the visitors and associated infrastructure and activities. Moreover, they note that many natural-area systems around the world have encountered severe financial difficulties as the number of national parks and other areas has grown, while funding often has remained stable or declined (Eagles, 1995; Wescott, 1995). Thus, even if funding were ideally to come from government, fiscal austerity may force a choice between implementing user fees or jeopardizing conservation objectives, as funding to maintain visitor services is drawn away from conservation activities. Lastly, supporters note that the increased fiscal independence resulting from fees can help generate political support as well as political autonomy for natural areas.

Ultimately, the question of whether to charge fees at public natural areas—and, if so, at what level—is a political one that depends on management objectives, as well as legal and administrative constraints. Various management objectives may exist, including:

- *Cost Recovery*—Generation of revenue to at least cover tourism's financial costs (e.g., for facility construction and maintenance) and possibly tourism's other costs (e.g., environmental damage).
- *Generation of "Profit"*—Generation of revenue in excess of costs, with the excess being used to finance traditional conservation activities (at the destination or at other sites) or to achieve other objectives.
- *Generation of Local Business Opportunities*—Would typically involve low or no fees in an effort to maximize number of visitors.
- *Generation of Foreign Exchange and/or Tax Revenues From Tourist Purchases*—As with business opportunities, would typically involve low or no fees in an effort to maximize number of visitors.
- *Provision of Maximum Opportunities for Learning and Appreciation of Natural Resources*—Again, may involve low or no fees, though overall learning and appreciation might be increased by charging fees and using resulting revenue to enhance education programs.
- *Visitor Management*—Implementation of use fees to reduce/redistribute visitor numbers or reduce depreciative behavior, thereby decreasing congestion, user conflict or environmental damage; however, achievement of this objective may necessitate relatively high fees.

Of course, a combination of objectives may exist. For example, in the case of a developing country, cost recovery or profit generation may be the primary objective for foreign visitation while maximum learning opportunities may be the primary objective for domestic visitation.

Regardless of the chosen objective, assertions by proponents or opponents of fees should be critically evaluated. For example, as with government programs generally, non-users (e.g., those who do not visit ecotourism sites) subsidize users (visitors) when fees are not charged. A decision must be made regarding whether it is appropriate to subsidize a specific activity, and this decision may be affected by various considerations. For instance, subsidies are often proposed to ensure that low-income groups are able to visit natural areas. However, for those sites visited primarily by high-income groups (common for sites distant from population centers), the poor may be worse off with a free entry system, as they subsidize rich visitors through taxes (Knapman and Stoeckl, 1995). Indeed, a survey in the U.S. found that low income, elderly and rural groups favored user fees (Harris and Driver, 1987; Stevens et al., 1989). Moreover, it is generally possible to devise fee systems to facilitate visitation by groups that might be disadvantaged, such as through lower fees for students or the elderly or through "open" days with no fee, which implicitly favors local residents.

In addition, one should consider the appropriateness of taxpayers subsidizing foreign visitors, particularly when the foreign visitors are wealthier than the taxpayers, as generally occurs when visitors from developed countrys travel to developing country destinations. Several countries, including Peru, Ecuador and Kenya have raised fees for foreigners while maintaining low fees for residents (Olindo, 1991). Moreover, in a survey conducted at three Costa Rican parks, Baldares and Laarman (1990) found that both residents and foreigners agreed that foreigners should pay more than residents. Such differential pricing across market segments is common within the tourism industry. For example, the price of airline tickets is often differentiated across the business and holiday market segments, with the former paying higher prices than the latter (differentiation is achieved through mechanisms such as advanced purchase and "Saturday night stay" requirements).

One should question whether fees truly represent a "double-charge." Fees are typically implemented precisely because funding from tax revenue is insufficient to achieve recreation and conservation management objectives. Industry concerns regarding the effect of fees on visitor levels should also be critically evaluated. Though the inverse relationship between price and demanded quantity is a fundamental economic principle, past experience suggests that modest fees (e.g., up to $5) have little or no long-term impact on visitation levels at most sites; that is, visitation is price inelastic at modest fee levels (Knapman and Stoeckl, 1995; Lindberg et al., 1996; Walsh, 1986). Much higher fees can be sustained at unique sites with little or no effect on visitation level. Fees may even increase visitation if the resulting revenue is used to enhance visitor experience. However, price elasticity will vary widely, and at some sites with nearby substitutes, fees may significantly reduce demanded quantity (Stevens et al., 1989).

Implicit in industry opposition to fees is the assumption that taxpayers should subsidize visitation by industry clients, and thus subsidize tourism businesses (whether this constitutes a subsidy of the business or the visitor depends on the extent to which the business can pass the cost of the fee on to clients). As with subsidies for foreign visitors, this may be deemed appropriate, but its desirability should be addressed. Finally, low fees for certain visitor services (e.g., campgrounds) may reduce opportunities for private providers of these services who must compete with public equivalents.

If the management objective is to provide ecotourism in the most economically efficient manner (i.e., in the manner that maximizes social welfare), then fees should be set at the point where demand (marginal benefit) equals marginal cost (more detail is provided in Lindberg and Enriquez, 1994; Rosenthal et al., 1984). Unfortunately, rarely is there sufficient information on demand—or, especially, on cost—for a precise determination of efficient fees. Nonetheless, economic efficiency does provide one possible basis for price determination. In addition, it highlights the issue of ecotourism-related costs and the economic losses that occur when fees are set on different bases (Walsh, 1986, discusses additional bases on which to set prices).

UNDERSTANDING DEMAND AND SETTING FEES

Effective achievement of cost recovery and other objectives requires information regarding ecotourism demand and costs. For example, if a site is to set fees to maximize profits, it must first identify both the demand curve (how many people will visit at each price) and the supply curve (the cost of providing the experience for each level of visitation). This section outlines some of the factors that affect demand, as well as techniques for gaining information about demand and costs. This presentation is based primarily on "economic theory" approaches. For additional discussions of "business" approaches, see Meidan (1982) and McKercher (1998). For "social psychology" approaches, see McCarville et al. (1992), and McCarville et al. (1996).

The demand for an ecotourism site will depend on a variety of factors (see Lindberg and Huber, 1993, for more detail), including:

- ᦲ visitor income and other demographic characteristics;
- ᦲ tastes and trends;
- ᦲ destination image;
- ᦲ availability and prices of competing attractions;
- ᦲ cost of travel (time and money) to the destination country;

∽ quality of the attraction;

∽ quality of general trip experience;

∽ political and economic stability;

∽ complementary attractions; and

∽ cost of travel (time and money) from the destination gateway to the attraction.

There are various methods for estimating demand for an ecotourism site. Perhaps the most common is *market evaluation*, in which fees and visitation levels at equivalent sites are analyzed. This method provides a common basis for determining whether investments in the private sector will be worthwhile. However, care must be taken when evaluating new destinations, as they will expand the supply of destinations, thereby putting downward pressure on prices. Unfortunately, lodges and other businesses typically do not share information on visitation levels and prices, so comparison is difficult. In addition, few national parks and other public facilities have historically charged fees; when fees have been charged, they have rarely been based on business considerations such as the cost of providing the service and the willingness of consumers to pay for the service. Moreover, there is rarely the necessary variability in fees and resulting visitation levels to enable estimates of visitor responsiveness to different fee levels.

Even when information is obtained from similar sites, it must be adjusted to take into account differences in demand factors, such as the quality of attraction and travel cost. Because there has been little systematic analysis of demand factors for ecotourism, especially in the international context, the importance of each factor must be largely based on intuitive judgment by those familiar with the industry (Walsh, 1986, discusses factors in the U.S. recreation context). However, it is hoped that future research will help identify the importance of each factor, thus facilitating more effective application of this strategy. Such research would also facilitate identification of cost-effective means for increasing demand (such as resources being devoted to enhancing visitor centers, if they were identified as being particularly important).

A second method is to estimate demand using *non-market valuation* techniques, such as the TCM and CVM techniques described above (see Walsh, 1986, for further discussion). However, when used for pricing purposes, the relationship between fee and visitation level is of interest, rather than average or total WTP. It should be stressed that though these techniques have been widely used, the accuracy of results may depend heavily on the quality of survey design and administration (the examples provided in this chapter are used to illustrate concepts, and research quality has not been evaluated specifically). In addition, psychological and other factors may mean that visitors are willing to pay less "on-the-ground" than is indicated by non-market valuation estimates. For these reasons, results from such studies should be used with some caution.

Related to non-market valuation techniques are *market research* techniques, such as conjoint analysis and choice modeling (Hair et al., 1995). These techniques measure the importance of attributes (e.g., the demand factors listed above) in consumer decisions. They can be used to estimate the probability that consumers will choose a particular product (e.g., will visit a particular park) based on the attributes of that product relative to those of others in the market. Because price can be one of the attributes, these techniques can be used to estimate the responsiveness of visitation levels to price changes.

A third method is the use *flexible management and/or auctions*. Because of the inherent difficulty in estimating demand, and due to the fickleness of the industry,

---

Example
USING TCM TO ESTIMATE DEMAND CURVES
KAKADU NATIONAL PARK, AUSTRALIA

Knapman and Stoeckl (1995) used the travel cost method and data from a 1990 survey to estimate demand curves for Kakadu National Park in Australia. Based on their "Model B," which includes an allowance for the cost of travel time, they estimated the following relationship between entry fees, estimated visitation and estimated fee revenue for Kakadu (numbers are rounded).

FEE (AU$)	ESTIMATED VISITATION	ESTIMATED FEE REVENUE (Fee x Visitation)
$ 0	244,000	$ 0
4	239,000	56,000
8	235,000	1,880,000
16	227,000	3,632,000
40	205,000	8,200,000
80	173,000	13,840,000
121	147,000	17,787,000
161	125,000	20,125,000
444	31,000	13,764,000

As it turns out, a fee of AU$10 per adult (rather than per visitor) was levied in 1993/94 and generated AU$1,900,000 from 205,000 visitors. This suggests that the estimates are reasonably accurate, at least at the lower fee levels.

this method is an important supplement to the others. For example, fees might be raised to $10 based on a CVM study or evaluation of equivalent attractions. However, if the number of visitors decreases more than predicted, the fees might be adjusted downward. Alternatively, if the number of visitors decreases less than predicted, the fees might be raised. In short, fees can be adjusted using "informed trial and error" until objectives, such as cost recovery, are met. However, significant fee changes should be phased in slowly.

Auctioning permits or other tourism fees will typically align fees with demand since tour operators would be expected to bid their maximum willingness to pay for the permit (provided that there are several bidders and the auction is administered effectively). However, auctions are generally appropriate only when there is a limited number of permits or allowable entries and when the price of such permits is relatively high. This will typically be the case with hunting, and such high-value tourism opportunities as viewing mountain gorillas.

Example

ESTIMATING COSTS AT ECOTOURISM SITES
BELIZE

Most of this chapter has focused on demand and benefits. However, cost recovery and some other objectives require knowledge of costs. This is difficult to obtain, as many costs incurred by natural areas relate to both ecotourism and conservation. Often, management, and other, costs are allocated to conservation in general, and only the costs specifically attributable to ecotourism (e.g., guides employed by the natural area) are allocated to ecotourism. However, Lindberg et al. (1996) applied cost-accounting techniques in order to generate more realistic cost estimates at three ecotourism sites in Belize.

Based on the medium scenario, they estimated tourism-related costs of BZ$46,894 ($23,447) at Cockscomb Basin Wildlife Sanctuary during the period April 1991 to April 1993. Estimated ecotourism-related revenue, primarily from bunk fees and donations, was BZ$42,213, for a deficit of BZ$4,681. If a cost-recovery objective were to be pursued, these figures allow one to estimate the necessary entrance fee. In this case, using 1992 visitation of 2,968 foreign visitors, an entrance fee of BZ$1.60 ($0.80) for foreigners (no fee for residents) would lead to cost recovery. Because this fee is so low, it would not be expected to reduce visitation. This estimate is based on single points for demand and cost, rather than full demand and supply curves, yet it illustrates how such information can be used to set fees. More extensive use of cost data has been recommended for natural area pricing and budget allocation decisions (e.g., New South Wales National Parks and Wildlife Service, 1997).

TYPES OF FEES

Once overall fee policies have been determined, managers must determine the goods and services for which fees should be charged, as well as how they should be collected. Although there is some overlap in terminology, the following are some of the common fee categories:

- *Entrance Fee*—Collected when tourists enter the area.
- *Admissions Fee*—Charged for admission to specific facilities, such as visitor centers.
- *Use Fee*—Charged for use of specific objects (such as rented equipment), or opportunities (such as camping sites).
- *License and Permit Fee*—Similar to a use fee; includes hunting and fishing permits.
- *Sales and Concessions*—Includes profits from direct sales of souvenirs, lodging and other goods or services; fees from concessions to private businesses for selling these goods and services; and revenues from licensing natural-area logos and trademarks.

In addition to different types of fees, there are also different methods for collecting them. The most obvious method is through direct on-site collection, such as upon entry to a site or as the good or service is being purchased. The benefits of this method include: 1) the direct connection between the fee payment and the service provided, and 2) the opportunity to inform, regulate and count visitors. A drawback of direct collection is the expense.

For sites with multiple entry points and/or low volumes of visitors, direct collection may not be practical. Instead, an honor system, with drop boxes for payment, or a pass system may be appropriate. For example, the state of Tasmania in Australia uses an entry pass for visitor access to any of the state's 14 national parks. Spot-checks may be necessary to enforce compliance under such systems.

Another method is to collect the fees indirectly through tour operators, with the cost usually being passed along to tourists as part of the tour package price. This option often is used in conjunction with direct collection. The benefits of indirect collection include: 1) the potential to enhance communication between the park and the local tourism industry, 2) reduced administrative costs for the natural area while still allowing visitation levels to be monitored, and 3) the potential to hide fees in the cost of the tour package, thus possibly reducing the effect of higher fees on visitation levels. A drawback of indirect collection is the reduced contact between park personnel and visitors.

Another alternative is to collect revenue from other sectors of the tourism industry. This option is usually based on hotel or transportation taxes and provides advantages similar to tour operator fee collection. For example, in the state of Montana, 6.5% of the hotel bed tax revenue goes to management of state parks. However, in order to gain industry acceptance, it may be critical for fees to be levied only when there is a strong correlation between the fees and natural-area use.

Example

THE PROTECTED AREA CONSERVATION TRUST
BELIZE

The Protected Areas Conservation Trust (PACT) involves a $3.75 conservation fee for all foreign visitors, which is added to the pre-existing $11.25 airport departure tax. Based on an estimated 140,000 foreign visitors per year, this recently implemented program is expected to generate more than $500,000 annually. The trust is independent of the government and is supervised by a board comprised of both governmental and non-governmental representatives. PACT funding can be used for a variety of purposes, including training, environmental education, protected-area planning, and institutional support, but it is not intended to replace core government funding.

The difficulty of establishing such a fund should not be underestimated—the program was five years in development, with the final differing substantially from the initial proposal. Moreover, because Belize's tourism is heavily dependent on natural and cultural attractions, there is a relatively clear justification for levying such a fee on tourists. This will not be the case for all countries. Nonetheless, the PACT represents an excellent example of creative finance for conservation, and other countries are exploring similar programs. More information on the PACT is provided by Spergel (1996).

OTHER FEE POLICY ISSUES

This last section outlines other general issues and recommendations relevant to fee policy. First, the best fee system for any particular area will depend on the type and level of visitation, level of cooperation with the industry, bureaucratic efficiency and many other factors. Thus, within overall objectives, flexibility should be provided for each site to implement the fee structure most appropriate to local conditions (since a single fee structure for the entire park system may not be efficient); for example, the advance-purchase entrance fee for Costa Rican parks, ranging from $5 for the least visited parks to $10 for the most visited (Chase, 1996; Costa Rica TravelNet, 1997).

If fee policy authority remains with the central administration, the ability to change fees should at least remain as flexible as possible. For example, the executive branch, such as a parks agency, can generally respond more quickly than can the legislative branch, such as a parliament or congress (Barborak, 1988). Also, experience suggests that earmarking at least a portion of ecotourism fee revenue back to the site itself increases managerial efficiency in fee collection, as well as responsibility in expenditure.

Second, fee revenue should be viewed as a supplement to, rather than replacement for, existing budget allocations. If the existing budget allocation is reduced as tourism revenue increases, the financial benefit of fees is lost. Indeed, the infra-structure and management costs brought on by implementing the fee system may reduce available funding. Moreover, tourism is inherently fickle, and the instability of tourism revenues may be greater than the instability of government funds. For this reason, trust funds should be established where feasible to ensure continued funding during low points in tourism cycles (these may be difficult to establish given that government agencies are accustomed to annual budget cycles). Opportunities for increasing non-fee revenues for natural areas, such as through donation programs or through souvenir sales, should be evaluated, as they can often provide additional substantial amounts of funding.

Third, fees and other ecotourism prices not only are affected by demand, but also can affect demand, insofar as they act as signals of product quality to visitors who are unfamiliar with the product. For example, a high-priced lodge may be more attractive than a low-priced lodge to visitors who are seeking a relatively high level of comfort. Likewise, high fees for Galápagos National Park are associated with a high-quality visitor product. Of course, if the lodge or site does not provide quality commensurate with the price, it jeopardizes return visits and word-of-mouth referrals.

Fourth, opposition to fees results in part because visitors may view them as unfair, or feel that they will not receive benefits from paying such fees (McCarville et al., 1996). Sites may be able to increase visitor acceptance of fees by explaining their purpose, with particular attention on whether, and how, fees will be used to enhance visitor services. For example, the Tasmania, Australia, national parks and reserves visitor's guide (1993) noted that "all funds raised from fees will be re-invested to ensure improved facilities such as better roads, shelters, picnic areas, toilets and walking tracks." However, information on fee purpose may not always affect willingness to pay the fee. For example, Laarman and Gregersen (1996) report a study by Barry (1992) at Tikal, Guatemala, in which no relationship was found between willingness to pay higher fees and information on fee purpose.

Fifth, communication with affected industry and other user groups may reduce opposition from those sources. It is unrealistic to expect total agreement and acceptance of fees, but acceptability can be improved by meaningful collaboration with user groups. A likely outcome of such collaboration is awareness of the importance of phased implementation of fees (or fee increases) so that industry can adjust their prices accordingly. For example, in 1996 the "environmental maintenance charge" on commercial tours for ecotourists visiting Australia's Great Barrier Reef was increased from AU$1.00 ($0.70) to AU$5.00 ($3.50). The industry strongly opposed the increase. In part, the opposition resulted from the magnitude of the increase, but it also resulted from the timing, which did not allow operators to incorporate the change into prices of tours that sell a year or more in advance (a similar problem occurred in Costa Rica, where fees were changed suddenly after election of a new government). A common industry recommendation is an advance notice of 18 months. In some countries, the industry opposes fee collection

---

Example
SIUSLAW NATIONAL FOREST
OREGON, USA

Historically, the U.S. Forest Service has been authorized by the U.S. Congress to charge only camping fees. Management objectives focused primarily on not undercutting the private sector, so a market evaluation was made, and fees were set at approximately the same level as comparable private sector campgrounds.

In 1996, Congress authorized the Forest Service, as well as other federal agencies, to conduct visitor fee "demonstration projects" for three years (Public Law 104-134). This allowed the service to charge non-camping fees, including entrance fees. At the Siuslaw National Forest, the management objective was partial recovery of operating costs. The management studied fees charged at other sites (primarily Oregon State Parks sites), and made evaluations of the fee amounts it would have to charge for full cost recovery. The full cost recovery fee was considered too high, so partial recovery was settled upon. This illustrates the dynamic nature of objectives and knowledge of visitor demand; this demand can constrain achievable objectives.

The fee structure includes a fee of $3 per car ($3 per person at one site that attracts visitors in buses) or an annual pass for $25. The site retains 80% of the revenue (traditional government funding allocation has not been reduced as a result of implementing these fees, though it may possibly be reduced due to general budgetary reductions). The additional revenue will be used to improve services and facilities and this is being explained to visitors to reduce resistance to entrance fees at sites that historically have not charged such fees. This project not only illustrates how fees can be implemented, but also how natural-area management agencies can take a "business approach" to ecotourism, including development of business plans (Siuslaw National Forest, 1996).

because management of revenues is perceived to be corrupt. As would visitors, the industry would like to see benefits resulting from collected revenues.

Sixth, the fact that fees potentially reduce visitation means that fees can be used as a management tool. Higher fees might be charged at popular sites, during periods of high use, to encourage people to visit less popular and less expensive sites. Of course, this will be effective only insofar as fees reduce visitation. (As noted earlier, fees may need to be raised to high levels to have much of an effect.) They may be more effective when applied within a natural area system that includes several substitutes, in which case fees may have a relatively large effect at individual sites.

Lastly, the development and maintenance of accurate accounting and financial management systems for both revenues and expenditures provides the information needed to make effective decisions in the future. Relatedly, monitoring of the fee system, including revenues and visitation levels, enables appropriate changes to be made when objectives are not being achieved. (See "Siuslaw National Forest," page 100.)

ECOTOURISM AND ECONOMIC DEVELOPMENT

Ecotourism has been embraced by many as an opportunity to generate income and employment in areas relatively untouched by traditional development efforts, and to generate tangible economic benefits from natural areas. There are at least three reasons for generating such local benefits. First, it is equitable insofar as conservation of the area designated for ecotourism may reduce or eliminate traditional resource use. Second, the ecotourists, as consumers, may support the importance of tourism benefiting local residents (Eagles et al., 1992). Third, when residents receive benefits they are more likely to support tourism and conservation, even to the point of protecting the site against poaching or other encroachment. For example, Lindberg et al. (1996) found that ecotourism-related benefits were an important basis for positive resident attitudes toward adjacent natural areas (Wunder, 1996; 1998). Conversely, if residents bear the costs without receiving benefits, they may turn against tourism and conservation, and may intentionally or unintentionally damage the site. Whether ecotourism benefits lead to increased support for conservation and, ultimately, to changes in resource use is dependent on a variety of circumstances (Brandon, 1997; Brandon and Wells, 1992).

Ecotourism's contribution to local economic development has been varied, and there is general recognition that this contribution could be increased at many sites. Moreover, tourism also can generate economic costs, such as inflation, and these costs may affect all residents, including those who do not receive benefits. This section briefly reviews concepts and the current contribution of ecotourism to economic development, and then describes opportunities for increasing this contribution.

An understanding of ecotourism's contribution to economic development requires an understanding of the ecotourism "industry." Ecotourism is, of course, tremendously variegated; it encompasses everything from paying travel agents thousands of dollars for trips to the furthest reaches of the globe, to simply walking to a nearby park. However, to simplify matters, it is useful to think of ecotourism as comprised of three components. The first is the outbound operator who sells tours to international tourists in the source country. The second is the inbound operator who actually organizes and leads the trip in the destination country. The third is the attraction that is being visited.

Consider the example of an American tourist wishing to visit Amboseli National Park in Kenya. She might buy a tour from a U.S. outbound operator, which in turn has arranged for an inbound operator to lead the trip in Kenya. The inbound operator will in turn purchase admission to the park, which is managed by the Kenyan Wildlife Service. Alternatively, the tourist may choose to arrange the trip directly with an inbound operator, either to save money or because she is already in Kenya. Or, she might forego using an operator in favor of traveling to the park by herself.

Many observers voice the concern that much of the trip cost, and thus the economic benefit, remains with outbound operators and source country airlines. To some extent, this is simply due to the nature of the tourism industry; substantial funds are spent on marketing, commissions and transport before tourists even reach the destination.

Example
OUTBOUND OPERATOR FINANCES
MASSACHUSETTS, USA

Sorenson (1991) presents a case study of Overseas Adventure Travel (OAT), an outbound operator in Massachusetts. In 1989, OAT sales totaled $4,525,000 (all figures are rounded), of which $1,400,000 was for air transport and $3,027,000 for land tours. The land tours cost $1,962,000 to supply, with a resulting gross profit from this product of $1,065,000 (approximately 86% of the total company gross profit). Much of this gross profit remained in the U.S. through allocation to salaries ($714,000), related sales and marketing ($496,000), and administrative/general ($264,000). Using preliminary 1990 budget figures, the major sales and marketing budget items were media advertising (6% of sales and marketing budget), catalogues and other sales tools (43%), postage (10%), telephone costs (6%) and travel agent commissions (18%). Though the proportion of total sales revenue actually spent "in-country" at destinations is not estimated, the revenue allocated to land tours represents less than half of total sales.

Similarly, Brown et al. (1995) estimate that 40% of foreign visitor expenditure for trips to the Hwange and Mana Pools National Parks in Zimbabwe is lost to the country because of international air travel costs. There may be opportunities for increasing the portion of trip cost that reaches the destination by, for example, using destination country airlines and bypassing outbound operators through direct marketing by inbound operators or attractions (e.g., via the World Wide Web). However, more attention has been paid to increasing spending once in the destination country, as well as increasing the impact of this spending on local communities in particular.

ECONOMIC IMPACT ESTIMATES AND CONCEPTS

Several studies of ecotourism's national, regional and local economic impacts have been conducted. For example, Aylward et al. (1996) estimated that nature tourism in Costa Rica generated over $600 million in foreign exchange in 1994 (Wells, 1993). Driml and Common (1995) estimated that visitors to the Australia's Great Barrier Reef World Heritage Area spent AU$776 million ($543 million) in 1991/1992. Lindberg et al. (1996) estimated that visitors to the Hol Chan Marine Reserve and adjacent marine tourism sites provided jobs for 44% of the households in San Pedro and 26% of the households in Caye Caulker.

Ecotourism's economic contribution depends not only on how much money flows into the region of interest (the country, state, province or local community), but also on how much of what comes into the region stays in the region, thereby producing multiplier effects. The impact of ecotourism, or any economic activity, can be grouped into three categories: direct, indirect and induced. Direct impacts are those arising from the initial tourism spending, such as money spent at a restaurant. The restaurant buys goods and services (inputs) from other businesses, thereby generating indirect impacts. In addition, the restaurant employees spend part of their wages to buy various goods and services, thereby generating induced impacts. Of course, if the restaurant purchases the goods and services from outside the region, then the money provides no indirect impact to the region—it leaks away. Figure 4.1 is a simplified illustration of some of these impacts and leakages (Nourse, 1968; Walsh, 1986).

A consistent finding of economic impact studies, particularly in developing countries, is the high level of leakage. Much of the initial tourist expenditure leaves the host country (and especially the destination site itself), to pay for imported goods and services used in the tourism industry. The following examples are estimates of the percentage of tourism spending leaking away from host country economies: Nepal (70%), Thailand (60%), typical developing country (55%), Zimbabwe (53%) and Costa Rica (45%) (Brandon, 1993; Brown et al., 1995; Lindberg, 1991; Smith and Jenner, 1992).

FIGURE 4.1
IMPACTS AND LEAKAGES

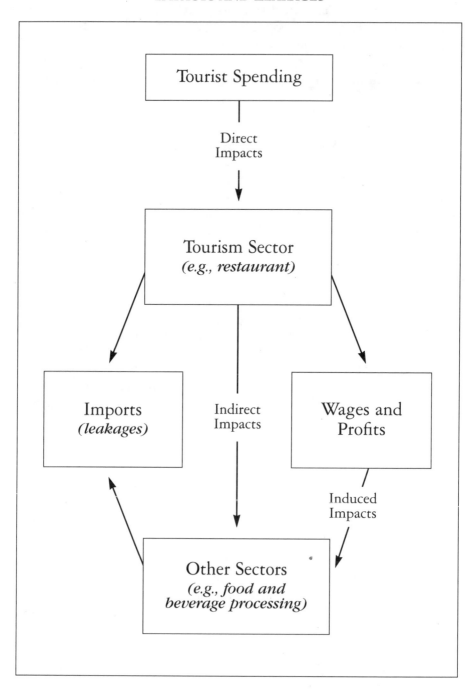

Example
ESTIMATING DIRECT, INDIRECT AND INDUCED IMPACTS FOR DORRIGO NATIONAL PARK
NEW SOUTH WALES, AUSTRALIA

Powell and Chalmers (1995) used visitor surveys and input-output (IO) analysis to estimate the impact of visitor spending at two national parks in New South Wales, Australia. The visitor surveys were used to estimate the direct impacts of ecotourism. IO analysis involves compilation of tables that show the size of each sector within the region of interest, as well as how these sectors are linked to each other. For example, it shows how much money the Personal Services sector, which includes hotels and restaurants, spent on inputs from all other sectors in the region. This information is used to estimate the indirect and induced impacts of ecotourism.

The study generated an estimate of AU$3.2 million in annual visitor expenditure plus AU$342,000 in annual agency expenditure (AU$1.00=U.S.$0.70). Accounting for indirect and induced impacts, it was estimated that Dorrigo National Park, with approximately 160,000 visitors per year, contributes almost AU$4.0 million in regional output, AU$1.5 million in regional household income, and payments to 71 employees. These represent 7%-8% of regional totals for each category. IO has also been widely used in the U.S. to provide similar types of information (Dawson et al., 1993; Johnson et al., 1989).

More than 90 percent of tourism spending is thought to leak away from communities near most nature tourism sites. For example, Baez and Fernandez (1992) estimate that less than 6 percent of the income generated by tourism at Tortuguero National Park, in Costa Rica, accrues to the local communities. Similar figures have been estimated for the Annapurna region of Nepal (Panos, 1997) and lower figures for whale watching in Baja California, Mexico (Dedina and Young, 1997). In Tangkoko DuaSudara, in Indonesia, the benefit distribution is 47% to the major tour company, 44% to hotels, and only 7% to guides (of which the head reserve guard receives 20%). Guides and food are usually brought from the provincial capital, so few benefits are retained at the village level (Kinnaird and O'Brien, 1996).

The wide variation in estimated leakage across sites is partially a result of differing assumptions, definitions and methods used. However, it also is affected by the size and sophistication of the economy being evaluated, the types of tourists and tourism development, and the policies and efforts of individual tourism businesses. Smaller economies will have more leakages than larger economies because a lower diversity of goods is produced; however, small-scale nature tourism tends to use more local goods than does large-scale traditional tourism.

Following are examples of linkages and leakages from two ecotourism businesses.

Example
LINKAGES AND LEAKAGES
AT MANA POOLS LODGE
ZIMBABWE

Brown et al. (1995) have estimated the distribution of revenues for trips involving the Mana Pools Lodge in Zimbabwe (see also Kangas et al., 1995). The following figures show how revenues from a typical Harare/Mana Pools/Harare trip costing $700 are used to purchase various local, national and international inputs (trip cost does not include international airfare to Harare). All figures are in U.S. dollars and are rounded to nearest dollar. The leakage column shows the percentage of payment for each item that leaks away from the Zimbabwean economy. Of the total leakage, slightly more than half, in dollar terms, results from commissions.

ITEM	COST	LEAKAGE AS % OF ITEM COST
Retail Agent Commission	$ 140	72%
Staff	82	0%
Food/Drink	68	2%
Administrative Overhead	60	0%
Advertising and Marketing	60	80%
Repairs and Maintenance	47	24%
Energy	42	43%
Depreciation	28	43%
Communications	5	0%
Insurance	5	0%
Housekeeping	3	0%
Freight and Transport	1	50%
Printing and Stationery	1	2%
Travel [a]	1	20%
TAXES	27	0%
PROFIT	131	0%
TOTAL	**$700**	**27%**

NOTE: [a] Though not specified in the report, this presumably represents staff travel

Example
LINKAGES AND LEAKAGES
AT SEA CANOE
THAILAND

Sea Canoe, an operator based in Thailand, provided the following figures. They illustrate the company's expenditure on various purchases, together with the linkages and leakages associated with those purchases.

ITEM	ITEM AS % OF SALES	LINKAGE (% REMAINING IN THAILAND)	LEAKAGE (% LEAVING THAILAND)
Staff (incl. training)	35%	(a) 35%	0%
Commissions	15%	13%	2%
Local Services	15%	(b) 15%	0%
Overhead	4%	4%	0%
Equipment	3%	0%	3%
Communication	3%	3%	0%
Distribution	3%	0%	(c) 3%
Travel	3%	1%	2%
Welfare	2%	2%	0%
Marketing	2%	1.5%	0%
Food	1%	1%	0%
Repairs	0.5%	0.5%	0%
Postage	0.5%	0.5%	0%
TAXES	6%	6%	0%
PROFITS	7%	7%	0%
TOTAL	100%	89.5%	10.5%

NOTES: (a) Represents staff, including Westerners who live and pay taxes in Thailand

(b) Represents boat hire from locals

(c) Represents payment to the holding company that pays for international marketing, research and development costs (the company spends money on travel and services in potential, new destinations)

The issue of leakage is very complex, and comparisons across sites and types of trips can be misleading. In addition, the ultimate level of local economic benefit depends not only on the level of leakage, but also on the amount of spending (Lindberg and Enriquez, 1994). For example, the importance of leakage level is illustrated by the Ecuadorean Amazon Napo region described by Wunder (1998) citing the work of Drumm (1991). The upper Napo region received $357,000 per year in local income from tourist spending of $1,340,000 per year. Due to a higher level of leakage, the exclusive and pristine lower Napo region received less local income ($339,000 per year) despite higher tourist spending ($3,860,000 per year).

On the other hand, Wunder (1998) presents the case of the Madre de Dios region in the Peruvian Amazon, based on Groom et al. (1991). In this case, there is a relatively high local share (25%) in tourism expenditure in the "backpacker" area of Puerto Maldonado, and a relatively low local share (11%) in the virgin but remote Manu Biosphere Reserve. Nonetheless, Manu generates so much more tourism revenue than does Puerto Maldonado ($1,700,000 versus $172,000, respectively) that it also generates more local income ($192,695 versus $42,910, respectively), despite having higher levels of leakage (lower local share).

Thus, though much attention has been paid to leakage estimates, it is more productive to focus on sources of leakage and how to "plug" them (as well as to the applaud the efforts of companies that actively do so). Knowledge of the leakages, or conversely the linkages, within the economy can be used to identify what goods are needed, but not being produced, in the region, how much demand there is for such goods, and what the likely benefits of local production would be. This enables policy makers to determine priorities for developing inputs for use by the tourism, and other, industries. For example, in Belize, many of the agricultural products used by the tourism industry are imported. By identifying the extent of this leakage, an estimate can be made to determine the benefits of developing a local supply of agricultural products for the tourism industry. This estimate would include not only the benefits to the agricultural sector, but also to other sectors through indirect and induced impacts of increased production in agriculture (Healy, 1997b; Lindberg and Enriquez, 1994; Telfer and Wall, 1996). Such information enables policymakers to determine priorities for reducing leakage by developing inputs for use by the tourism and other, industries and enhances ecotourism's potential to promote economic development.

INCREASING LOCAL BENEFITS

A common priority in ecotourism is to increase local economic benefits, and the traditional approach is to increase the number of visitors. Given that negative impacts (environmental, experiential, sociocultural and economic) correspond, to varying degrees, to visitor numbers, it is generally preferable to increase local benefits by:

- increasing spending per visitor;
- increasing local participation in the tourism industry;
- increasing backward linkages with related local industries (reducing leakages);
- implementing/increasing revenue sharing and direct payment programs; and/or
- increasing local control and ownership.

To some extent, these mechanisms overlap. For instance, overall benefits from employment may be directly related to how tourism is managed and controlled. If tourism is locally owned and controlled, leakages will likely be reduced, and linkages to other sectors of the local economy will likely be greater than would otherwise be the case. It is worth noting that these mechanisms may not always be desirable. For example, increased local control and ownership also means increased local risk. Moreover, the degree of local benefits will result from several factors beyond the level of local ownership (Wunder, 1996; 1998).

In practice, the most appropriate mechanism, or group of mechanisms, will depend on local cultural, political and economic conditions. In addition, to some extent these mechanisms will develop spontaneously to meet immediate needs. For example, a new lodge might seek local agricultural inputs simply because local farmers may be the best source of such inputs. However, concerted efforts by the ecotourism industry, government agencies, non-governmental organizations (NGOs) and others may be necessary to achieve ecotourism's potential to provide local benefits. For example, the industry can work with local communities to identify opportunities for employment in the industry or to provide goods such as food and handicrafts. Indeed, inbound operators currently and potentially play a critical role in providing domestic and local benefits at many destinations.

Government agencies and NGOs can play important roles in providing the capital availability, and entrepreneurial and business development training, necessary for wide distribution of benefits. Training programs are appropriate not only for direct participation in the tourism industry (e.g., as guides or providers of accommodation), but also for indirect participation by ancillary industries (e.g., training in the agricultural sector with respect to new product development and maintenance of hygiene standards). Without such programs, benefits may be limited to non-locals or to local elites who have the requisite capital and skills to provide goods and services needed by ecotourists. For example, studies in Nepal suggest that only those who are village elites have been able to capture ecotourism benefits (Sowers et al., 1994; Wells and

Brandon, 1992). Various publications cover business and skill development relative to ecotourism (Bushnell, 1994; Cotterill, 1995; McKercher, 1998; Pedersen, 1995; Pond, 1993), and examples of employment and training approaches are presented in *Ecotourism: A Guide for Planners and Managers,* Volume 1 (Lindberg and Huber, 1993).

Revenue sharing and local control will depend on a variety of factors, including political support and the goodwill of the tourism industry. Often, legislative action is necessary. For example, the 1993 amendment to Nepal's Wildlife Conservation Act provides for the distribution of 30% to 50% of protected area revenue to surrounding communities (Brandon, 1996). In the Caribbean nation of Dominica, the Alien Land Holding Act gives Dominicans greater control of land than is often the case in other countries. Hotels are small-scale, and over 62% of facilities and 70% of units are fully-owned by local people (Panos, 1997). However, this ownership and control may be jeopardized by both a recently announced "economic citizenship" program and plans to build an international airport.

Often, there are opportunities for increasing visitor spending on infrastructure and services at ecotourism destination areas. These might include lodgings, restaurants or snack bars, souvenir shops, visitor centers, cultural performances and so on. Of course, careful planning is vital prior to substantial investments being made in accommodations and other sizeable infrastructures. However, in many cases only a modest investment will be necessary, such as for small-scale handicraft development.

Handicrafts can be a significant, and sometimes the primary, source of ecotourism-related income for local communities (Healy, 1994). For example, Lindberg and Enriquez (1994) report that ecotourism-related handicraft sales in Maya Center, Belize, generated an average of BZ$2,336 ($1,168) per household for the year ending March, 1993. This revenue is particularly impressive when one considers that Belize's GDP per capita was BZ$3,124 at the time, and that most of the materials used to construct the crafts were collected locally.

In some cases, opportunities to develop and sell handicrafts will be obvious. However, various information-gathering techniques, such as visitor surveys and focus groups, can be used to identify potential interest in new handicrafts (or other local goods and services) and to obtain feedback on existing handcrafts. For example, Healy (1997a) notes that focus groups, which might involve discussion and evaluation by 8-10 tourists, can be an excellent way of finding out about tourist desires ("inexpensive but interesting gifts for people in my office"), questions ("what's so special about natural dyes?"), and concerns ("it looks too fragile"). They also can be used to evaluate alternative designs (the colors and patterns of a tablecloth), sizes (when a garment is made to sell in children's sizes), prices and packaging.

Perhaps the most obvious opportunity for local residents to benefit from is employment and income in the tourism industry itself (though there are often issues of seasonality and low wages). However, frequently, there are opportunities for increasing local benefits through employment in related industries. For example, residents might provide local transportation, ranging from the traditional to the modern. Likewise, there may be opportunities to increase tourism-related purchases from the local agricultural sector (Lindberg and Enriquez, 1994; Telfer and Wall, 1996).

One of the most important considerations is the level and type of control that local people have during development. Local involvement and control can include ownership, management, co-management and participation in planning. Though distinct, revenue sharing and local ownership and control are often implemented in a single program. Several models for such programs exist. For example, the Bwindi Impenetrable Forest in Uganda is a new (1991) park that contains about half (300) of the world's remaining mountain gorilla population. Uganda National Parks, in conjunction with the International Gorilla Conservation Programme (a consortium of NGOs), developed a plan to establish ecologically sound tourism while creating a source of revenue through gorilla viewing. Communities benefit directly through employment and through a campground owned and operated by local residents directly outside the park gates. A revenue sharing program allocates a portion of all receipts from gorilla viewing to community projects in the twenty-one parishes touching the park boundary.

Another model, as practiced in Rio Blanco, Ecuador, is that the community jointly operates an ecotourism project. Sixty percent of profits are reinvested into the project, with the remaining profits being divided equally among households (Schaller, 1996). Numerous other cases of local ownership and revenue sharing exist, including the oft-cited examples of the CAMPFIRE program in Zimbabwe, the Kenya Wildlife Service revenue sharing program, and the ACAP project in the Annapurna region of Nepal (Lindberg and Huber, 1993).

SUMMARY

Ecotourism's popularity in the conservation and development fields stems in large part from its potential to generate economic benefits, including revenue for natural-area management and employment for people living near these areas. Nonetheless, there is substantial debate regarding the extent to which this potential has been realized. The purpose of this chapter has been to present general economic principles as they relate to ecotourism, and relevant results from the research that has been conducted. In addition, several strategies and tools for increasing benefits have been discussed.

There is substantial variability across ecotourism sites, such that the importance and relevance of these principles and strategies will also vary. Nonetheless, two principles relevant across sites are that: 1) economic concepts and economic research can provide valuable information to be used in decision making processes;

and 2) the decisions themselves are sociopolitical in nature and ultimately reflect the priorities and values of decision makers, domestic and foreign businesses, agencies and other stakeholders.

ACKNOWLEDGEMENTS

Katrina Brandon made a significant contribution to the development of this chapter. Sea Canoe provided financial data from their operations. These contributions are greatly appreciated.

REFERENCES

Aylward, B., K. Allen, J. Echeverria, J. Tosi. 1996. "Sustainable Ecotourism in Costa Rica: The Monteverde Cloud Forest Reserve," *Biodiversity and Conservation*, vol. 5, pp. 315-343.

Baez, A.L., L. Fernandez. 1992. "Ecotourism as an Economic Activity: The Case of Tortuguero in Costa Rica," paper presented at the First World Congress of Tourism and the Environment, Belize.

Baldares, M.J., J.G. Laarman. 1990. "User Fees at Protected Areas in Costa Rica," Forestry Private Enterprise Initiative Working Paper No. 48., Research Triangle Park, North Carolina.

Barborak, J.R. 1988. "Innovative Funding Mechanisms Used by Costa Rican Conservation Agencies," paper presented at the IUCN General Assembly, San Jose, Costa Rica.

Barry, C.C. 1992. "Nature Tourism and Its Development in Guatemala: Assessing Current Trends and Future Potential," master's thesis, University of North Carolina, Chapel Hill, North Carolina.

Bennett, J. 1995. *Economic Value of Recreational Use: Gibraltar Range and Dorrigo National Parks*, New South Wales National Parks and Wildlife Service, Hurstville, New South Wales, Australia.

Brandon, K. 1993. "Basic Steps Toward Encouraging Local Participation in Nature Tourism Projects," in Lindberg, K., D. Hawkins, eds., *Ecotourism: A Guide for Planners and Managers, Volume 1*, The Ecotourism Society, North Bennington, Vermont.

Brandon, K. 1996. "Ecotourism and Conservation: A Review of Key Issues," World Bank Environment Department Paper No. 033, World Bank, Washington, D.C.

Brandon, K. 1997. "Policy and Practical Considerations in Land-Use Strategies for Biodiversity Conservation," *Last Stand: Protected Areas and the Defense of Tropical Biodiversity*, Oxford University Press, Oxford.

Brandon, K., M. Wells. 1992. "Planning for People and Parks: Design Dilemmas," *World Development*, vol. 20, no. 4, pp. 557-570.

Brown, G., M. Ward, D.J. Jansen. 1995. "Economic Value of National Parks in Zimbabwe: Hwange and Mana Pools," report prepared for the ZWMLEC project, coordinated by the World Bank.

Bushnell, S. 1994. "Pacific Islands Ecotourism: A Business Planning Guide," Honolulu: Pacific Business Center, University of Hawaii at Manoa.

Chase, L.C. 1996. "Capturing the Benefits of Ecotourism: The Economics of National Park Entrance Fees in Costa Rica," master's thesis, Cornell University, Ithaca, New York.

Costa Rica TravelNet. 1997, March. "National Parks Entrance Fees," www:http://catalog.com/calypso/cr/parks/parkfees.htm.

Cotterill, D. 1995. "Developing a Sustainable Ecotourism Business," proceedings of the 1995 Ecotourism Association of Australia Conference. Ecotourism Association of Australia, Brisbane, Australia.

Dawson, S.A., D.J. Blahna, J.E. Keith. 1993. "Expected and Actual Regional Economic Impacts of Great Basin National Park," *Journal of Park and Recreation Administration*, vol. 11, no. 4, pp. 45-59.

Dedina, S., E. Young. 1997, "Conservation and Development in the Gray Whale Lagoons of Baja California Sur, Mexico," www:http://scilib.ucsd.edu/sio/guide/z-serge.html

Dixon, J.A., P.B. Sherman. 1990. *Economics of Protected Areas: A New Look at Benefits and Costs*, Island Press, Washington, D.C.

Driml, S., M. Common. 1995. "Economic and Financial Benefits of Tourism in Major Protected Areas," *Australian Journal of Environmental Management*, vol. 2, no. 1, pp. 19-29.

Drumm, A. 1991. "Integrated Impact Assessment of Nature Tourism in Ecuador's Amazon Region," study for FEPROTUR-NATURALEZA, Quito, Ecuador.

Eagles, P.F.J. 1995. "Tourism and Canadian Parks: Fiscal Relationships," *Managing Leisure*, vol. 1, no. 1, pp. 16-27.

Eagles, P.F.J., J.L. Ballantine, D.A. Fennell. 1992. "Marketing to the Ecotourist: Case Studies from Kenya and Costa Rica," unpublished manuscript, Department of Recreation and Leisure Studies, University of Waterloo, Canada.

Groom, M.J. et al. 1991. "Tourism as a Sustained Use of Wildlife: A Case Study of Madre de Dios, Southeastern Peru," *Neotropical Wildlife Use and Conservation*, University of Chicago Press, Chicago, Illinois.

Hair, J.F., R.E. Anderson, R.L. Tatham, W.C. Black. 1995. *Multivariate Data Analysis With Readings*, Prentice Hall, Upper Saddle River, New Jersey.

Harris, C.C., B.L. Driver. 1987. "Recreation User Fees: Pros and Cons," *Journal of Forestry*, May, pp. 25-29.

Healy, R. 1994. "Tourist Merchandise as a Means of Generating Local Benefits from Ecotourism," *Journal of Sustainable Tourism*, vol. 2, no. 3, pp. 137-151.

Healy, R. 1997a. "Market Research for Tourist Crafts," December, unpublished manuscript. WWW: http://www.env.duke.edu/faculty/healy/CRAFT_1.html

Healy, R. 1997.b "Food As Tourist Merchandise: A Contribution Toward Sustainable Development in Protected Areas," December, unpublished manuscript. WWW: http://www.env.duke.edu/faculty/healy/healy.html.

Johnson, R.L., E. Obermiller, H. Radtke. 1989. "The Economic Impact of Tourism Sales," *Journal of Leisure Research*, vol. 21, no. 2, pp. 140-154.

Kangas, P., M. Shave, P. Shave. 1995. "Economics of an Ecotourism Operation in Belize," *Environmental Management*, vol. 19, no. 5, pp. 669-673.

Kinnaird, M.F., T.G. O'Brien. 1996. "Ecotourism in the Tangkoko Duasudara Nature Reserve: Opening Pandora's Box," *Oryx*, vol. 30, no. 1, pp. 65-73.

Knapman, B., N. Stoeckl. 1995. "Recreation User Fees: An Australian Empirical Investigation," *Tourism Economics*, vol. 1, no. 1, pp. 5-15.

Kramer, R.A., N. Sharma, M. Munasinghe. 1995. *Valuing Tropic Forests: Methodology and Case Study of Madagascar*, World Bank Environment Paper Number 13, World Bank, Washington, D.C.

Laarman, J.G., H.M. Gregersen. 1996. "Pricing Policy in Nature-based Tourism," *Tourism Management*, vol. 17, no. 4, pp. 247-254.

Lindberg, K. 1991. *Policies for Maximizing Nature Tourism's Ecological and Economic Benefits*, World Resources Institute, Washington, D.C.

Lindberg, K., J. Enriquez. 1994. *An Analysis of Ecotourism's Economic Contribution to Conservation and Development in Belize, Volume 2*, World Wildlife Fund, Washington, D.C.

Lindberg, K., J. Enriquez, K. Sproule. 1996. "Ecotourism Questioned: Case Studies From Belize.," *Annals of Tourism Research*, vol. 23, no. 3, pp. 543-562.

Lindberg, K., R.M. Huber, Jr. 1993. "Economic Issues in Ecotourism Management," *Ecotourism: A Guide for Planners and Managers, Volume 1*, The Ecotourism Society, North Bennington, Vermont.

Maille, P. , R. Mendelsohn. 1993. "Valuing Ecotourism in Madagascar," *Journal of Environmental Management*, vol. 38, pp. 213-218.

Mak, J, M.E.T. Moncur. 1995. "Sustainable Tourism Development: Managing Hawaii's 'Unique' Touristic Resource—Hanauma Bay," *Journal of Travel Research*, vol. 33, no. 4, pp. 51-57.

McCarville, R.E., B.L. Driver, J.L. Crompton. 1992. "Persuasive Communication and the Pricing of Public Leisure Services," *Influencing Human Behavior: Theory and Applications in Recreation, Tourism, and Natural Resources Management*, Sagamore, Champaign, Illinois.

McCarville, R.E., S.D. Reiling, C.M. White. 1996. "The Role of Fairness in Users' Assessments of First-time Fees for a Public Recreation Service," *Leisure Sciences*, vol. 18, pp. 61-76.

McKercher, R.D. 1998. *The Business of Nature-based Tourism*, Hospitality Press, Melbourne, Australia.

Meidan, A. 1982. "Marketing Strategies for Hotels," *International Journal of Hospitality Management*, vol. 1, no. 3, pp. 169-177.

Mitchell, R.C., R.T. Carson. 1989. *Using Surveys to Value Public Goods: The Contingent Valuation Method*, Resources for the Future, Washington, D.C.

Navrud, S., E.D. Mungatana. 1994. "Environmental Valuation in Developing Countries: The Recreational Value of Wildlife Viewing," *Ecological Economics*, vol. 11, pp. 135-151.

New South Wales National Parks and Wildlife Service (NSW, NPWS). 1997. "Draft Nature Tourism and Recreation Strategy," NSW NPWS, Sydney, Australia.

Nourse, H. 1968. *Regional Economics: a Study in the Economic Structure, Stability and Growth of Regions*, McGraw-Hill, New York.

Olindo, P. 1991. "The Old Man of Nature Tourism: Kenya," *Nature Tourism: Managing for the Environment*, Island Press, Washington, D.C.

Panos. 1997. *Ecotourism*, March, www:http://www.oneworld.org/panos/panos_eco2.html.

Pedersen, A. 1995. "Promotion of Community-based Ecotourism in the Maya Forest," report prepared for Management Systems International, Washington, D.C.

Pond, K. L. 1993. *The Professional Guide*, Van Nostrand Reinhold, New York.

Powell, R., L. Chalmers. 1995. *Regional Economic Impact: Gibraltar Range and Dorrigo National Parks*, New South Wales National Parks and Wildlife Service, Hurstville, New South Wales, Australia.

Price Waterhouse (Harare). 1994. "The Lowveld Conservancies: New Opportunities for Productive and Sustainable Land-Use," report to the Savé Valley, Bubiana, and Chiredzi River Conservancies.

Rosenthal, D.H., J.B. Loomis, G.L. Peterson. 1984. "Pricing for Efficiency and Revenue in Public Recreation Areas," *Journal of Leisure Research*, vol. 16, no. 3, pp. 195-208.

Schaller, D. 1996. "Indigenous Ecotourism and Sustainable Development: The Case of Rio Blanco, Ecuador," master's thesis, Department of Geography, University of Minnesota.

Siuslaw National Forest. 1996. "Fee Demonstration Business Plan," unpublished manuscript, Siuslaw National Forest, Corvallis, Oregon.

Smith, C., P. Jenner. 1992. "The Leakage of Foreign Exchange Earnings From Tourism," *Travel and Tourism Analyst*, vol. 3, pp. 52-66.

Sorenson, R. 1991. Overseas Adventure Travel, Inc. Case Study 9-391-068. Harvard Business School, Cambridge, Massachusetts.

Sowers, F., M. Walters, B.N. Upreti. 1994. "Assessment of USAID Biological Diversity Protection Programs: Nepal Case Study," *USAID Country Report*, United States Agency for International Development, Washington, D.C.

Spergel, B. 1996. "Summary of the Protected Area Conservation Trust," World Wildlife Fund, Washington, D.C.

Stevens, T., T. More, P.G. Allen. 1989. "Pricing Policies for Public Day-use Outdoor Recreation Areas," *Journal of Environmental Management*, vol. 28, pp. 43-52.

Telfer, D.J., G. Wall. 1996. "Linkages Between Tourism and Food Production," *Annals of Tourism Research*, vol. 23, no. 3, pp. 635-653.

Tisdell, C. 1996. "Ecotourism, Economics, and the Environment: Observations From China," *Journal of Travel Research*, vol. 34, no. 4, pp. 11-19.

Walsh, R.G. 1986. *Recreation Economic Decisions: Comparing Benefits and Costs*, Venture, State College, Pennsylvania. (Note: A second edition of this book, with J. Loomis as lead author, appeared in 1997, after this chapter was written.)

Wells, M. 1993. "Neglect of Biological Riches: The Economics of Nature Tourism in Nepal," *Biodiversity and Conservation*, vol. 2, pp. 445-464.

Wells, M. 1997. "Economic Perspectives on Nature Tourism, Conservation and Development," World Bank Environment Department Paper No. 55., World Bank, Washington, D.C.

Wells, M., K. Brandon. 1992. *People and Parks: Linking Protected Area Management With Local Communities*, World Bank, U.S. Agency for International Development, and World Wildlife Fund, Washington, D.C.

Wescott, G. 1995. "Victoria's National Park System: Can the Transition from Quantity of Parks to Quality of Management Be Successful?" *Australian Journal of Environmental Management*, vol. 4, no. 2, pp. 210-223.

Wunder, S. 1996. *Ecoturismo, Ingresos Locales y Conservación: El Caso de Cuyabeno, Ecuador*, Unión Mundial Para La Naturaleza (UICN/IUCN), Quito, Ecuador.

Wunder, S. 1998. "Forest Conservation Through Ecotourism Incomes? A Case Study from the Ecuadorean Amazon Region," CIFOR special paper, CIFOR, Bogor, Indonesia.

National Planning Limitations, Objectives and Lessons

The Development of Australia's National Ecotourism Strategy

Jill Grant and Alison Allcock

INTRODUCTION

This chapter describes the process whereby Australia's National Ecotourism Strategy was developed, as well as its translation into practice through the National Ecotourism Program. The consultative process, which was a key to the success of the finished document, is discussed, and recommendations are made on how this process could be adapted to other countries.

The *National Ecotourism Strategy* (NES) was a policy statement that outlined specific objectives and actions for the sustainable development of ecotourism in Australia. The NES is no longer official government policy following the election and change of government in March, 1996. A National Tourism Action Plan has been prepared, which addresses sustainable tourism development generally, rather than ecotourism specifically. However, the principles contained in the strategy have provided the impetus for many ongoing activities, including the current focus on sustainable tourism and the improvement in environmental performance for the tourism industry as a whole, not just in specialized niche markets.

In Australia there are three tiers of government (federal, state and local), each with discrete areas of responsibility and jurisdiction. The federal government is responsible for broad policy development and strategic planning, and through budgetary allocations, directs significant funding to programs that address national priorities. The development of the NES represented a new direction for the government in that it formally addressed an emerging market segment and provided leadership in an area in which it was important to achieve balance between the objectives of industry development and protection of the environment.

BACKGROUND

There were three parallel initiatives that contributed to the development of the NES: the *National Tourism Strategy*, the *National Strategy for Ecologically Sustainable Development* and the Pacific Asia Travel Association Policy on Endemic Tourism.

In June 1992, the federal government released the *National Tourism Strategy* (NTS), which was formulated to provide direction for future government policy and industry planning. The NTS provided an overview of the tourism environment in Australia and identified directions for ensuring that the political and economic climate was conducive for the tourism industry to prosper. This was to be achieved without increasing government intervention in the industry. The NTS signaled recognition by the federal government that emerging service industries, in particular tourism, may require different policies than "traditional" Australian export earners such as agriculture and mining.

The NTS identified four goals, including an environmental goal to "provide for sustainable tourism development by encouraging responsible planning and management practices consistent with the conservation of our natural and cultural heritage" (Commonwealth Department of Tourism, 1992a). This goal was to be achieved through a number of strategies addressing environmental and social issues, including the promotion and development of ecotourism, which was identified as an area of the tourism industry with significant growth potential.

Work on the NTS was undertaken concurrently with a separate but related policy initiative, the *National Strategy for Ecologically Sustainable Development* (ESD), which was released in December 1992, and included the recommendations of its Tourism Working Group. Integral to the ESD strategy was the philosophy that the environment must be conserved for the tourism industry to be viable in the long term. The federal government considered the formulation of an overall ecotourism policy framework as a vital step towards achieving sustainable tourism in natural areas.

The NTS was released in 1992, and work began on an ecotourism strategy later that year. The aim of the NES was to provide an overall framework to guide the integrated planning, development and management of Australia's ecotourism, on a sensitive and sustainable basis. It also provided an action plan for achieving ecotourism's full potential.

The Pacific Asia Travel Association (PATA) released a policy statement entitled *Endemic Tourism: A Profitable Industry in a Sustainable Environment* in November 1992. This policy provided a vision for the region which recognized that the cultural characteristics of communities have great value as tourism assets. To promote this concept PATA planned to organize workshops throughout Australia in early 1993. Work had already commenced on the NES and, as it was important to obtain a cross-section of views from around the country, a series of joint workshops was convened by the Commonwealth Department of Tourism (now Office of National Tourism) and PATA.

THE STRATEGY DEVELOPMENT PROCESS

The decision to formulate an ecotourism strategy was made in response to growing international interest and the increasing profile of Australia's natural environment as a tourism asset. Although there was no set process for development of the NES when work began, it was understood that the project would be a two-stage process. The first stage was to be a review of academic and popular literature on ecotourism; the second stage was to garner and incorporate input from the community.

The consultative approach (usually involving public advertisements calling for input, as well as workshops or meetings), is common in Australian public sector management and policy development. Indeed, some of the workshops for the NTS were chaired by the Minister for Tourism and attracted the support and attention of the most senior industry representatives in Australia. There are numerous benefits of adopting a consultative approach, the two greatest for the NES being the gathering of information from a wide range of interest groups and encouraging "ownership" of the final strategy.

INFORMATION GATHERING

An extensive literature review in late 1992 and early 1993 revealed a small but growing interest in ecotourism worldwide. New articles continued to appear throughout the time the NES was developed. However, much of the literature focused on environmental tourism in developing countries, and there was little research that could be directly applied in the Australian context. For instance, information relating to the economic imperatives associated with ecotourism development was less relevant to Australia than to developing countries. Similarly, the base level of tourism infrastructure was more established in Australia, making it easier for ecotourism enterprises to operate. On the other hand, unlike smaller countries, the very size of the Australian continent created problematic internal transport logistics that became a major impediment to ecotourism in some areas. Issues such as the training required to develop appropriate business skills, and equity of access to ecotourism opportunities, were common to most countries, including Australia.

Though the lack of relevant research created a problem, it also presented an opportunity to usher Australia's ecotourism in a completely new direction—one designed to serve the tourism industry, protect the natural environment and provide a product strongly identifiable with Australia in the international marketplace.

PUBLIC CONSULTATION

The literature review was supplemented by a process of national public consultation whereby the views of other interested parties could be incorporated into the debate alongside academic opinion and media discussion. There is a perception in

Australia that federal government public servants in the national capital, Canberra, are removed from the reality of the rest of the country. To counter this impression, it was also useful to obtain input from travel and tourism industry representatives as well as state and local governments.

As the success of the NES rested on achieving broad consensus between various levels of government (federal, state and local) and private-sector interests, there was a need to seek involvement from a range of individuals and organizations, particularly from local government agencies, natural resource managers, tour operators, tourism marketers, planners, conservation and community groups, developers and indigenous Australians.

Workshops were convened to gather information about issues, opportunities and impediments to ecotourism in Australia. The enthusiasm with which the industry, conservation groups, governments and others contributed to the process, and the wealth of information they brought to the discussion changed the direction of the NES by developing its community and industry focus. Issues identified here helped direct subsequent expenditure and provided a practical focus to the reality of running an ecotourism business under Australian conditions.

The workshops were held in major cities and some regional centers. The programs included short presentations by representatives of various interest groups. The sharing of their perspectives proved to be a very useful approach for stimulating discussion. Issues identified by the presenters were then fleshed out during the day. The workshops provided a forum for the discussion of local issues, even those not always relevant for development of a national strategy. However, local issues did provide useful examples of the costs and benefits of ecotourism in a wide range of climactic and regional locations.

A call for written submissions was placed in the national press in response to concerns from operators who had been unable to attend the workshops but wished to contribute. The over 250 written submissions provided an additional avenue for debate, and included valuable facts, case studies and stakeholder perspectives that were largely incorporated into a final document. This process encouraged "ownership" of the final strategy by the industry and other interested parties; this was reflected in the widespread adoption of many of the strategic principles and actions of the NES.

Ultimately it was the consultative process that inspired and stimulated the direction of the document. The definition of ecotourism, the key issues discussed in the final NES, and decisions about the direction of program funding, were all based on issues raised through the workshops and public submissions. Development of the NES coincided with increasing interest in ecotourism within the community. If time had been available it would have been possible to consult further. There was a demand for more consultation (even though it was conducted over a full year), while other groups felt that the consultation process was too extensive and that implementation was more important. Ultimately, there was a need to balance the time given to public consultation with the finalization of the document and implementation of its recommendations.

The NES was developed in close consultation with Australia's states and territories. Prior to its commencement, only one state, Victoria, had completed an ecotourism strategy of its own. South Australia and Queensland were also working on ecotourism or nature-based tourism plans, working closely with the federal government and using the NES as a basis for their own state strategies. Although this brought about delays in the process, the benefit was that there were strong commonalities in the content and direction of the documents.

The consultation process was highly visible and functioned to reconcile points of view and address contentious issues. Where points of view were not fully reconciled, all submissions were documented so that the reader could formulate a balanced perspective. The NES benefited from this investment of time and resources. Concerns, issues and priorities were not always homogeneous throughout Australia, and many would not have been identified at all had the process been developed centrally. In planning community input, practical outcomes can be ensured by:

- having discussions extend beyond the most prominent aspects of ecotourism;
- sensitively managing potential conflicts between participants;
- making certain all participants are aware of the process at the end of the workshop; and
- recognizing the input of all participants.

If the process were to be conducted again, it would be useful to prepare a comprehensive issues paper and circulate it prior to the workshops. It is the synthesis of local issues that gives a strategic document its strength; a document which can be studied in advance by the participants will help to focus discussions (especially in the event of competing agendas and time constraints) and will also provide a framework for written responses by those who are unable to attend.

COST OF THE PROCESS

The major costs of NES development were staff salaries and overhead, travel, workshop venue hire, advertising, printing and distribution of the draft and final strategies. Many of these costs are difficult to isolate and will vary from country to country. A project team of four people worked almost exclusively on the NES for about 12 months, and contract staff were engaged as needed at key times. Besides salary costs, there were associated office costs and some relatively high telephone and communication expenses.

Due to Australia's large geographic size and relatively expensive domestic travel, the cost of convening or attending workshops was significant. Public interest and equity considerations necessitated visits in all states and territories. Return visits were subsequently required to meet with states that were developing their own ecotourism strategies, and to present workshops and conference papers to professional organizations. Although state governments and industry associations assisted with the organization of workshops, the establishment and maintenance of communication with so many interest groups was expensive and required considerable staff time and energy. Although there was no charge to attend the workshops in Australia, it might be possible to organize such workshops on a cost recovery basis if funds are not available for similar projects in other parts of the world.

Written submissions were invited through an advertisement placed in all major metropolitan newspapers. Radio interviews conducted at the time of the workshops also helped to raise awareness of the process and led to additional submissions being received.

Printing costs were met by the government. Three thousand copies of the draft and ten thousand of the final NES were printed. There was no charge for either the draft or final, as policy documents produced by the federal government are usually distributed free of charge. In this way the government encourages participation in policy development.

KEY ISSUES IDENTIFIED IN THE NES

Agreement on the definition of ecotourism was one of the most difficult issues to reconcile. The final definition focused on the natural environment, ecological and cultural sustainability, education and interpretation, and local and regional benefits. A strict definition would have excluded operators who, for whatever reason, did not meet best practice standards in all of their business activities; a very loose definition would have allowed any operator to use the ecotourism label for marketing advantage.

The final definition was framed to encourage entry into ecotourism by new operators and to encourage existing operators to adopt environmentally sustainable practices wherever possible, even if they were not specifically seeking ecotourism business. The broad definition proved successful as many "mainstream" Australian operators have now reviewed and improved their environmental practice, with the added advantage of substantial cost savings.

The major issues affecting or likely to affect the development of the industry were identified through the consultation process as:

- ecological sustainability
- integrated regional planning
- natural resource management
- regulation
- infrastructure
- impact monitoring

- marketing
- industry standards and accreditation
- ecotourism education
- involvement of indigenous Australians
- viability and equity considerations

These are discussed more fully in the *National Ecotourism Strategy* (Commonwealth Department of Tourism, 1994).

NATIONAL ECOTOURISM PROGRAM

The National Ecotourism Strategy was translated into practice through the National Ecotourism Program (NEP). The federal government committed AU$10 million ($7 million) over the four years from 1993-94 to 1996-97. The NEP aimed to sustainably develop ecotourism through innovative projects that would increase Australia's competitiveness as an ecotourism destination, enhance visitor appreciation of natural and cultural values, and contribute to the long-term conservation and management of ecotourism resources. Following the change of government in 1996, the remaining NEP funds were incorporated into the National Tourism Development Program, which commenced in the 1996-97 financial year and included the category, "Managing Tourism in Natural Environments."

The aims of the NEP were addressed by a range of competitive grants and several consultancies. Grants were offered to community groups and government agencies for projects designed to implement the NES in rural Australia. Agencies were required to apply against a set of common guidelines. Projects were then assessed, and those which best met the goals of the program (outlined in the NES) were funded. Hence the grants were not automatic; organizations had to compete for funding.

Specialist consultants were commissioned to undertake aspects of the strategy that involved development of issues for national application. These included encouraging better energy and waste minimization practices in the industry, an investigation into the development of a national ecotourism accreditation scheme, a needs analysis for ecotourism education, the development of comprehensive ecotourist profiles, and a study into methods to improve the business skills and practices of ecotourism operators.

COMPETITIVE GRANTS

These grants were divided into three major categories:

INFRASTRUCTURE DEVELOPMENT—Provided for visitor access to ecotourism destinations and offered assistance with the management of environmental impacts and physical protection of natural resources. Projects that utilized innovative eco-design and environmentally friendly technology were particularly encouraged, including protective boardwalks with interpretive signs, visitor education facilities such as wildlife viewing platforms, and alternative power systems for remote sites.

BASELINE STUDIES AND MONITORING—Assessed and contributed to the management of changes to natural environments caused by, or likely to occur as a result of, tourism activities. The research conducted under this element of the program aimed to provide a more informed basis for decisions by tourism planners, operators and natural resource managers. These studies included: assessing the impact of tourist infrastructure on environmental processes in Central Australia; the impacts, economics and management of recreational scuba diving in marine-protected areas; and the monitoring of freshwater ecosystems in response to bushwalking and camping activities.

REGIONAL ECOTOURISM PLANNING—Aimed at improving the capacity of regions to attract foreign and domestic tourists to natural areas and to encourage planning processes that recognize ecosystems as their basis. The grants encouraged the involvement of local participation in the planning and decision making process, including consultation with local government, regional development and tourism bodies, natural resource managers, and indigenous and community groups to ensure a wide commitment to a regional plan. Examples of successful projects included the development of a community ecotourism planning handbook and a number of regional ecotourism strategies that have now been successfully implemented.

CONSULTANCIES

The Energy and Waste Minimization Study provided a comprehensive investigation of best practices and a demonstration of the economic and marketing benefits of adopting environmentally responsible practices. The result of the consultancy was the publication, *Best Practice Ecotourism: A Guide to Energy and Waste Minimisation* (Commonwealth Department of Tourism, 1995), which has been widely used by ecotourism operators. The accommodation sector has also adopted many of the principles contained in this document.

The study also provided the impetus for a project conducted in conjunction with the main national industry association, Tourism Council Australia, and the World Travel and Tourism Council to provide the tourism industry with a comprehensive overview of sustainable energy technologies. The resulting report, *Tourism Switched On* (Office of National Tourism, 1996), was designed to help tourism businesses with making informed choices about energy use. It highlights the cost savings of renewable energy use and promotes the concept that good environmental practice is also good business practice.

The Ecotourism Education Consultancy aimed to promote an increased level of awareness and understanding of the principles and practices of ecotourism to a range of audiences including the media, the tourism industry, education and training bodies, and consumers. Current and future education needs of the industry were identified, and a series of communication strategies was prepared. An ecotourism education directory was also prepared which lists training courses, education resource materials and useful contacts for ecotourism in Australia (Commonwealth Department of Tourism, 1996).

A public awareness program was developed in direct response to the recommendations of the report and resulted in a series of short videos with the theme "Australia: Worth Looking At, Worth Looking After." These videos were used as part of in-flight entertainment programs and elsewhere within the tourism industry (including hotels, backpacker establishments and bus companies). Another feature of the program was information on the Office of National Tourism Internet home page, which communicated environmental care messages both to Australia-bound international visitors and domestic tourists.

The Business Development Consultancy was aimed at improving the overall business skills of ecotourism operators. This study was undertaken in response to finding that many operators were well-qualified in regard to environmental knowledge, but had little formal training in business management. An investigation of networks and alliances for cooperative marketing, purchasing and skill-sharing were conducted, and mechanisms were determined to improve the business performance of ecotourism operators who were generally located outside capital cities and worked unusual hours. Several major recommendations of this report were put into practice through the establishment of pilot networks that fostered cooperative approaches to ecotourism business development and collective marketing by small operators.

The Market Research Consultancy was undertaken by the Bureau of Tourism Research (a federal government agency) to assess the nature and level of demand for ecotourism experiences. A market profile of ecotourists and information on their expectations was also prepared to enable the industry to develop new ecotourism products and target new markets with increased effectiveness. The findings were published in *The Nature of Ecotourism* (Blamey, 1995). The results of focus group studies using a cross section of the market were distilled in the booklet *Ecotourism Snapshot: A Focus on Recent Market Research* (Office of National Tourism, 1997). This research has addressed a major information gap identified by the NES consultation process and has assisted ecotourism operators in tailoring their product and service to meet visitor expectations.

CONFERENCES AND WORKSHOPS PROGRAM

Another component of the NEP was the provision of funds to a number of high-profile conferences and workshops that focused on sustainable industry development. The first of these was the Sustainable Design and Ecotourism Seminar, held in conjunction with the World Congress on Ecotourism and Adventure Travel in November, 1994. Funding was also provided in 1995 and 1996 to the Ecotourism Association of Australia to sponsor seminars at their annual conference, with an Applied Technology Forum and a People, Parks and Profitable Partnerships seminar. Assistance was also provided to the Australian Nature Conservation Agency for the 1995 Encounters with Whales Conference and for a follow-up consultancy to investigate the feasibility of forming a national whale- and dolphin-watching association. This study and a subsequent national meeting led to the formation of the "Cetacea Australia" association in April 1997.

These industry-directed initiatives have done much to raise the profile of ecotourism principles and have led to stronger links between land management agencies and operators. Based on written responses and comments received during the NEP evaluation process, there has also been a notable increase in the uptake of new technologies and innovative approaches to management by the broader industry.

NATIONAL ECOTOURISM ACCREDITATION PROGRAM

In response to the need identified by industry for a system to assess and promote genuine ecotourism operations in Australia, a National Ecotourism Accreditation Program (NEAP) was developed. The program was developed by industry over a two-year period of extensive consultation. Funding was made available from the NEP to investigate the feasibility of, and operator response to, accreditation. Funding was then provided for a set of assessment criteria to be jointly developed and tested by the Ecotourism Association of Australia, the Australian Tourism Operators Network and Tourism Council Australia.

The assessment criteria were then distributed to a group of 50 Australian operators representing a sample of geographical locations, operation sizes and types. Since November 1996 the program has been accepting applications from ecotourism operators and protected area agencies—there were 110 ecotourism products accredited as of June 1998. This response has largely met expectations, and as the program becomes more widely known, participation will likely increase further.

The program provides a benchmark for best environmental practice and allows for continuous improvement in the provision of environmental tourism products. Sustainable practice and interpretation of the natural environment is a requirement for accreditation. Accreditation will help consumers to make informed decisions, reduce environmental impacts, and provide benefits to natural areas and local communities. To promote the program, a series of workshops has been held at various locations around Australia. In addition, articles in the press and tourism industry newsletters have helped to explain the accreditation program.

To date there have been no comprehensive consumer awareness activities due to cost considerations. As membership grows, however, it should be possible to let consumers know more about the NEAP and the quality of services offered by accredited ecotourism operations.

THE IMPORTANCE OF NATIONAL PLANNING

Most public policy developed by the Australian government is based on voluntary participation rather than regulation. Aside from the attendant political and social aversion, regulatory mechanisms are expensive and difficult to enforce. The NEP offered incentives rather than regulation, arguing that marketing benefits accrue from adoption of standards, and that financial benefits accrue from use of environmentally friendly technologies.

National planning is one way to bring people together to seek common solutions, thereby avoiding direct confrontation, such as through possible litigation against tourism developers who breach environmental regulations. The adoption of environmental safeguards reduces the possibility for conflict. National planning also gives the ecotourism segment of the tourism and travel industry some cohesion by focusing on how best to achieve its philosophy of sustainability. It helps to develop an industry agenda and set priorities by providing a focus for funding. There are also long-term environmental impacts for the entire industry, in that "green" practices may well be eventually adopted throughout the sector. (As visitation to Australia increases, this focus on sustainability of the industry as a whole, not just on specific sectors, will become increasingly important. A large part of Australia's international reputation is based on the quality of its environment. It will be important to maintain this through best practice environmental management.)

EVALUATING THE SUCCESS OF THE NES

The NES encountered no major criticisms after its publication, although there was resistance to accreditation initiatives because the industry was divided on the approach and uncertain of the implications for their businesses. It took two years after the release of the NES for the National Ecotourism Accreditation Program to become a reality. However with the added time and consultation, the level of support and commitment within the industry was sufficient to make it a success. Without the impetus of the NES in identifying the importance of accreditation and the subsequent funding under the NEP, it is doubtful that it would have been possible to establish such an initiative.

It was apparent during the consultation process that different issues varied in importance depending on local conditions. Getting the industry to participate in the consultation process was not always easy in terms of timing, availability, cost and location of the workshops. Although there may have been some bias in the workshops and submissions (as only certain groups made themselves available to participate or took the time to prepare a submission), on a national basis, a representative sample of operators did contribute at various stages of the process, and their response to the finished document was positive.

Policy development in Australia is an evolutionary process, and policy is revised as prevailing attitudes and conditions change. In retrospect, the key to the widespread acceptance of the NES was in the development of the draft strategy. By allowing comment on this document and incorporating a diversity of views within its framework, there were no major surprises when the document was finalized. As a result, the industry and other government agencies that were identified as having responsibility for its implementation were ready to accept the NES. When the NEP was launched in 1994 there was already a good understanding of the types of projects that would best meet the aims of the NES.

Another critical success factor was that funds were available to develop the NES and deliver on its initiatives. The NEP provided support to state and local governments and to community groups, many of which have been able to continue with their own implementation plans after the initial injection of funds. The NEP made a significant contribution to the infrastructure, planning and research base of ecotourism (and regional tourism in general). As a direct result of the NEP's competitive grants, Australia now has a greater number and variety of quality ecotourism facilities—such as protective boardwalks, interpretive signs, and information centers—and an increased level of baseline research on tourism impacts.

Also as a direct result of the program, a higher percentage of local governments have now recognized the potential offered by the tourism industry for employment generation and diversification of their economic base, and have strategic plans in place for the development of ecotourism in their region.

Another tangible outcome of the NES and NEP has been the change in the nature of the industry—it has become more cohesive and has forged a strong identity in the marketplace. The growth in membership of the Ecotourism Association of Australia and the success of the National Ecotourism Accreditation Program are evidence of this. Other industry associations, such as the Australian Tourism Operators Network and Tourism Council Australia, have also played strong roles in increasing the professionalism and viability of the industry.

In recognition of the importance of sustainable tourism, the Australian government has committed AU$14.72 million ($10.3 million) over seven years (beginning in 1997) to the Cooperative Research Center for Sustainable Tourism, which will provide an industry-focused research agenda to assist management decision making and prepare for the next century. Moreover, there has been a proliferation of ecotourism-related tertiary courses and vocationally based training that are meeting the need for highly skilled planners, policy makers and operators.

In early 1997, a survey of previous grant applicants (including both successful and unsuccessful cases) was conducted to evaluate the NEP. Comments received demonstrate that both the NES and the NEP are considered to be world leaders in government involvement in a niche market. The results also show that these initiatives have attracted considerable international interest. They have provided Australia with a competitive edge internationally by minimizing the factors inhibiting the growth of ecotourism, and establishing an industry framework that should facilitate the growth of the industry on a competitive and sustainable basis.

CONCLUSION

The development of the NES was a major commitment by the former Department of Tourism, both in terms of resources and subsequent funding through the NEP. The NEP's success was due to the strategic framework provided by the NES. By addressing key priorities, a significant boost was given to the ecotourism industry; this influence has spread to the entire industry through adoption of ecotourism principles and practices. Without the planning and analysis provided by the NES, this funding would not have been as well targeted, and some of the major industry requirements, at a crucial stage of development, would not have been identified. The many positive outcomes of the NES have demonstrated the benefits of strategic thinking at a national level.

Ideas and directions generated from this experience also contributed to the development of the *National Tourism Action Plan* (to be released in June 1998), and will no doubt impact resulting future programs. The principles contained in the NES are widely researched and accepted. Other countries may benefit from the Australian experience and could easily adapt this approach to their own country. Specific recommendations for others attempting such a process include the following:

- Prepare an issues paper to focus discussions and stimulate thinking.
- Conduct extensive consultation through well-publicized and promoted public meetings.
- Allow sufficient time for comment on draft documents in the form of written submissions.
- Try to acknowledge all views received within the strategic context.
- Allocate funds for implementation in response to specific needs identified by the consultation and, wherever possible, sponsor projects that demonstrate best practice in terms of ecologically sustainable development.

Even though the NES is no longer official government policy, the process through which it was developed remains relevant to planning and managing tourism in natural areas and can provide a useful guide to others involved in national planning.

REFERENCES

Blamey, R.K. 1995. "The Nature of Ecotourism," Occasional Paper 21, Bureau of Tourism Research, Canberra, Australia.

Commonwealth Department of Tourism. 1992a. *National Tourism Strategy*, Australian Government Publishing Service, Canberra, Australia.

Commonwealth Department of Tourism. 1992b. *National Tourism Strategy*, Australian Government Publishing Service, Canberra, Australia.

Commonwealth Department of Tourism. 1994. *National Ecotourism Strategy*, Australian Government Publishing Service, Canberra, Australia.

Commonwealth Department of Tourism. 1995. *Best Practice Ecotourism: A Guide to Energy and Waste Minimisation*, Australian Government Publishing Service, Canberra, Australia.

Commonwealth Department of Tourism. 1996. *Ecotourism Education—A Directory of Training Courses, Education Resource Materials and Useful Contacts for Ecotourism in Australia*, Australian Government Publishing Service, Canberra, Australia.

Office of National Tourism. 1996. *Tourism Switched On, Department of Industry, Science and Tourism*, Canberra, Australia.

Office of National Tourism. 1997. *Ecotourism Snapshot: A Focus on Recent Market Research*, Department of Industry, Science and Tourism, Canberra, Australia.

Office of National Tourism. 1998. *Tourism—A Ticket to the 21st Century: National Action Plan*, Department of Industry, Science and Tourism, Canberra.

Pacific Asia Travel Association. 1992. *Endemic Tourism: A Profitable Industry in a Sustainable Environment*, PATA Think Tank, Sydney, Australia.

Copies of many of these publications may be obtained from: The Information Officer, Office of National Tourism, GPO Box 9839, Canberra, ACT 2600, Australia

ADDITIONAL READINGS

Commonwealth of Australia. 1992. *National Strategy for Ecologically Sustainable Development*, Australian Government Publishing Service, Canberra, Australia.

Office of National Tourism. 1996. *Projecting Success—Visitor Management Projects for Sustainable Tourism Growth*, Department of Industry, Science and Tourism, Canberra, Australia.

Office of National Tourism. 1996. *Developing Tourism—Projects in Profile*, Department of Industry, Science and Tourism, Canberra, Australia.

Protected Area Planning Principles and Strategies

William T. Borrie, Stephen F. McCool and George H. Stankey

INTRODUCTION

Protected areas play an important role in the evolving challenge of maintaining a sustainable world. Not only do they provide refuges for biological diversity, but they play an equally significant role in the changing economic and social basis of local communities and nations. That protected areas are increasingly becoming a source of tourist revenue is not surprising. In many cases, such as the community baboon sanctuary in Belize or Kinabalu Park in Malaysia, entrance fees and other revenues from visitors not only offset the cost of management but also provide the local community with additional income that then provides incentive for continued protection. The income derived from the protected area, and the attachments people form with the area, often become an important component of the local community. However, the cultural and economic effects of protected areas and their management may disproportionately impact the local community, perhaps leading to resentment toward the park. Actions affecting the protected area may be controversial because of those effects. Therefore, conducting consultations and achieving the support of local constituencies will be essential to the success of any protected area planning effort.

These social, cultural and economic dimensions remind us that natural resource planning and management, and protected area management in particular, occur within highly politicized contexts. The objective of preserving natural areas is frequently impacted by the desire to encourage recreational use, particularly with respect to government goals for economic development and the role of nature-based tourism or ecotourism within those programs. The two goals of preservation and use are frequently in conflict, with disagreement about which should receive priority. Protected areas represent a legitimate and important source of income and stability, but the increasing recognition and capacity of protected areas to generate revenue can lead to economic dependency, which in turn increases pressures to maximize financial returns. In the face of this pressure, protected area managers must act as guardians of the values for which the area was established, mitigating the negative biophysical and social impacts of increased tourism. These are the kinds of contentious contexts in which protected area managers increasingly, but inevitably, conduct and implement planning processes. It is through planning that managers can provide not only technical expertise, but also interact collaboratively with affected publics to ensure support and implementation of actions to protect the natural resource values of protected areas.

Designating and identifying boundaries does not guarantee protection of the values for which the areas were established. A significant body of literature has shown the myth of the non-consumptive visitor, demonstrating that use of an area will impact many of the values for which the area was established (Cole, 1987, Hammitt and Cole, 1987; Hendee et al., 1990; Speight, 1973; Wall and Wright, 1977; Wilkes, 1977). Understanding how to manage the impacts that come with increased visitation is therefore an essential component of any protected area's obligation to conserve its significant resources. Various planning and management frameworks have been developed to explicitly consider the issues of visitation.

The concept of "carrying capacity" is one such framework dealing with the issue of visitor impact (most recently, see Butler, 1996). However, despite a substantial history of attempts to apply it as a management framework, as well as the existence of a large body of research literature, carrying capacity has provided protected area managers with little practical direction. In large part, this is because both ecological and social impacts of recreation and tourism use are often influenced by variables other than amount of use. Moreover, the predominant focus on carrying capacity has unfortunately misdirected attention almost solely to controlling numbers of visitors, deflecting attention away from many more useful actions based on an understanding of relationships between visitation levels, impacts, area goals and local community expectations (Lindberg et al., 1997; McCool, 1996; Stankey and McCool, 1989). Essentially, carrying capacity focuses attention on the question, "How many is too many?" when the question confronting protected area managers is, "What are the appropriate or acceptable conditions for visitation and how do we achieve them?"

In this chapter, the challenges of protected area planning are explored by addressing the latter question. The chapter focuses on maintaining protected area values in the face of increasing recreational pressure, although these general concepts and principles can be applied to other "threats" as well (Machlis and Tichnell, 1985). Outlined first are the social and political contexts within which such planning occurs. It is in these complex contexts that an interactive, collaborative learning-based planning process would seem most appropriate. Next, an overview of eleven principles of visitor management is presented. These principles must be acknowledged and incorporated in any protected area planning system. Following this section, the conditions needed to implement a carrying capacity approach are reviewed; these requisite conditions lead us to conclude that, despite a resurgence of interest, the carrying capacity model does not adequately address the needs of protected area management. The final section briefly outlines the *Limits of Acceptable Change* planning system, an example of an approach that can incorporate the eleven previously described principles, and has a demonstrated capacity to respond to the needs of protected area managers. Though this chapter focuses on the U.S. context and experience, it is relevant in other countries. The ideas in this chapter have been variously presented in Malaysia, Venezuela, Canada, Puerto Rico and elsewhere (McCool, 1996; McCool and Stankey, 1992; Stankey and McCool, 1993) and have benefited from the positive interactions and feedback received from protected area managers in those countries.

PROTECTED AREA PLANNING IN AN ERA OF CHANGE

That protected area planning has moved from a time of apparent stability to an era of social and political change, and turbulence should come as no surprise to protected area managers. The growing diversity of communities claiming interest in management of protected areas translates into new voices articulating an ever-widening range of visions and functions for protected areas. These new voices are increasingly apparent in a political system that not only allocates funds for protected area management, but also must resolve complex management problems.

Cultural and spiritual values that once were considered inconsistent with the protected area's mandate for protection are now often accommodated. For example, areas which were originally established to exclude many extractive uses now recognize pre-existing and legitimate claims of indigenous peoples for subsistence. This legitimization of prior uses and values has made the protected area manager's job more complex and difficult. Managers are now confronted with balancing these uses with the objective of preserving biological diversity, ecological processes and habitats for threatened and endangered species.

Incorporation of a wider variety of goals into protected area management creates a tension or conflict for which traditional rational-comprehensive models of planning are ill-equipped (see Briassoulis, 1989, for a description of various planning models). Such models are well-suited for identifying the most technically efficient path to a single goal founded upon substantial social consensus. However, when one confronts the wide array of goals currently attributed to protected areas and the frequent lack of consensus over these competing goals, the appropriateness and utility of such traditional planning models is questioned. Increasingly, today, there exists a shift in conditions to which planning models must respond—from one in which scientific and technical expertise dominate, to one in which affected publics play the significant role. In the latter context, quality scientific and technical information remains essential, for it can describe current conditions and ecological processes, help provide understanding of causation, identify consequences and implications, and define alternative solutions. However, progress on implementation cannot begin until there is agreement on goals, which are fundamentally social-political statements of desired ends. The specification of goals is not a scientific or technical matter. Thus, while rational-comprehensive and scientific methods of inquiry are necessary to the planning process, they are not sufficient. In fact, it is not uncommon that traditional rational-comprehensive approaches to planning (McCool et al., 1986), conducted in a comprehensive and technically competent manner, lead to more, not less, disagreement. At the root of this lies conflicting values among various interests.

In these situations, the principal planning problem is not so much how to achieve a particular vision of the future, but rather which future to select. Expert-driven models of planning do little to help resolve this conflict, because the choice of a desired future is fundamentally political and social, not technical. These "wicked problems" are ones in which there are no right or wrong answers, just more or less useful ones (Allen and Gould, 1986). Technical approaches to planning require managers to provide scientifically proven answers to justify decisions. "Wicked problems," conversely, cannot be resolved solely through science.

Political conflicts are resolved through a process of negotiation. This process incorporates learning, representation of interests, and dialogue, and must ultimately lead to a consensus (here defined as "grudging agreement") about a desired future and appropriate pathways to it. However, while the tension created by the presence of conflicting goals provides an excellent impetus for mutual learning, such learning also requires acceptance of others, multiple types of knowledge, and opportunities to test and evaluate ideas. Learning is an important objective because our level of knowledge concerning management of recreation in protected areas is limited. Actions undertaken to reduce impacts are, by and large, experiments—particularly at the larger spatial scales and longer time frames. Learning provides the feedback necessary to change actions when outcomes do not occur as expected (Lee, 1993). As the future of protected area management unfolds, it may be that these outcomes were not as attractive as originally conceived.

Given this context, approaches to protected area management must combine technical-scientific data with social learning in order to develop plans that can be effective. While the following sections focus on the more technical aspects of protected area management, it should be noted that this discussion occurs only within the context of engaging affected publics in dialogue about these areas. In the recreation and ecotourism context, these publics might include residents of local communities, tourism businesses, the tourists themselves, and so on.

PRINCIPLES OF VISITOR MANAGEMENT

The following discussion of protected area planning begins with an examination of eleven guiding principles which have emerged from research on visitor impacts and from the management of protected areas to minimize those impacts. These principles provide a sound basis for any systematic planning system for natural-area management. They illustrate important concepts of planning, such as the need for an explicit statement of management objectives, that are even more applicable within an era of change.

This chapter then goes on to examine two visitor management approaches that aspire to protect the ecological and social conditions of protected areas. Whereas the *Limits of Acceptable Change* approach has proven to be a highly adaptable and applicable framework, the carrying capacity approach, while seemingly explicit and rational, can be seen as less useful. While intuitively attractive, the implementation of a recreational carrying capacity too casually assumes workable conditions for its application. We describe some of the severe limitations of the carrying capacity approach as an illustration of the implications of the eleven principles of visitor management. The *Limits of Acceptable Change* process is then presented as a more useful approach to protected area management.

PRINCIPLE 1: APPROPRIATE MANAGEMENT REQUIRES EXPLICITLY STATED OBJECTIVES—Explicitly stated objectives are of utmost importance in natural-area management. The need for such objectives has been a clear and consistent theme throughout the literature on visitor management in protected areas (Brown et al., 1987; Schomaker, 1984). Objectives provide definitive statements of desired social and environmental conditions, recreational opportunities, and benefits from managing the area (Stankey and McCool, 1984). These objectives derive from legislative or administrative policy direction, or from explicit assertions in the management plan for the area. Formally stated objectives will help identify the appropriateness of various management actions and provide managers criteria by which to judge the success of management actions they have been using to resolve protected area issues and problems. According to Manning (1986):

> *Management objectives provide an answer to the question of how much change is acceptable by deciding what types of recreation experience a particular recreation area should provide, the feel of naturalness of environmental conditions, the kind of experience offered and the intensity of management practices.*

Good objectives are time-bound, specific, quantifiable and attainable (Schomaker, 1984). However, writing good objectives is not easy. While people tend to agree about general values and concepts, specific and explicit objectives are likely to evoke considerable disagreement about what is to be accomplished or produced at a protected area. It should be noted that the process of establishing objectives is an intrinsically political one. Methods that include interaction with affected parties will help the manager develop objectives upon which a consensus can be developed and enhance the likelihood of their successful implementation.

PRINCIPLE 2: DIVERSITY OF RESOURCE, SOCIAL AND MANAGERIAL CONDITIONS IN AND AMONG PROTECTED AREAS IS INEVITABLE AND MAY BE DESIRABLE—Visitors to a particular protected area often expect the area to satisfy a variety of recreation activities, specific recreation experiences, and various beneficial outcomes from their recreation. However, it is unlikely that their demands for such a wide variety of recreation opportunities can be met by a uniform set of conditions across the area. Further, it is unlikely that resource and social conditions within any relatively large protected area will be uniform. Biophysical conditions, use impacts, use levels, and expectations of appropriate conditions tend to vary (for example, see Martin et al., 1989, concerning variability in acceptable campsite impact conditions in the periphery versus the center of a wilderness). Visitor use is frequently unevenly distributed and development unevenly focused at particular sites. Topography, vegetation and access influence use densities and level of impact.

The diversity of conditions is inevitable, and can be desirable. The availability of a variety of settings provides visitors with a choice and allows them to consider their requirements and expectations for a site. Furthermore, providing a diversity of opportunities influences future use and may provoke demands for a broader array of recreation opportunities. It is a means of protecting uniqueness and suitability in the management of protected areas. For example, in large protected areas it would generally not be desirable to have development spread evenly throughout the area, but to have, instead, the interior of protected areas display fewer human-induced impacts than the periphery. Managers can identify this diversity and then make decisions on its desirability, based on such considerations as visitor preferences, environmental values and relative availability, thus separating technical decisions from judgmental ones. Finally, Haas et al. (1987) argue that managing for diversity through some type of explicit zoning is more likely to lead to preservation of protected area values rather than existing implicit or de facto zoning.

PRINCIPLE 3: MANAGEMENT IS DIRECTED AT INFLUENCING HUMAN-INDUCED CHANGE—Many protected areas were established to protect unique and valuable natural features and conditions, and natural processes. Rather than directly managing these natural processes, protected area managers usually work to minimize and manage human-induced impacts on these natural processes. Human-induced changes can lead to both environmental and social conditions that visitors and/or managers find unacceptable or inappropriate. In addition to helping determine how much change is acceptable, managers should concern themselves with actions that are effective in influencing the amount, type, time and location of these impacts.

PRINCIPLE 4: IMPACTS ON RESOURCE AND SOCIAL CONDITIONS ARE INEVITABLE CONSEQUENCES OF HUMAN USE—A variety of research has shown that relatively small amounts of use produce most of the biophysical impact that occurs on any site (Cole, 1987). Any recreational use of a protected area has some environmental impact, the severity of which depends on the environment's ability to resist and recover from such impact. Typically, the ability to resist and recover is rapidly outpaced by the frequency, intensity and nature of recreational use. Thus, the decision for allowing human use in a particular area is a de facto decision to accept relatively high levels of visitor impact. The principal question that managers must therefore ask is, "How much impact is acceptable in this area?" Once this question has been addressed, managers must then deal with the appropriateness of various techniques or actions in managing this level of impact. In a similar way, social impacts often occur with relatively small amounts of use. For example, a few people behaving in a rowdy manner can impact another visitor's experience far more than many people being quiet might.

PRINCIPLE 5: IMPACTS CAN BE TEMPORALLY OR SPATIALLY DISCONTINUOUS—Impacts from visitor use or management activities can occur off site and/or might not be visible until a later time. Displacing the management problem temporally or spatially can create two problems. First, a management strategy eliminating camping around a lake, for example, might simply displace impacts to other, perhaps more environmentally sensitive, areas, thereby creating two sets of impacts needing attention. Second, impacts can have effects that only become evident long after recreationists leave the site. For example, soil and vegetation impacts can have long-term implications such as increased soil erosion or reduced tree vigor. Both temporal and spatial displacement of impacts make the understanding and managing of impacts significantly more difficult, demand substantial knowledge about use-impact relationships at different scales, and require managers to carefully design appropriate monitoring strategies.

PRINCIPLE 6: THE USE/IMPACT RELATIONSHIP IS NONLINEAR AND INFLUENCED BY MANY VARIABLES—The relationship between visitor use levels and degrees of impact is an exceedingly complex, non-linear one. That is, managers cannot simply assume that as use levels increase so, too, will impacts, or conversely, that reductions in use levels will lead to proportionate reductions in impact. Moreover, a variety of other variables affects the use/impact relationship. It has long been observed that the behavior of recreationists heavily influences the amount of their impact. For example, in marine settings, snorkelers treading water with flippers can break fragile coral and stir up sand which then impacts coral and other marine life. Similarly, changes to the rules and regulations imposed upon visitors will change the degree of impact. For example, requiring or educating visitors to camp a certain distance away from lakes and streams not only lowers the impacts at the immediate lakeside or streamside, but also lowers the visual and social impacts upon other visitors, both human and animal. Other variables, such as travel method, group size, season of use, length of stay, and a variety of soil and vegetation characteristics, will influence the use/impact relationship as well.

Furthermore, even under simplified conditions, the use/impact curve has been found to be more curvilinear than linear (Hammitt and Cole, 1987). For instance, while per-visitor impacts on campsite conditions might initially be very low, they can rapidly increase until reaching a plateau at which most of the damage has already been done; thereafter, per-person impacts become incrementally small. This complexity of the use/impact relationship suggests that attempts to control human-induced impacts solely through use limits or carrying capacities have only a low probability of success. Education and information programs, and rules and regulations aimed at changing visitor behavior might be more effective. For instance, encouraging use concentration on already impacted sites is one well-known technique for limiting visitor impacts.

PRINCIPLE 7: MANY MANAGEMENT PROBLEMS ARE NOT USE-DENSITY DEPENDENT—There are only a few management problems that directly relate to the number of people using the area. These issues, such as sewage, water supply and parking problems, tend to have relatively simple technological solutions. However, with respect to the provision of social conditions, focusing on density of use might not be useful in solving management problems. For example, many visitors to backcountry areas of nationally protected areas may not be seeking solitude (Stankey and McCool, 1984). Thus, in this situation, controlling use levels to optimize solitude would be inappropriate. This is further exacerbated by different visitors having different perceptions of solitude, different expectations of crowding, and different tolerances for privacy.

PRINCIPLE 8: LIMITING USE IS ONLY ONE OF MANY MANAGEMENT OPTIONS—Controlling use should not necessarily be the first management tactic chosen to manage visitor impacts. Other management actions that should be considered include those that focus on improving visitor behavior, redistributing or containing use to less sensitive locations, and enhancing resource durability. Even if controlling use levels is the primary concern, efforts should be made to discourage use (e.g., through fees or more inconvenient access) rather than enforcing outright limits on use. Simply controlling the input of visitors into a park system will not necessarily lead to the optimum mix of outputs or the best achievement of the protected area's objectives. The costs (social, economic and ecological) to implement use limits might be greater than the benefits gained. A use-limit policy is one of the most intrusive and disruptive approaches a manager can use.

The emphasis on controlling use levels as a means for limiting impacts stems from the carrying capacity approach, originally adopted from the range management literature (Stankey and McCool, 1991). Because carrying capacity invokes the question, "How many is too many?" it tends to view imposition of use limits as an end in itself. Use-limit policies have historically carried with them a host of additional problems, such as choosing appropriate allocation and rationing techniques. These techniques have been among the most controversial actions protected area managers in the United States have ever taken (McCool and Ashor, 1984), in large part because they involve distribution and equity questions relative to who gets what.

PRINCIPLE 9: MONITORING IS ESSENTIAL TO PROFESSIONAL MANAGEMENT—Monitoring can be defined as the periodic and systematic measurement of key indicators of biophysical and social conditions. Historically, it has been an important component of the protected area manager's job. However, monitoring generally has been conducted informally, with little systematic planning and implementation. Monitoring performs two major functions. First, it allows managers to maintain a formal record of resource and social conditions over time. In serving this function, data points can inform managers of changes in these conditions rather than relying solely on informal perceptions of changes that might have occurred. This is particularly important in situations where managers are frequently transferred to different areas or where effects are slow to develop. Second, monitoring helps assess the effectiveness of management actions, thus helping managers understand, in a relatively objective way, if actions address the problem. (It should be noted that there may be factors other than management actions that influence the changes in conditions identified through monitoring programs.) However, despite its acknowledged importance, support for, and execution of, monitoring programs is often poor.

PRINCIPLE 10: THE DECISION MAKING PROCESS SHOULD SEPARATE TECHNICAL DECISIONS FROM VALUE JUDGEMENTS—Many decisions confronting protected area managers are simply technical in nature, such as the number of toilets needed in a campground, the ecologically preferred location of a trail, or the design of a visitor center. However, many other decisions reflect judgments about values, such as objectives for an area, optimal spacing between campsites, and the types of facilities or kind of recreation opportunities to be provided. It is important in decision making that these means-versus-ends decisions are not confused. Decision processes should separate questions of "what is" from "what ought to be." For example, the task of identifying the range of diversity in resource or social conditions that exists within a protected area defines "what is." On the other hand, determining the preferred range of diversity defines "what ought to be." Existing conditions may influence preferred conditions, but the two tasks should be kept separate. Even those decisions that are seen as largely technical are seldom value-neutral. Deciding "what ought to be" should be an explicit process, open to public examination and negotiation.

PRINCIPLE 11: CONSENSUS AMONG AFFECTED GROUPS ABOUT PROPOSED ACTIONS IS NEEDED FOR SUCCESSFUL IMPLEMENTATION OF PROTECTED AREA MANAGEMENT STRATEGIES—In many situations, political polarization and conflict over natural resource management has hindered progress in planning and management. Within the highly charged social and political contexts that protected area managers frequently work, technical planning processes often create more disagreement than agreement. Technical solutions may adversely affect well-defined values expressed by a group within the public. The ensuing lawsuits, decision appeals, protests and other disruptive activities can lead to increased stagnation and uncertainty of outcomes. Therefore, successful planning needs to incorporate public participation as a fundamental and on-going component. Moreover, the citizenry expect to be involved and to be noticed. As the public grants the authority for an agency to operate in a protected area, so too is the political power ultimately held by the wider public. This necessitates their involvement in, and commitment to, agency planning processes and decisions. An inclusive and collaborative approach builds understanding so that everyone can make progress.

THE USE OF CARRYING CAPACITY
FOR PROTECTED AREA MANAGEMENT

One popular approach to visitor management is carrying capacity. Borrowed from the range and wildlife management professions, it was hoped that a maximum number of visitors could be specified, above which appropriate ecological and social conditions could not be sustained. For a good number of reasons, determining recreational carrying capacity is neither simple nor particularly useful (Hammit and Cole, 1987). Part of the problem is that managers using a carrying capacity approach are mixing means with ends. Carrying capacity is viewed as a means of guarding protected area resources. Frequently, however, it becomes an end in itself. Limitations on visitor use are then implemented as a means towards achieving the set carrying capacity. Whether these limitations are effective in protecting ecological and social conditions in the park is overlooked or forgotten.

The resurgent interest in carrying capacity as a management framework has its roots in several factors: 1) the increasing complexity of management, 2) accelerating demands on natural resources to provide a wider diversity of goods and services, and 3) the search for a defensible answer that can be implemented in a wide variety of settings. For example, Butler (1996) argues, "to avoid at least some of the negative impacts associated with visitation, it must be ensured that capacity limits are identified and not exceeded." But establishing such capacities still represents a simplistic and inappropriate response to a "wicked problem," a problem that is more social and political than technical and, therefore, requires a social rather than technical solution.

Given the resurgence of interest in carrying capacity, we now introduce some of the trade-offs which must be made for successful application to protected area management. It is rare that all of these conditions for implementation would be met. However, it is important for managers to be aware of the limitations and assumptions they are adopting by setting recreational carrying capacities. It will become obvious that many of the previously presented principles are not well met by a carrying capacity approach. Stankey and McCool (1992) and Shelby and Heberlein (1986) describe the necessary conditions for the application of carrying capacities and subsequent use limits in recreational settings. These conditions have been modified somewhat to make them more appropriate for the variety of resources and social conditions found in national parks and protected areas. The first five describe conceptual conditions; the last four pertain to practical conditions. All nine not only point out the limitations of the carrying capacity approach, but also expose the level of thought that managers must bring to their planning efforts.

CONDITION 1: THERE MUST BE AGREEMENT ON THE TYPE OF DESIRED SOCIAL AND RESOURCE CONDITIONS, INCLUDING THE TYPE OF RECREATION OPPORTUNITY—Relevant stakeholders (e.g., managers, users) must agree on the types of opportunities to be provided. If, for example, one group feels that the area should provide opportunities for motorized recreation on roads and another argues for non-motorized recreation without roads, no carrying capacity can be established because of the immense differences in allowable use levels. Agreements on type of recreation or desired conditions are essentially political decisions, in which science's role is limited to understanding the consequences and range of alternative choices. Following Principle 1, these agreements on desired conditions should be explicitly stated at the outset.

CONDITION 2: THE RECREATION ACTIVITIES AND/OR EXPERIENCES TO BE PROVIDED MUST BE DENSITY DEPENDENT—As Wagar's seminal report (1964) on recreational carrying capacity noted over 30 years ago, and as has been documented on numerous occasions since, many recreational experiences are either independent of, or even positively associated with, use level. For some opportunities, such as sunbathing at the beach, use level might have no effect whatsoever upon the experience. Indeed, if the sunbathers are teenagers, it is likely "the more, the better." However, other opportunities, such as visiting wilderness areas to enjoy solitude or watching wildlife in natural settings, might be very sensitive to changes in use density.

CONDITION 3: THERE MUST BE AGREEMENT ON THE ACCEPTABLE LEVEL OF IMPACT—With any recreational use in an area, some impact occurs. That is, impacts cannot be eliminated or avoided, only managed. Thus, the key question is, "How much impact is acceptable, given agreement on the type of recreation opportunity to be provided?" For example, this question might focus on the amount of vegetation loss permitted at campsites, the level of diver-caused damage to coral, or how much development is acceptable on an island or cay. Although science can provide information on the consequences of vegetation loss or development, acceptability is inherently a judgmental decision based on a complex set of political, social and ecological trade-offs. It is likely that the various groups with an interest in the protected area will have different perspectives on what would be an acceptable level of impact.

CONDITION 4: A CLEAR, SPECIFIC AND KNOWN RELATIONSHIP MUST EXIST BETWEEN USE LEVELS AND SOCIAL AND RESOURCE CONDITIONS—In order to answer the question, "How many is too many?" the relationship between use and impact (or use and conditions) must be known, explicit and specific. That is, managers must develop explicit measures that quantify the link between amount of recreational use and level of biophysical or social impacts. Such measures would indicate increases or decreases in impact given changes in amounts of recreational use. Simply assuming increasing impacts given increasing use is insufficient. As stated in Principles 6 and 7, the relationship between use level and degree of impact upon the experience (or upon the environment) is rarely linear. In many cases, such a relationship may not exist at all.

CONDITION 5: USE LEVEL MUST BE MORE IMPORTANT THAN VISITOR BEHAVIOR IN DETERMINING THE AMOUNT OF IMPACT—For carrying capacity to work well, the relationship between use and impact must be relatively simple, with a minimum of other variables influencing impact levels. Unfortunately, the literature now documents many situations where the relationship between use and impact is non-linear, complex, variant and influenced more strongly by the behavior of the individual or group rather than by the numbers of visitors (Cole, 1987; Graefe et al., 1987).

CONDITION 6: THE PROTECTED AREA MANAGEMENT AUTHORITY MUST CONTROL ACCESS IN THE AREA— Even if conditions one through five are fulfilled, the agency must still have control over access to the area in order for a carrying capacity limit to be implemented. Without such control, the agency possesses little capacity for influencing entry into the protected area, and the carrying capacity figure represents little more than a number on paper. Although such control is found in many North American protected areas, the extent to which it exists in many countries is questionable.

CONDITION 7: THE PROTECTED AREA MANAGEMENT AUTHORITY MUST HAVE THE RESOURCES (PERSONNEL, FINANCIAL, INFORMATION, ETC.) TO ADMINISTER THE CARRYING CAPACITY LIMIT— Ultimately, a recreational carrying capacity is implemented by imposition of a limit on recreational use. In North America, the financial and personnel resources required to administer use limits have proven considerable; indeed, they are formidable enough to prevent many organizations from implementing limits even when they have been identified in management plans (Washburne and Cole, 1983). Clearly, implementation of carrying capacity implies a long-term, sustainable financial commitment that many organizations are unable or unwilling to make. In addition, the level of political understanding and support for implementing use limits is often not forthcoming.

CONDITION 8: THERE MUST BE AGREEMENT ON THE OBJECTIVES OF A RATIONING SYSTEM IN IMPLEMENTING CARRYING CAPACITY—In situations where the demand exceeds capacity, use must be rationed through some management action (Stankey and Baden, 1977). Objectives for this rationing system must be explicitly identified prior to design of the system (Shelby and Danley, 1979). For example, it must be decided whether the purpose of the system is to make the allocation of opportunities for entry equitable or, alternatively, to make sure the opportunities are awarded to those for whom they are most beneficial. Principle 11 describes the importance of a process by which to achieve consensus on management actions. The lack of such agreement on clearly specified objectives has been one reason for the significant litigious and political activity initiated against carrying capacities in North America. In other social-political systems, such consensus might not be as important.

CONDITION 9: THERE MUST BE AGREEMENT THAT THE CARRYING CAPACITY LIMIT REPRESENTS EITHER THE MAXIMUM OR THE OPTIMUM NUMBER OF PEOPLE VISITING AN AREA—Although this condition never has been explicitly addressed in North American settings where capacities/limits have been established, it carries significant implications for administration of the limit. For example, if the carrying capacity level represents the maximum number of visitors permitted, and capacity exceeds actual demand (use), then any inefficiencies in how the rationing system operates can be easily tolerated. If, on the other hand, the capacity level represents a measure of optimum use, then managers would need to take action to ensure that the protected area is filled to capacity whenever possible. This question is particularly significant for protected areas that are strongly dependent on user and entrance fees, for there will always be pressure to increase visitation and revenue.

THE LIMITS OF ACCEPTABLE CHANGE (LAC) PLANNING SYSTEM

The *Limits of Acceptable Change* (LAC) planning system was developed in response to an increasing recognition in the U.S. that the conditions under which recreational carrying capacities could be defined and implemented were few and far between. The LAC system, in contrast, focuses on identifying acceptable and achievable resource and social conditions. LAC acknowledges the value judgments involved in determining appropriate levels of impact and use intensity, understanding that these levels are derived from social judgments about appropriate conditions, and the amount of change that will be allowed (or not allowed) to occur. The decision making process thereby separates technical decisions from value judgments, and makes the process leading to those judgments open, explicit and accessible. LAC recognizes the need for crystallization of judgments among various stakeholders before management can proceed. In this way, the LAC approach matches and endorses the eleven principles of visitor management mentioned earlier. It is a process through which many of the conditions (e.g., #1, #3 and #8) can be met.

In the U.S., LAC was first implemented in designated wilderness managed by the USDA Forest Service. Since that time, additional work has been conducted in other protected areas and with other land management agencies. Similar systems have been developed, such as the *Visitor Activity Management Process* (VAMP) used by Parks Canada (Graham, 1989), the *Visitor Impact Management* (VIM) framework of Graefe et al. (1990), and the *Visitor Experience and Resource Protection* (VERP) planning process (Manning et al., 1995) developed by the USDI National Park Service. Each of these systems emphasizes the conditions desired for the protected area rather than how much use an area can tolerate. This provides interesting validation of the conclusion that a simple numerical solution fails to meet the needs of protected area managers.

As originally conceived, and described in greater detail in Stankey et al. (1985), LAC consists of nine steps designed to incorporate the idea of "acceptability" and diversity in resource and social conditions. While not an entirely new idea, LAC sought to improve wildland recreation management by defining and managing towards more explicit, measurable objectives (Stankey et al., 1985). LAC seems well placed to face the complexities of protected area management, particularly in this era of social and political change. The nine steps presented below demonstrate LAC to be a planning system that is well suited to modification for current and specific needs; its potential for contributing to improved management of nature-based tourism seems high.

STEP 1: IDENTIFY AREAS' SPECIAL VALUES, ISSUES AND CONCERNS—Citizens, managers and others with a vested interest in the area meet to identify what special features or distinctive qualities within the protected area require attention, what management problems or concerns have to be dealt with, what legal and administrative constraints exist for the area, what issues the public considers most important in the area's management, and what role the area plays in both a regional and national context. Scientists can help provide and compile information not readily available to managers and the public. This step encourages a better mutual understanding of the natural resource base (such as the sensitivity of particular environments to recreation use and tourism development), a general concept of how the resource can be managed, and a focus on principal management issues. LAC is very much an issue-driven process. Issues identified in this step will need addressing throughout the planning process.

STEP 2: IDENTIFY AND DESCRIBE RECREATION OPPORTUNITY CLASSES—Most protected areas contain a diversity of biophysical features, as well as a range of human occupation and use. As mentioned earlier, the type of management appropriate for these differing features and areas will likely vary throughout the area. Opportunity classes describe subdivisions or zones where different social, resource, or managerial conditions will be maintained. The classes that are developed represent a way of defining a range of desired conditions within the protected area. The definition of opportunity classes might follow the basic specifications of the *Recreation Opportunity Spectrum* system, commonly utilized by the U.S. Forest Service (Clark and Stankey, 1979) to produce narrative descriptions of resource, social, and managerial conditions defined as appropriate and acceptable for each opportunity class.

The *Recreation Opportunity Spectrum* specifies six classes ranging from the primitive (a fairly large area characterized by an essentially unmodified, natural environment) to the urban (an area characterized by urbanization and substantial modification). Each class describes a consistency between the social, managerial, and environmental conditions. For example, high levels of visitation would correspond to a highly visible management presence and to a more developed recreation site. Managers seek to not only describe the conditions within each class, but also the distribution of these recreation opportunity classes across the protected area. As expressed in Principle 3, previously, a diversity of opportunities is an important objective of protected area management.

STEP 3: SELECT INDICATORS OF RESOURCE AND SOCIAL CONDITIONS—Indicators are specific elements of the resource or social setting selected to represent (or be "indicative of") the conditions deemed appropriate and acceptable in each opportunity class. Because it is impossible to measure the condition of, and change in, every resource or social feature within a protected area, a few indicators are selected as measures of overall area health, just as blood pressure is often monitored to gauge physical health. Indicators should be a direct measure of the conditions specified by the opportunity classes and, therefore, reflect the unique and important qualities of the visitor experience and environmental resource. Indicators should be dependable, reliable and repeatable. They should also be easily subject to quantitative, nondestructive measurement, and adequately reflect and respond to changes in recreational use. Indicators are an essential part of the LAC framework because their state is taken to reflect the overall condition found throughout an opportunity class area. An individual indicator might not adequately depict the condition of the whole area. Rather, a bundle of indicators can be used to monitor conditions and assess the effectiveness of various management practices.

STEP 4: INVENTORY EXISTING RESOURCE AND SOCIAL CONDITIONS—Inventories can be time-consuming and expensive components of planning. In the LAC process, the inventory is guided by the indicators selected in Step 3. For example, level and type of development, use density and human-induced impacts on park resources might be measured. Other variables, such as location of different features, facilities, and access points, can also be inventoried to develop a better understanding of area constraints and opportunities. Inventory data are mapped so that the condition of indicators in different locations are known. The inventory also helps provide a shared database of known conditions which can help in the establishment of realistic and attainable standards.

STEP 5: SPECIFY STANDARDS FOR RESOURCE AND SOCIAL CONDITIONS FOR EACH OPPORTUNITY CLASS—In this step, the specific, measurable range of conditions for each indicator is identified. Defining those conditions in measurable and specific terms provides the basis for establishing a distinctive and diverse range of recreational settings. Standards serve to define the "limits of acceptable change." They represent the maximum level of impact judged acceptable in a specific opportunity class; they are not necessarily objectives to be attained. While the standards defining the range of acceptable conditions in each opportunity class must be realistic, they must also do more than mimic existing (perhaps unacceptable) conditions. They are not to be seen as explicit standards of degradation; rather, if existing conditions are minimally acceptable, they should be seen as an opportunity to improve conditions through the establishment of more stringent standards (Stankey et al., 1985).

STEP 6: IDENTIFY ALTERNATIVE OPPORTUNITY CLASS ALLOCATIONS—Most protected areas can be managed in several different ways. Parks and protected areas often differ significantly in the amount of development, human density (both residents and visitors), and recreational opportunities available. In this step, different types of alternatives are identified. Using information from Step 1 (area issues and concerns) and Step 4 (inventory of existing conditions), managers and citizens can begin to jointly explore how well different opportunity class allocations address the various contending interests, concerns and values. Different combinations and permutations should be considered as a means for making explicit the allocation preferences. This is a prescriptive step—like other steps which establish what should be—and therefore ought to involve input from policy makers, managers and the public. The provision of allocation alternatives will allow follow-up review, evaluation and selection.

STEP 7: IDENTIFY MANAGEMENT ACTIONS FOR EACH ALTERNATIVE—The alternative allocations proposed in Step 6 are only the first step in the process of developing a preferred alternative. Both managers and citizens need to know what management actions will be required to achieve or maintain the desired conditions. In a sense, Step 7 requires an analysis of the costs (broadly defined) that will be imposed by each alternative. For example, people might wish to protect a specific area from all development and restore any impacts that might compromise the area's pristine condition. However, this alternative might require such a huge commitment of funds for acquisition and enforcement (e.g., virtual closure to public use for an extended time) that the alternative might not seem as attractive. Note that management actions should be specific and consistent with the opportunity classes previously identified and the conditions inventoried. Managers might choose to provide protection in part of an opportunity class above and beyond the minimum standards mentioned previously. As Stankey et al. (1985) suggest, "by maintaining conditions better than the standard requires, further diversity" is achieved. Cole et al. (1987) provide a useful assessment of alternative actions for managing wilderness recreation use.

STEP 8: EVALUATE AND SELECT PREFERRED ALTERNATIVE—With the various costs and benefits of the several alternatives before them, managers and citizens can proceed to the evaluation stage. The managing authority, based on guidance from the public, can then select a preferred alternative. Evaluation must take into account many factors, but examples would include the responsiveness of each alternative to the issues identified in Step 1, management requirements from Step 7, and public preferences. It is important that the factors figuring into the evaluation process and their relative weight be made explicit and available for public review. It is also essential to analyze the various costs and benefits, and to whom they would accrue.

STEP 9: IMPLEMENT ACTIONS AND MONITOR CONDITIONS—With an alternative finally selected and articulated as policy by decision makers, the necessary management actions are put into effect and a monitoring program instituted. Often, an implementation plan detailing actions, costs, staffing, timetables and responsibilities, will be needed to ensure timely implementation. The monitoring program should focus on the indicators selected in Step 3 and compare their condition with those identified in the standards. This information can then be used to evaluate the success (or lack thereof) of actions, and provide systematic feedback regarding performance of the management program. If conditions are not improving, the intensity of the management effort might need to be increased or new actions implemented. Cole (1989) and Marion (1991) provide methods for monitoring wilderness campsite conditions.

In summary, the LAC process provides a framework for thinking about issues of recreation development and management. It is a framework that recognizes the intrinsic complexity of development issues, yet provides a process for dealing competently with this complexity without being excessively reductionist. By combining the technical expertise of planners and scientists with valuable personal knowledge held by the local public, together with an explicit recognition of the importance of public involvement in the decision making process, LAC can result in more defensible decisions that have greater chances of implementation.

LAC has proven to be a highly adaptable framework that has seen application in a variety of protected areas. The procedure laid out in LAC was not meant to be mandated for every situation. Rather, managers have found it to be an appropriate statement of principles from which to develop their own similar or derivative planning systems. By wrestling with the conditions under which the planning approach must operate, managers avoid being naive about the complexity and consequences of the planning process. By grounding their own planning process in the principles described in this chapter, managers can still develop a process that fits the capacity and/or ability of their organization and setting.

An example of a planning system that builds upon the framework of LAC is the *Tourism Optimization Management Model* (TOMM) developed in Australia (Manidis Roberts Consultants, 1997). TOMM is a management approach designed to monitor and manage tourism on Kangaroo Island, a resort and farming island off the coast of South Australia that attracts some 150,000 visits per year. Like LAC, the first component of TOMM is an analysis of the context in which the planning must occur. Just as Step 1 of LAC identifies the social values, issues and concerns, the first phase of TOMM identifies the community values as well as the policy and planning directives of the various stakeholders. TOMM's contextual analysis also includes examination of the island's tourism products and the trends and opportunities for the tourism market, much as Step 2 of LAC maps out recreational opportunities. While LAC emphasizes the quality of the environment and visitor experience, TOMM places more emphasis on the sustainability of the tourism industry. Towards that end, TOMM goes on to identify and inventory potentially optimal conditions for tourism to occur (economic, market, environmental, experiential and socio-cultural). The second component of TOMM then sets up indicators and acceptable ranges for those indicators within an annual performance monitoring program, similar to LAC's Step 3. In response to the data generated by the monitoring program, TOMM's third component generates management response options for the tourism industry.

TOMM, like LAC was designed to meld the technical expertise of industry and government with community and conservation group knowledge and was intended to serve a multitude of stakeholders with a multitude of interests (Manidis Roberts Consultants, 1997). TOMM also demonstrates the ability of a planning process that follows the principles laid out in this chapter to operate at a regional level over a multitude of public and private land tenures. Both TOMM and LAC move from setting limits or carrying capacities to a focus on desired conditions and an open and explicit process towards achieving and maintaining those conditions.

CONCLUSION

The *Limits of Acceptable Change* planning process, and its derivative approaches like TOMM, represent an effective evolution of problem conceptualization compared to the recreational carrying capacity approach. However, in and of itself, LAC provides only a framework for identifying appropriate management actions. It does not determine what should be done, by whom, or where. Managerial, public, and scientific expertise is still required. LAC helps frame management questions more effectively than in the past. Understanding the principles upon which LAC is based, and the conditions under which visitor management of protected areas must operate, will help lead to planning systems more compatible with specific agency needs and capability, and more suited to the complexities of protected area planning in this era of social and political change.

REFERENCES

Allen, G.M., and E.M. Gould. 1986. "Complexity, Wickedness and Public Forests," *Journal of Forestry*, vol. 84, no. 4., pp. 20-24.

Briassoulis, H. 1989. "Theoretical Orientations in Environmental Planning: An Inquiry Into Alternative Approaches," *Environmental Management*, vol. 13, pp. 381-392.

Brown, P.J., S.F. McCool, M.J. Manfredo. 1987. "Evolving Concepts and Tools for Recreation User Management in Wilderness: A State-of-Knowledge Review," proceedings at the National Wilderness Research Conference: Issues, States-of-Knowledge, Future Directions, 1985, July 23-26, Fort Collins, Colorado. Forest Service, General Technical Report INT-220, Ogden, Utah. USDA Forest Service, Intermountain Research Station.

Butler, R.W. 1996. "The Concept of Carrying Capacity for Tourism Destinations: Dead or Merely Buried?" *Progress in Tourism and Hospitality Research*, vol. 2, pp. 283-293.

Clark, R.N., G.H. Stankey. 1979. "The Recreation Opportunity Spectrum: A Framework for Planning, Management, and Research," U.S. Forest Service, General Technical Report PNW-98, Portland, Oregon. USDA Forest Service, Pacific Northwest Forest and Range Experiment Station.

Cole, D.N. 1987. "Research on Soil and Vegetation in Wilderness: A State-of-Knowledge Review," Proceedings—National Wilderness Research Conference: Issues, States-of-Knowledge, Future Directions, 1985, July 23-26, Fort Collins, Colorado. U.S. Forest Service, General Technical Report INT-220, Ogden, Utah. USDA Forest Service, Intermountain Research Station.

Cole, D.N. 1989. "Low-Impact Recreational Practices for Wilderness and Backcountry," U.S. Forest Service, General Technical Report, INT-265, Ogden, Utah. USDA Forest Service, Intermountain Forest and Range Experiment Station.

Cole, D.N., M.E. Peterson, R.C. Lucas. 1987. "Managing Wilderness Recreation Use: Common Problems and Potential Solutions," U.S. Forest Service, General Technical Report. INT-230, Ogden, Utah. USDA Forest Service, Intermountain Forest and Range Experiment Station.

Graefe, A.R., M.P. Donnelly, J.J. Vaske. 1987. "Crowding and Specialization: A Re-examination of the Crowding Model," proceedings at the National Wilderness Research Conference: Current Research, 1985, July 23-26, Fort Collins, Colorado. U.S. Forest Service, General Technical Report INT-212, Ogden, Utah. USDA Forest Service, Intermountain Research Station.

Graefe, A.R., F. R. Kuss, J.J. Vaske. 1990. "Visitor Impact Management: The Planning Framework," Washington D.C. National Parks and Conservation Association.

Graham, R. 1989. "Visitor Management and Canada's National Parks," *Towards Serving Visitors and Managing Our Resources*, Tourism Research and Education Center, University of Waterloo, Waterloo, Ontario.

Haas, G.E., B.L. Driver, P.J. Brown, R.C. Lucas. 1987. "Wilderness Management Zoning," *Journal of Forestry*, vol. 85, no. 12, pp. 17-21.

Hammitt, W. E., D.N. Cole. 1987. *Wildland Recreation: Ecology and Management*, Wiley, New York.

Hendee, J.C., G.H. Stankey, R.C. Lucas. 1990. *Wilderness Management*, North American Press, Golden, Colorado.

Lee, K. N. 1993. *Compass and Gyroscope: Integrating Science and Politics for the Environment*, Island Press, Washington, D.C.

Lindberg, K., S.F. McCool, G.H. Stankey. 1997. "Rethinking Carrying Capacity," *Annals of Tourism Research*, vol. 24, no. 2, pp. 461-464.

Machlis, G.E., D.L. Tichnell. 1985. *The State of the World's Parks: An International Assessment for Resource Management, Policy, and Research*, Westview Press, Boulder, Colorado.

Manidis Roberts Consultants. 1997. "Developing a Tourism Optimisation Management Model" (TOMM), A Model to Monitor and Manage Tourism on Kangaroo Island, South Australia. (Final Report). Manidis Roberts Consultants, Surry Hills, New South Wales.

Manning, R.E. 1986. *Studies in Outdoor Recreation: Search and Research for Satisfaction*, Oregon State University Press, Corvallis, Oregon.

Manning, R.E., D.W. Lime, M. Hof, W.A. Freimund. 1995. "The Visitor Experience and Resource Protection (VERP) Process: The Application of Carrying Capacity to Arches National Park," George Wright Forum, vol. 12, no. 3, pp. 41-55.

Marion, J.L. 1991. *Developing a Natural Resource Inventory and Monitoring Program for Visitor Impacts on Recreation Sites: A Procedural Manual*, Natural Resources Report NPS/NRVT/NRR-91/06, USDA National Park Service, Denver, Colorado.

Martin, S., S.F. McCool, R.C. Lucas. 1989. "Wilderness User Perceptions of Campsite Impacts," *Environmental Management*, vol. 13, no. 5, pp. 623-629.

McCool, S.F. 1996. "Limits of Acceptable Change—A Framework for Managing National Protected Areas: Experiences from the United States," unpublished paper, School of Forestry, University of Montana, Missoula, Montana.

McCool, S.F., J.L. Ashor. 1984. "Politics and Rivers: Creating Effective Citizen Involvement in Management Decisions," National River Recreation Symposium Proceedings, 1984 October 31-November 3; Baton Rouge, Louisiana, Louisiana State University, Baton Rouge, Louisiana.

McCool, S.F., J.L. Ashor, G.L. Stokes. 1986. "An Alternative to Rational Comprehensive Planning," proceedings at the National Wilderness Research Conference: Current Research, 1985, July 23-26, Fort Collins, Colorado. U.S. Forest Service, General Technical Report INT-212, Ogden, Utah. USDA Forest Service, Intermountain Research Station.

McCool, S.F., G.H. Stankey. 1992. "Managing for the Sustainable Use of Protected Wildlands: The Limits of Acceptable Change Framework," paper presented at IV World Congress on National Parks and Protected Areas, February 10-21, 1992, Caracas, Venezuela.

Schomaker, J.H. 1984. "Writing Quantifiable River Recreation Management Objectives," National River Recreation Symposium Proceedings, 1984, October 31-November 3, Baton Rouge, Louisiana, Louisiana State University, Baton Rouge, Louisiana..

Shelby, B., M.S. Danley. 1979. "Scarcity, Conflict and Equity in Allocating Public Recreation Resources," paper presented at the annual meeting of the Rural Sociological Society, August, Burlington, Vermont.

Shelby, B., T.A. Heberlein. 1986. *Carrying Capacity in Recreation Settings*, Oregon State University Press, Corvallis, Oregon.

Speight, M.C.D. 1973. "Outdoor Recreation and its Ecological Effects: A Bibliography and Review," discussion paper in conservation, University College, London.

Stankey, G.H., J. Baden. 1977. "Rationing Wilderness Use: Methods, Problems, and Guidelines," U.S. Forest Service, Research Paper INT-192, Ogden, Utah. USDA Forest Service, Intermountain Research Station.

Stankey, G.H., D.N. Cole, R.C. Lucas, M.E. Peterson, S.S. Frissell. 1985. "The Limits of Acceptable Change (LAC) System for Wilderness Planning," U.S. Forest Service, General Technical Report INT-176, Ogden, Utah. USDA Forest Service, Intermountain Research Station.

Stankey, G.H. S.F. McCool. 1984. "Carrying Capacity in Recreational Settings: Evolution, Appraisal, and Application," *Leisure Sciences*, vol. 6, no. 4, pp. 453-473.

Stankey, G.H., S.F. McCool. 1989. "Beyond Social Carrying Capacity," *Understanding Leisure and Recreation: Mapping the Past Charting the Future*, Venture Publishing, State College, Pennsylvania.

Stankey, G.H., S.F. McCool. 1991. "Recreational Use Limits: The Wildland Managers Continuing Dilemma," *Western Wildlands*, vol. 16, no. 4, pp. 2-7.

Stankey, G.H., S.F. McCool. 1992. "Managing Recreation Use of Marine Resources Through the Limits of Acceptable Change Planning System," unpublished paper, School of Forestry, University of Montana, Missoula, Montana.

Stankey, G.H., S.F. McCool. 1993. "Managing Tourism and Recreation in Protected Habitats: Prerequisites for Effective Strategies," paper presented at Second World Congress on Tourism for the Environment, September 26-October 2, 1993, Porlamar, Isla de Margarita, Venezuela.

Wagar, J. A. 1964. *The Carrying Capacity of Wild Lands for Recreation*, Forest Science Monograph 7, Society of American Foresters, Washington, D.C.

Wall, G., C. Wright. 1977. "The Environmental Impact of Outdoor Recreation," Department of Geography Publication Series No. 11, University of Ontario, Waterloo, Ontario.

Washburn, R.F., D.N. Cole. 1983. "Problems and Practices in Wilderness Management: A Survey of Managers," U.S. Forest Service Research Paper INT-304, Ogden, Utah. USDA Forest Service, Intermountain Research Station.

Wilkes, B. 1977. "The Myth of the Non-consumptive User," *The Canadian Field Naturalist*, vol. 91, no. 4, pp. 343-349.

Managing Ecotourism Visitation in Protected Areas

Jeffrey L. Marion and Tracy A. Farrell

INTRODUCTION

Ecotourism is expanding worldwide, generating substantial revenues and providing potential incentives for protecting natural environments. Ecotourism management seeks to integrate and balance several potentially conflicting objectives: protection of natural and cultural resources, provision of recreation opportunities and generation of economic benefits. In the absence of effective planning and management, ecotourism can lead to significant negative impacts on vegetation, soil, water, wildlife and historic resources, cultures (such as loss of interest in traditional practices), and even visitor experiences (such as visitor crowding and conflicts). Such impacts can be both ecologically and culturally significant and may negatively affect visitor satisfaction. Visitation may then diminish, along with economic benefits and resource protection incentives (Mieczkowski, 1995).

This chapter provides a brief overview of visitor-related natural resource and experience impacts associated with ecotourism within protected areas. Ecotourism impacts may result from the development and management of visitor facilities (e.g., roads, lodges, visitor centers and campgrounds) and from visitation to developed or undeveloped protected areas. The focus of this chapter is on managing the effects of protected area visitation, which is comprised of local, regional, national and international use. The term recreation often refers to in-country visitation while the term ecotourism more frequently refers to international visitation dependent upon natural and cultural resources. Most ecotourism definitions include a stipulation that the visitation be environmentally and culturally sensitive, adhering to a low-impact ethic. However, ecotourists still hike, camp and have measurable impacts on protected areas—impacts that are often confounded with those of tourists, recreationists and even local residents. Managers are rarely able to differentiate among these differing sources of visitor impacts, so they are grouped together into the more general terms visitors, visitation and visitor impacts. Where possible, international examples are used to illustrate these impacts and highlight their implications.

A traditional response to visitor impacts has been the establishment of carrying capacities that limit visitation. However, research reveals that many factors influence the extent of such problems and that reducing visitation is often not an effective or preferred management response. Thus, this chapter also reviews the effect of other influential factors, including type of use and visitor behavior, the variable resistance and resilience of environmental attributes such as vegetation and soil types, and the role of management in shaping visitation, resources and facilities to support visitation while minimizing associated impacts. Effective management requires identification of the type and extent of impacts and of the role and influence of various mediating factors. Decision making frameworks, such as *Limits of Acceptable Change*, also require that managers first identify the potential causes of impacts to aid in the selection of effective management interventions. A final section of this chapter reviews and provides guidance in selecting appropriate actions from a diverse array of management strategies and tactics shown to be effective in reducing visitor impacts.

THE NATURE AND SIGNIFICANCE OF VISITOR IMPACTS

Visitor resource and experience impacts are increasingly important concerns for the managers of protected areas. Though there are significant "external" threats to protected areas (e.g., land use practices of park neighbors). Environmental degradation caused by facility development and visitation represent important "internal" threats (Machlis and Tichnell, 1985). These resource impacts and social or experiential impacts, such as visitor crowding and conflict, can also negatively affect visitor experiences. In popular protected areas, high visitation, coupled with insufficient funding and staffing, can lead to pronounced human disturbance and degraded visitor experiences. Government and non-government mandates and management policies for these areas commonly require managers to facilitate visitation while preserving natural resources and processes. Allowing visitor use makes a certain amount of impact unavoidable. This section briefly reviews some common visitor resource and visitor experience impacts and discusses their significance for protected areas.

VISITOR RESOURCE IMPACTS

There is limited empirical literature on the environmental degradation caused directly by ecotourists within developing country protected areas. Much of this research has been conducted in developed countries, in parks and wilderness areas not managed specifically for ecotourism. This body of literature, often referred to as recreation ecology (Cole, 1987), is directly applicable to ecotourism management. Recreation ecology studies describe the types, amounts and rates of ecological changes resulting from visitor use, including use-related environmental and managerial factors that influence these changes (Marion and Rogers, 1994). Knowledge gained from this discipline can aid protected area managers in documenting and monitoring the effects of visitor use, understanding the relationships and relative influence of factors that affect the character and severity of resource impacts, and selecting effective strategies and actions to sustain expanding ecotourism while minimizing associated resource impacts.

The development of lodges, visitor centers and other structures (distinct from visitor use of these facilities) is one form of ecotourism-related impact occurring within protected areas. Many such facilities, often extensive in size, have been developed in ecologically sensitive areas. A wide variety of ecotourism use-related activities (including hiking, camping, wildlife viewing, boating, snorkeling, diving and horseback riding) then follows, also contributing to resource impacts. Studies of recreation ecology typically focus on resource impacts associated with these common activities. For more comprehensive reviews of recreation ecology literature refer to Cole (1987), Hammitt and Cole (1987), Knight and Gutzwiller (1995), Kuss et al. (1990), Liddle (1997) and Mieczkowski (1995).

The types of resource impacts experienced in protected areas depends on the visitor activity. For example, vegetation and soil disturbance are caused by trampling associated with hiking, horseback riding and camping. Low levels of such disturbances reduce ground vegetation height, cover and biomass, and may alter the composition of flora by eliminating fragile species (Cole, 1995a; Sun and Liddle, 1993). Higher levels of trampling cause more complete ground vegetation loss and compositional change, as well as loss of tree seedlings, saplings and shrubs (Cole, 1995b; Marion and Cole, 1996). Trampling also pulverizes soil leaf litter and humus layers, which are either lost through erosional processes or intermixed with underlying mineral soils. These soils then become exposed and vulnerable to wind or water erosion and compaction (Cole, 1982; Marion and Merriam, 1985a; Monti and Mackintosh, 1979). The compaction of soils decreases soil pore space and water infiltration, which in turn increases water runoff and soil erosion.

The creation, proliferation and condition of trails and campsites are potential management concerns related to hiking, horseback riding and camping activities. In addition to the trampling effects previously described, trail impacts include excessive tread widening, muddiness, erosion and development of multiple treads within the trail corridor (Cole, 1983; Marion et al., 1993). Additional concerns related to camping include campsite proliferation, excessive campsite densities in popular areas, expansion of campsite sizes, and particularly severe instances of vegetation loss and soil erosion (Cole, 1990). Often these activities simultaneously affect multiple categories of resources. For example, two worldwide surveys of parks revealed the common occurrence of vegetation loss, excessive trail tread width and erosion, wildlife harassment and loss of habitat, and water resource impacts (Giongo et al., 1994; Machlis and Tichnell, 1985).

Wildlife viewing, one of the most popular activities associated with ecotourism, also contributes to a variety of direct and indirect impacts to the wildlife itself. Trampling or vehicle traffic can directly degrade wildlife habitats, and the presence of tourists may disrupt essential wildlife activities such as feeding, sleeping or reproduction and the raising of young (Knight and Cole, 1995a). In the Galápagos Islands, trail use altered nesting locations and disrupted displaying behaviors of nesting, blue- and red-footed boobies (Burger and Gochfield, 1993). Feeding and harassment of wildlife also causes unnatural behavioral changes including learned responses such as attraction, habituation (waning of a response), or avoidance (Knight and Cole, 1991) and can lead to the establishment of unnatural and unhealthy food dependencies. In addition, the attempt to avoid humans can lead to displacement of wildlife from certain places (spatial displacement) during certain times (temporal displacement), often resulting in lower quality food sources, inferior cover, and increased competition and predation. At Amboseli National Park in Africa, cheetahs avoided tourism activity areas or delayed hunting and other activities in response to trail use and vehicle concentration (Haysmith and Hunt, 1995).

The management of wildlife viewing is complicated by the fact that wildlife responses to recreation activities are highly variable, dependent upon the recreationists' behaviors, the context of the disturbance, and the wildlife's learned responses (Knight and Cole, 1995b). These responses are often inconsistent, even within a single species and population. Significant disturbance can be serious enough to lead to the alteration of wildlife population structure or size by decreasing natality or increasing mortality—species may become locally extinct, or new species, even non-natives, may move in.

Water resource impacts include both physical and biological forms of pollution. Examples of physical impacts include increased suspended matter and turbidity from eroded soils or disturbance of bottom sediments, nutrient input from soaps or fecal material, and oil and gas residues from boat engines (Hammitt and Cole, 1987, Kuss et al., 1990; Liddle and Scorgie, 1980). Biological impacts associated with visitation include, pathogenic bacteria, viruses and protozoa—all potentially present in human waste (Hammitt and Cole, 1987; Kuss et al., 1990). The presence of such pathogens is commonly evaluated based on the presence of fecal coliform and streptococcus bacteria, which are non-pathogenic but act as indicators of human or animal waste contamination. (Pathogenic organisms, such as the protozoan Giardia lamblia, however, cause disease and have the potential to create serious public health problems.)

Snorkeling and scuba diving are increasingly popular ecotourism activities that may result in physical damage to coral reefs (from both visitors and boat anchors), harassment or artificial feeding of fish, and collection of reef organisms. According to Salm (1986), the degree of impact for coral reefs depends on reef size and shape, activities, and level of user experience. In a study of snorkeling and diving impacts on coral reefs near a resort in Egypt, heavily used areas along the reef exhibited decreased coral sizes and total percentage of live coverage of coral colonies, and greater numbers of live coral fragments (Hawkins and Roberts, 1993). Lightly used areas were also degraded, demonstrating significant reductions in coral height and average diameter. Also noted in this study was the impact on other recreationists of seeing the damaged coral. Based on its visual appearance, recreationists were concerned that visitor use was degrading the coral.

VISITOR EXPERIENCE IMPACTS

Visitor crowding and conflict are the two primary social or experiential impacts. Wagar (1964) first reported that crowding can decrease aesthetic enjoyment and diminish opportunities for solitude. Crowding was originally based on physical components measured in terms of visitor density, but later came to be conceptualized as psychological evaluations of visitor density (Gramann, 1982). Early research efforts reported that as user density increased, satisfaction decreased (Heberlein and Shelby, 1977), leading managers to focus on determining the permissible numbers of visitors that would prevent crowding.

Later research revealed that increases in visitor numbers did not always, or directly, diminish visitor satisfaction (Absher and Lee, 1981; Shelby, 1980). In fact, density is not negatively evaluated as crowding by visitors until it is perceived to interfere with or disrupt desired recreation objectives or outcomes (Fishbein and Ajzen, 1975; Gramann and Burdge, 1984). For example, visitor enjoyment of wildlife in the Maasai Mara may be negatively affected by the practice of vehicles surrounding big game species, apart from the actual number of vehicles or visitors. Goal interference depends on the personal characteristics of visitors, including their motivations, preferences and expectations, and level of experience with the area, as well as the characteristics or behaviors of other visitors, and attributes of the setting (Manning, 1985).

Visitor expectations, preferences and motives may be more important determinants of perceived crowding than actual visitor densities. To illustrate, consider two tour groups of birders who travel to the same protected area. The first group consists of a few experienced birders who plan to observe quietly in selected habitats along a trail in hopes of sighting new bird species to add to their life lists. The second group is comprised of a large number of first-time birders whose objectives include bird observation, socialization with other group members, and exercise. Members of the first group might experience crowding upon encountering even a few other visitors, whereas members of the second group might not feel crowded on a trail where other visitors are within sight at all times. Potential consequences of perceived crowding are decreased visitor satisfaction and visitor displacement—visitors may go to other areas, change the timing of their visitation, or alter their behavior (Anderson and Brown, 1984). Visitors may also change their expectations or activities in order to better tolerate crowded conditions (Heberlein and Shelby, 1977).

Visitor conflict also has the potential to diminish visitor satisfaction, which may reduce a protected area's popularity or appeal. Conflict can occur between individual visitors or between groups of visitors, particularly when there are distinct differences between visitors or visitor groups, such as their modes of travel. Conflict can also occur between visitors and guides, land managers and local residents. Visitor conflict is caused by the interference with recreation goals resulting from someone else's presence or behavior (Jacob and Schreyer, 1980). To illustrate, consider hikers and horseback riders on a common trail. While hikers must step off the trail and wait for the horses to pass, this type of encounter is rarely more than a minor inconvenience. A more common source of conflict for hikers is the greater impact of horse use on trail conditions, which may lead to severe rutting or muddiness, and the presence of horse manure. Thus, conflict may occur without negative confrontational experiences or even direct personal contact.

Several factors influence the degree of conflict that may be experienced. Visitors who have greater experience and skills or are intensely involved in certain activities are more likely to experience conflict because they have stricter guidelines for appropriate behavior (Jacob and Schreyer, 1980). For example, an experienced scuba diver may be irritated by inexperienced snorkelers standing on a coral reef. Conflict may also result when other visitors are perceived as devaluing a resource perceived as irreplaceable. For example, a visitor exploring an archeological ruin may become angry with other visitors for moving or collecting pottery shards. Conflict with local residents or guides may also occur due to differences in cultures, lifestyles or traditional practices. For example, in northern Canada, conflict between visitors and local guides resulted from the killing of polar bears to feed sled dogs used to transport visitor supplies (Lawrence and Wickins, 1997).

SIGNIFICANCE OF VISITOR IMPACTS

The significance of visitor impacts may be addressed from three perspectives: ecological, visitor experience and managerial. Visitor resource impacts frequently affect only localized areas, often a relatively small percentage of the area within protected area boundaries. However, even localized impact can harm rare or endangered species, damage sensitive resources, or threaten ecosystem health.

Also, some environments like alpine meadows and coral reefs have low resource recovery rates, requiring many years to recover from even limited degradation. Visitor impacts may also contribute indirect or secondary effects that extend beyond localized areas or park boundaries (Cole, 1990). For example, stream sedimentation from trail tread erosion may reduce the quality of aquatic habitat for fish populations, or the presence of visitors may harm wildlife through habitat fragmentation or displacement. Natural systems are inherently complex, and visitor activities may disturb or disrupt any number of interconnected functions.

Even visitor resource impacts that have little ecological significance may have great recreational or social significance if the impacts are offensive to other visitors, provide a source of conflict between visitor groups, or reduce the functional value of trails or recreation sites. Visitors have varying perceptions of the existence and significance of recreation-induced resource impacts. Recent studies have found that even perceived impacts can degrade the quality of visitor experiences (Roggenbuck et al., 1993; Vaske et al., 1993). Perceptions are based on how visitors believe impacts affect the overall attributes of the setting, such as scenic appeal or solitude, and whether or not the impacts are believed to be undesirable (Lucas, 1979; Whittaker and Shelby, 1988). For example, littering was a commonly reported resource impact by visitors at Mt. Everest in Nepal, and at Gunung Gede Pangrango National Park in Indonesia (Ceballos-Lascuráin, 1996). Visitors appear to be sensitive to overt effects such as the occurrence of litter, horse manure or tree damage, and to particularly visible examples of physical impacts such as soil erosion. However, visitor responses can be quite variable. Lucas (1979), for example, found that visitor satisfaction was not diminished by trail and campsite impacts. In contrast, Roggenbuck et al. (1993) found that littering and human damage to campsite trees were among the most highly rated indicators affecting the quality of wilderness experiences. Hollenhorst and Gardner (1994) also found vegetation loss and bare ground on campsites to be important determinants of satisfaction by wilderness visitors. Finally, resource impacts such as soil muddiness or erosion can decrease satisfaction by increasing the difficulty of hiking or by reducing visitor safety.

Visitor experience impacts can also have great recreational or social significance. Visitor crowding and conflicts reduce visitor satisfaction and may lead to the spatial or temporal displacement of visitors. Over time, visitors who are particularly sensitive to such impacts will not return or may be replaced by less sensitive visitors. The social values of providing and sustaining high quality recreational experiences for visitors are thus compromised.

From a management perspective, visitor impacts are significant because they directly reflect management success in meeting two primary mandates: resource protection and recreation provision. These mandates commonly direct managers to protect natural resources and processes, while providing satisfying visitor experiences and incorporating the needs of local residents. Visitor resource impacts directly degrade resource conditions and the quality of visitor experiences. Visitor experience impacts directly degrade the quality of visitor experiences. Reductions in the quality of the visitor experience, from either resource or experience impacts, may affect the quantity of visitation. Reductions in the amount or growth of visitation can also have economic significance (e.g., lost revenue for the protected area and surrounding communities) as well as political significance (e.g., lost support for protected area preservation and management) (Ceballos-Lascuráin, 1996).

THE INFLUENCE OF USE-RELATED AND ENVIRONMENTAL FACTORS

To choose the most appropriate strategies and tactics to manage visitor resource impacts, managers need to determine the underlying causes of impact and understand the roles of influential factors. While the amount of visitation is an inherent determinant of resource impacts, research has demonstrated the importance of many other factors. Two general categories of influential factors—use-related and environmental—are briefly described.

USE-RELATED FACTORS

Studies of visitor impacts to campsites and trails have documented that most resource impacts are related to the amount of visitation in a curvilinear fashion (Cole, 1982, 1987, 1995b; Kuss et al., 1990). This curvilinear relationship is illustrated in Figure 7.1 by data from a study of campsites in the U.S. Boundary Waters Canoe Wilderness Area (Marion and Merriam, 1985b). Most resource impacts appear rapidly and are substantial even on campsites receiving only a dozen nights of camping per year. Numerous studies have also shown that further increases in use cause little additional change for most forms of impact. For example, moderate levels of trampling quickly destroy the majority of vegetation cover and organic litter on trails and campsites. The underlying soils are then highly prone to compaction and erosion. Further increases in visitation at this point will not substantially increase many types of impact since the damage is already at near maximum levels. Exceptions include tree damage and certain soil-related impacts such as the total area of exposed soil and amount of soil erosion.

One important implication of the curvilinear use/impact relationship is that visitation would have to be reduced or dispersed to extremely low levels to achieve significant reductions for most types of impacts. The opposite of dispersal is visitor containment or concentration, a more promising strategy for minimizing resource impacts in areas receiving moderate to heavy visitation. Trails represent a common form of visitor containment by concentrating visitor traffic on their resistant treads. Dispersal is difficult to achieve in practice because visitors often choose to engage in recreation activities in similar areas. For example, hiking routes and campsite locations are chosen based on proximity to water sources, as well as for aesthetic considerations, such as access to attractions and/or features. Thus dispersal strategies are commonly ineffective, and may result in increasing the total area of disturbance. However, dispersal policies permit the greatest degree of visitor choice and freedom and are often preferred in areas of low visitor use.

FIGURE 7.1
RELATIONSHIP BETWEEN VISITATION AND RESOURCE IMPACT AS ILLUSTRATED FOR SIX INDICATORS OF CAMPSITE CONDITION

(Source: Marion and Merriam, 1985b)

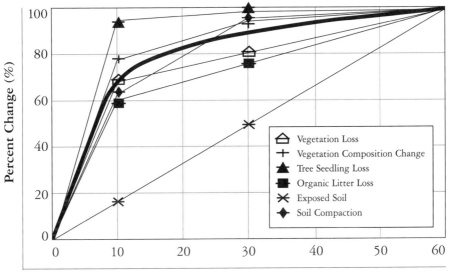

NOTE: Change is expressed as a percentage of change on high-use sites. Thus, approximately 70% of the vegetation loss that occurs at campsites receiving visitors for 60+ nights per year has already occurred at campsites receiving visitors 10 nights per year. The generalized curvilinear use-impact relationship is depicted by the thicker black line.

Based on a consideration of use-related factors, research has also shown that some types of use, such as horseback or off-road vehicle riding, create greater per capita impact than others, such as hiking or wildlife viewing (Weaver and Dale, 1978; Wilson and Seney, 1994). Higher impact activities could be more closely regulated, perhaps by restricting them to trails specifically designed and maintained to accommodate their higher impact. Uninformed or careless behavior may also result in avoidable resource impacts. For example, inexperienced snorkelers and divers damage coral by standing on reefs or by inadvertently breaking coral with their fins. Education or regulatory measures may be used to reduce these and other high impact behaviors, such as building fires or disturbing wildlife. Finally, large groups have a greater potential for damaging resources than the same number of individuals in smaller groups (Hammitt and Cole, 1987). Limits on group sizes are often encouraged or required to reduce such impacts.

ENVIRONMENTAL FACTORS

Environmental components, such as vegetation and soil types, can vary considerably in their relative resistance to visitor impacts or their ability to recover (resilience) following disturbance (Cole, 1988; Hammitt and Cole, 1987; Kuss et al., 1990; Sun and Liddle, 1993). In a study of trampling effects on mountain vegetation in four U.S. regions, Cole (1993) found considerable variation in the trampling resistance of different plant communities. Plant communities where grasses and sedges are dominant groundcover components were as much as 30 times more resistant than more susceptible community types comprised of fragile ferns or tall stemmed broad-leafed herbs. Liddle (1991) presents similar findings in a compilation of published data on 14 plant community types from around the world in which he reviews vegetative factors that explain their variation in trampling resistance. Studies have also shown that rates of vegetative and soil impact far exceed their rates of recovery (Bayfield, 1979; Boucher et al., 1991; Cole, 1988; Marion and Cole, 1996). The implication of this finding is that rest rotation schemes will be ineffectual, as recovery will proceed slowly in temporarily closed areas only to be followed by rapid deterioration when reopened. For example, campsite conditions following a single year of use at one U.S. park closely resembled conditions on long-established campsites. However, campsites that were closed to use required five or more years to recover to near-natural conditions, and these recovery rates were more rapid than in any other documented study (Marion and Cole, 1996).

Similarly, soils vary in their susceptibility to compaction and erosion (Hammitt and Cole, 1987; Pritchett, 1979). Soils with a wide range of particle sizes (e.g., loams), low organic content, and moderate-to-high moisture levels are the most prone to compaction. Soils most prone to erosion are those with a narrow range of particle sizes, particularly those high in silt and fine sands. Both soil compaction and erosion are accelerated by the absence of vegetation and litter cover; slope is also a critical factor influencing soil erosion. For example, a study of mountain footpaths in the Drakensberg Mountains of South Africa found that soil erosion was strongly affected by the loss of trailside vegetation (Garland, 1987). Similarly, in a study of horse paths at Chobham Common in England, decreases in ground vegetation cover, regeneration and vigor were found to increase trail susceptibility to wind erosion, leaching and runoff (Liddle and Chitty, 1981).

Resource resistance and resilience to visitor impacts is also modified by environmental factors such as climate, elevation and season (Cole, 1993; Leung and Marion, 1996). For example, vegetation and soils are more susceptible to disturbance during wet seasons, and vegetative recovery is greatly diminished in climates with short growing seasons. Through control over the location and use of trails and recreation sites, managers have the ability to minimize resource impacts by promoting visitation at resistant places and appropriate times, and by discouraging or prohibiting activity in sensitive environments. Knowledge of these and other environmental and use-related factors are critical to the selection of effective management actions.

SELECTING MANAGEMENT STRATEGIES AND TACTICS

An array of management strategies and tactics is available to prevent or minimize resource impacts and to enhance visitor experiences at protected areas. These are most effectively applied using a decision making framework that guides managerial selections and evaluates their success. The carrying capacity and *Limits of Acceptable Change* frameworks are briefly reviewed below. To choose the most effective intervention, managers need to determine the underlying cause(s) of a given problem as discussed previously, identify alternative strategies and tactics, select and implement one or more preferred actions, monitor their effectiveness, and evaluate the need for further action. Managers are often constrained in implementing such a process by limitations in funding and staffing (numbers, expertise), and concerns about restricting visitor freedom. Other management constraints include the linguistic and cultural diversity of ecotourism visitors, the needs of local communities, and other political and social issues.

MANAGEMENT FRAMEWORKS SHOULD GUIDE DECISIONS

As discussed in the chapter by Borrie, McCool and Stankey, carrying capacity has been the traditional decision making framework used to address visitor-related impacts. This approach emphasizes use-reduction strategies to resolve resource or visitor experience impacts. For example, in Rwanda's Volcanos National Park, numbers of tourists was chosen based on the health of the mountain gorilla population and visitor safety concerns. However, experience has shown that the carrying capacity approach is inherently restrictive on visitation, is often arbitrary, and dissuades managers from alternative actions that may have greater effectiveness and fewer "costs" to visitors (Stankey et al., 1990). This traditional model has been somewhat improved upon by incorporating managerial, biophysical and social factors. For example, tourist capacities for Carara Biological Reserve in Costa Rica and the Galápagos Islands are based on numbers of visitors that guides can manage, distance between groups, tourist space needed along the trail, and management capabilities and available resources (Cifuentes, 1992; Harroun and Boo, 1995).

With increasing frequency, managers are substituting decision making frameworks like *Limits of Acceptable Change* (LAC) (Stankey et al., 1985) or Visitor Experience and Resource Protection (VERP) (United States Department of the Interior, 1997a; 1997b) for more traditional methods (illustrated in Figure 7.2). These frameworks, which are similar to each other, offer more guidance and promote greater flexibility in addressing management problems. Protected area mandates are translated into prescriptive objectives that may vary by management zone. Objectives are then translated into numerical standards for selected indicators of resource or social conditions. Standards specify the limits of acceptable change, defining the critical boundary between acceptable and unacceptable conditions. If deterioration in resource or social conditions exceeds established standards, then managers must select and implement corrective actions.

Monitoring programs provide the mechanism to periodically evaluate resource conditions, management standards or the effectiveness of implemented actions (Marion, 1995). Resource monitoring may be defined as the systematic

FIGURE 7.2
SCHEMATIC ILLUSTRATING CONTEMPORARY PLANNING AND MANAGEMENT FRAMEWORKS

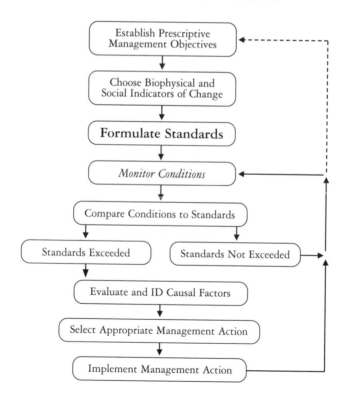

collection and analysis of data at regular intervals, in perpetuity, to predict or detect natural and human-induced changes, and to provide the basis for appropriate management response (United States Department of the Interior, 1991). Generally, data is collected by applying standardized procedures in order to assess various indicators of site condition (e.g., area of vegetation loss). The impact of visitation is often inferred through comparisons of indicator measures, taken on recreation sites, with measures taken on adjacent undisturbed (control) sites which have similar environmental attributes. Change over time may be inferred through comparisons of indicator measures taken on the same recreation site at different points in time, or, more appropriately, through comparisons of recreation site/control site differences over time. Sources of information guiding the development of visitor resource impact monitoring programs include Cole (1983; 1989b) and Marion (1991).

A principal benefit of visitor impact monitoring programs is that they provide an objective permanent record of resource conditions, even though individual managers may come and go. Managers may find this information valuable in preparing and justifying resource or visitor management actions or in preparing and justifying budget requests. Data may also be used to direct maintenance activities or set priorities for needed work. Trail and campsite condition monitoring programs are commonly applied in U.S. parks (Marion et al., 1993).

Monitoring programs allow managers to be proactive. Deteriorating conditions can be detected before severe or irreversible impacts occur, allowing time for implementing corrective actions. Relationships between specific impacts and other controlling factors may suggest effective management actions. For example, at Great Smoky Mountains National Park in the U.S., development of criteria for evaluating the impact resistance of existing and alternative campsite locations was based on analyses of the influence of environmental factors, such as topographic attributes and vegetation type and amount of cover (Marion and Leung, 1997). Similar relational analyses of trail monitoring data from this park revealed the relative influence of numerous use-related and environmental factors for five common indicators of trail condition (Marion, 1994). For example, excessively wide trail treads were highly correlated with wet soils. Excessively muddy trail treads were highly correlated with heavy horse use, valley bottom topographic positions, and locations where trails intercepted the runoff from springs.

Correlative analyses of monitoring data can suggest the causes of resource deterioration or improvement but cannot prove cause and effect. Only studies that include experimental designs can demonstrate cause and effect by controlling the influence of various confounding factors that may also alter resource conditions. Nevertheless, when interpreted through reference to other research and management experience such data provide a powerful tool for managers seeking to understand the underlying causes of impacts and the factors that affect them. Such knowledge is critical to the selection of effective management interventions and in the selection of resistant locations for new trails and campsites.

Protected areas differ tremendously in their legal and administrative protection, managing agencies, staffing and funding. These differences influence the readiness and capabilities of protected area managers for minimizing visitor impacts. In protected areas commonly known as "paper parks" there may be little or no on-site management even though visitation is occurring. Administrators may be most concerned with local community issues such as encroachment, poaching, loss of culture or discontentment with tourism. Historically, ecotourism has been promoted and developed without local consent and has altered local land uses or access, or has claimed lands required to sustain local populations. Relationships between managers and local residents have traditionally been poor due to a lack of communication and local involvement in protected area management. The LAC and VERP planning and management frameworks emphasize and facilitate a participatory decision making process to integrate local needs. Development of management plans using such frameworks can also help prepare parks for accommodating and managing rapid growth in visitation at the time when they become "discovered."

STRATEGIES AND TACTICS

Many management strategies and tactics have been applied to resolve resource impacts or visitor crowding and conflicts. Strategies are broad approaches that address underlying causes of problems (Manning, 1979). Tactics are the specific means or actions used to implement a strategy (Cole et al., 1987). The most common management strategies and tactics, presented and briefly reviewed in this section, are described in more detail in Brown et al. (1987), Cole et al. (1987), Hammitt and Cole (1987) and Hendee et al. (1990). Considerations for selecting "preferred" strategies and tactics are presented in a following section.

A comprehensive problem-oriented review of 37 specific tactics grouped by eight general strategies (Table 7.1) is provided by Cole et al. (1987). This review includes information on advantages and disadvantages, costs to visitors and management, and the effectiveness in addressing various problems. For example, the problem of wildlife harassment might be addressed by Strategy III, Modify the Location of Use Within Problem Areas (Example Tactic: Locate facilities such as trails and campsites away from critical areas) or by Strategy V, Modify Type of Use and Behavior (Example Tactic: Encourage behavior that minimizes wildlife disturbance). The following discussion is organized around these eight general strategies.

Strategies that reduce use of the entire area or of problem areas (Strategies I and II) address problems by limiting visitation through quotas, fees or other tactics. However, as previously described, the curvilinear use/impact relationship limits the effectiveness of use reduction and visitor dispersal in minimizing resource impacts. For social problems, many other factors, such as visitor behavior and

Table 7.1
Some Strategies and Tactics for Managing Resource Impacts or Visitor Crowding and Conflicts

I. **REDUCE USE OF THE ENTIRE AREA**
Limit number of visitors in the entire area
Limit length of stay in the entire area
Encourage use of other areas
Require certain skills and/or equipment
Charge a flat visitor fee
Make access more difficult throughout the entire area

II. **REDUCE USE OF PROBLEM AREAS**
Inform potential visitors of the disadvantages of problem areas and/or advantages of alternative areas
Discourage or prohibit use of problem areas
Limit number of visitors in problem areas
Encourage or require a length-of-stay limit in problem areas
Make access to problem areas more difficult and/or improve access to alternative areas
Eliminate facilities/attractions in problem areas and/or improve facilities/attractions in alternative areas
Encourage off-trail travel
Establish differential skill and/or equipment requirements
Charge differential visitor fees

III. **MODIFY THE LOCATION OF USE WITHIN PROBLEM AREAS**
Discourage or prohibit camping and/or stock use on certain campsites and/or locations
Encourage or permit camping and/or stock use only on certain campsites and/or locations
Locate facilities on durable sites
Concentrate use on sites through facility design and/or information
Discourage or prohibit off-trail travel
Segregate different types of visitors

IV. **MODIFY THE TIMING OF USE**
Encourage use outside of peak use periods
Discourage or prohibit use when impact potential is high
Charge fees during periods of high use and/or high-impact potential

V. **MODIFY TYPE OF USE AND VISITOR BEHAVIOR**
Discourage or prohibit particularly damaging practices and/or equipment
Encourage or require certain behavior, skills and/or equipment
Teach a wilderness ethic
Encourage or require a party size and/or stock limit
Discourage or prohibit livestock
Discourage or prohibit pets
Discourage or prohibit overnight use

VI. **MODIFY VISITOR EXPECTATIONS**
Inform visitors about appropriate uses
Inform visitors about conditions they may encounter

VII. **INCREASE THE RESISTANCE OF THE RESOURCE**
Shield the site from impact
Strengthen the site

VIII. **MAINTAIN OR REHABILITATE THE RESOURCE**
Remove problems
Maintain or rehabilitate impacted locations

(Source: Cole et al., 1987)

location of encounters, have been shown to be highly significant (Brown et al.,1987). Managers have traditionally favored use-reduction strategies, but research is demonstrating that many other strategies and tactics can be as effective while avoiding the need to reduce visitation. For example, tactics that modify the location of use (Strategy III) reduce impact and social problems by concentrating visitation at resistant locations or facilities, which can also be spatially arranged to separate conflicting uses and reduce crowding. For example, at Australia's Great Barrier Reef, recreation activity zones were designated in more resistant areas to minimize reef impacts (Kenchington, 1991). Visitor concentration tactics can decrease the extent of impact and sustain areas for greater use. This approach is favored over dispersal for managing campsite, trail and coral reef impacts when visitation is high (Hammitt and Cole, 1987; Liddle and Kay, 1987; Marion, 1995; Marion and Rogers, 1994). Containment has also been effectively applied to prevent wildlife impacts, as can be seen in an East African park where visitors observe wildlife from view sheds (Edington and Edington, 1986).

Similarly, modifying the timing of visitation (Strategy IV) can reduce use when soils, vegetation or wildlife are most sensitive to impact or can redistribute visitation away from peak use periods. Modifying the type of use and visitor behavior (Strategy V) is perhaps the most commonly used strategy. Visitor activity types or practices that are particularly damaging can be prohibited, restricted, or discouraged. For example, in Kenya's Maasai Mara Reserve tourist vehicles frequently surrounded the popular "big five" mammals, a practice that managers now discourage to reduce wildlife harassment impacts. Alternately, information and education can encourage adoption of low-impact hiking, camping, and wildlife-viewing practices (Cole, 1989a; Doucette and Cole, 1993; Hampton and Cole, 1995). Also in the Maasai Mara, education strategies and a code of ethics have been developed to alter the behavior of visitors and their drivers (Gakahu, 1992).

Altering visitor expectations (Strategy VI) is a strategy that can be used to reduce social crowding and conflict. Visitors can be informed about where they may encounter crowded conditions or uses that conflict with their own, so that these areas may be avoided. Local guides represent perhaps the best opportunity to alter visitor expectations. Guides know the park and its conditions and can relay valuable information, such as the trade-offs associated with alternative recreational opportunities (e.g., the ability to see wildlife versus the potential of encountering crowded conditions). Alternately, they may modify expectations by describing locations where their clients may encounter conflicting uses such as motorized recreation or local agricultural land-clearing practices.

Finally, recreation sites and trails may be shielded from impact by providing or modifying site facilities, or by site maintenance (Strategy VII). The removal and rehabilitation of problems, such as the cleanup of litter or trail work to drain muddy treads, comprise the final strategy (VIII). Site management efforts, including the selection, construction, maintenance, and rehabilitation of recreation sites and trails are a highly effective means for accommodating heavy visitation pressures. These tactics require sufficient funding and, therefore, have not been widely implemented in many developing countries (Giongo et al., 1994).

CONSIDERATIONS FOR SELECTING STRATEGIES AND TACTICS

This section provides guidance in identifying and selecting strategies and tactics that will permit ecotourism visitation while reducing associated resource impacts. Generally, a variety of strategies and tactics may be applicable for resolving any given visitor management problem. Selection of "preferred" actions must necessarily involve many considerations. Managers must evaluate the potential effectiveness of alternative strategies compared to their management costs (e.g., staffing and funding) and visitor costs (e.g., financial, loss of freedom, reduced quality of recreation experiences). For example, restricting use in sensitive wildlife areas may be highly effective in reducing wildlife impacts, yet entail high costs to visitors because viewing opportunities decrease, and high costs to managers because visitor management and enforcement needs increase. Surveys of protected area managers frequently identify limitations in staffing and funding as major management constraints (Giongo et al., 1994; Machlis and Tichnell, 1985). For example, due to inadequate funding, managers in the Galápagos Islands were unable to conduct monitoring to document deteriorating conditions that might justify changes in existing management (MacFarland and Cifuentes, 1995). Involving affected stakeholders in discussions of management problems and solutions can be a lower cost approach to modifying management and avoiding controversial decisions. Furthermore, local participation in protected area decision making is critical to ensure that ecotourism benefits local communities.

Costs to visitors may be minimized by favoring indirect strategies over more direct strategies. Indirect strategies influence, rather than regulate, visitor activity or behavior through tactics such as facility design or management, information dissemination or visitor education (Hammitt and Cole, 1987). Indirect actions are appropriate to prevent or reduce resource impacts. When successful, indirect strategies often have lower management costs, and research has shown that visitors prefer such light-handed approaches (Stankey and Schreyer, 1987). Direct strategies and tactics regulate and restrict visitor activities with actions that ration use, designate use areas, or limit group sizes. These actions are often both appropriate and necessary when indirect actions prove ineffective. They can also be effective in separating incompatible activities or preventing excessive resource impact in heavily visited areas (Lucas, 1990).

Park-related attributes such as level of development, accessibility and type and level of visitation also influence strategy selection. For example, Jaú Park in Brazil has few visitors, two rangers, no visitor center, and no designed or maintained trail system (Wallace, 1993). For parks like Jaú, it may be most logical to focus on the prevention of future impacts by planning the development of trails and facilities in resistant locations. In the absence of such facilities, managers might develop training programs for local guides and require visitors to obtain guide services. Guides can teach low-impact hiking, camping and wildlife-viewing practices, and monitor visitor activities to prevent impacts. Conversely, more highly developed and visited areas like the Galápagos Islands and Monteverde Cloud Forest Reserve will have greater success by maintaining or re-routing trails, and concentrating use on impact-resistant areas, and if necessary, regulating visitor behavior or numbers (Farrell and Runyan, 1991).

Often, a combination of strategies and tactics will prove most effective in addressing the underlying causes of management problems and avoiding unwanted secondary effects. For example, in the Galápagos Islands and at Monteverde Cloud Forest Reserve, a containment strategy restricts visitors to designated trails and requires that guides accompany groups to promote low-impact practices (Norris, 1994). These actions minimize vegetation and wildlife disturbance by restricting off-trail hiking. In this case, closure of designated areas might create additional problems such as increased visitation in adjacent areas with fragile soils or vegetation. Various management interventions have also been applied to reduce impacts associated with wildlife viewing, including temporal and spatial zoning of recreation activities, trail and recreation site management, design and provision of facilities, visitor education, and regulations and law enforcement (Knight and Temple, 1995; Larson, 1995).

A "success story" at Delaware Water Gap National Recreation Area in the U.S. illustrates the benefits of an integrated management approach. A visitor impact monitoring program documented a 50% reduction in the total area of disturbance associated with overnight and day-use activities on recreation sites from 1986 to 1991 as a result of this approach (Marion, 1995). Numerous actions were implemented, including: 1) closure of many visitor-created sites, particularly those in impact-susceptible locations, 2) designation of individual sites, 3) distribution of a river guide pamphlet showing recreation site locations and conveying site use regulations and low-impact practices, 4) placement of anchored fire grates on all sites, and 5) increased ranger patrols enhancing visitor contact and enforcement. Site designation and fire grate placement concentrated visitor traffic to core use areas around the fire grates, largely eliminating problems with multiple fire site construction and use. The closure of surplus sites reduced impact and enhanced visitor solitude by permitting greater spacing between sites. These educational efforts informed visitors of the new regulations and site use practices and, combined with the expanded ranger patrols, substantially reduced illegal site use.

Conclusion

In summary, this chapter has reviewed a wide variety of potential visitor impacts and presented alternative management strategies for mitigating and minimizing those impacts. Some of the key points which have been presented are:

- ◆ Visitor use can negatively affect vegetation, soil, water and wildlife resources, as well as the quality of visitor experiences.
- ◆ Visitor crowding and conflict can reduce the quality of visitor experiences.
- ◆ Environmental attributes such as vegetation and soil resistance and resiliency, influence the type and severity of visitor resource impacts.
- ◆ The use/impact relationship limits the effectiveness of visitor use reduction and dispersal strategies.
- ◆ Decision making frameworks can provide an explicit and flexible means of managing visitor impacts.
- ◆ Indirect management strategies are often less costly to implement and are preferred by visitors.

Ecotourism has been praised as an ideal land use alternative compared to more resource intensive industries like petroleum extraction or cattle grazing. The ecotourism industry has attracted considerable attention in recent years, leading to questions regarding how its success may be evaluated and how ecotourism benefits may be sustained. One important measure of both the success and sustainability of ecotourism is the management of visitor impacts to ensure the long-term protection of natural and cultural resources, as well as continued visitor enjoyment and use.

There is a wide variety of information available to aid in mitigating visitor impacts—from recreation ecology and social science research to recreation management experiences. Much of the literature cited in this chapter is derived from such research and experiences in protected areas of the United States. Environmental and cultural differences between countries and regions limits the applicability of some findings. However, managers can apply knowledge gained and solutions developed in other countries, and apply this knowledge, with flexibility to their unique circumstances.

According to Boo (1992), ecotourism management plans are frequently requested by areas that have recently experienced dramatic increases in visitation. Substantial resource impacts can occur rapidly in protected areas due to underdeveloped infrastructure (including visitor facilities and trail systems) and limited visitor education, regulation, and site-management programs. Managers frequently must first cultivate support for protected area operations from their constituencies and their agency to obtain the necessary support from local communities, government, the tourism industry or conservation groups. Unfortunately, such support is commonly linked to the amount of visitation and revenues, thereby making proactive planning and management difficult.

Limited staffing and budgeting for both newly discovered and well-known and developed areas severely restricts managers' efforts to minimize visitor impacts. For example, if resources are insufficient to implement a comprehensive LAC planning and management approach, then less costly options need to be developed. One alternative approach might involve enlisting the help of such experts as scientists and practitioners in the fields of ecotourism, protected area management, the social sciences, recreation ecology, wildlife management, and other disciplines, as well as representative area stakeholders. The incorporation of monitoring programs is also critical in evaluating the success of management strategies and determining if resource impacts have increased, decreased or remained the same. A panel of experts could be convened periodically to: 1) review monitoring data and evaluate management success in achieving stated objectives, 2) describe problems and their underlying causes, 3) identify and evaluate alternative strategies, and 4) make recommendations for addressing existing and future problems. Effective visitor impact management programs must therefore be pragmatic, making the most efficient use of available resources and emphasizing flexibility and innovation.

REFERENCES

Absher, J.D., R.G. Lee. 1981. "Density as an Incomplete Cause of Crowding in Backcountry Settings," *Leisure Sciences*, vol. 4, no. 3, pp. 231-247.

Anderson, D.H., P. J. Brown. 1984. "The Displacement Process in Recreation," *Journal of Leisure Research*, vol. 16, no. 1, pp. 61-73.

Bayfield, N. 1979. "Recovery of Four Montane Heath Communities on Cairgorm, Scotland, From Disturbance by Trampling," *Biological Conservation*, vol. 15, pp. 165-179.

Boo, E. 1992. "The Ecotourism Boom," WHN Technical Paper Series No. 2, World Wildlife Fund, Washington, D.C.

Boucher, D.H., J. Aviles., R. Chepote, O.E. Dominguez Gil, B. Vilchez. 1991. "Recovery of Trailside Vegetation from Trampling in a Tropical Rainforest," *Environmental Management*, vol. 15, no. 2, pp. 257-262.

Brown, P.J., S.F. McCool, M.J. Manfredo. 1987. "Evolving Concepts and Tools for Recreation User Management in Wilderness: A State of Knowledge Review," proceedings at the National Wilderness Research Conference, July 23-26, Fort Collins, Colorado, U.S. Forest Service, General Technical Report, INT-220, Intermountain Research Station.

Burger, J., M. Gochfield. 1993. "Tourism and Short-term Behavioral Responses of Nesting Masked, Red Footed, and Blue Footed Boobies in the Galápagos," *Environmental Conservation*, vol. 20, no. 3, pp. 255-259.

Ceballos-Lascuráin, H. 1996. *Tourism, Ecotourism, and Protected Areas*, IUCN: The World Conservation Union Gland, Switzerland.

Cifuentes, A. M. 1992. "Determinación de Capacidad de Carga Turística en Áreas Protegidas," CATIE, Turrialba, Costa Rica.

Cole, D.N. 1982. "Wilderness Campsite Impacts: Effect of Amount of Use," research paper INT-284, U.S. Forest Service, Ogden, Utah. USDA Intermountain Forest and Range Experiment Station.

Cole, D.N. 1983. "Assessing and Monitoring Backcountry Trail Conditions," research paper INT-303, U.S. Forest Service, Ogden, Utah. Intermountain Forest and Range Experiment Station.

Cole, D.N. 1987. "Research on Soil and Vegetation in Wilderness: A State of Knowledge Review," proceedings at the National Wilderness Research Conference, 1985, July 23-26, Fort Collins, Colorado. USDA Forest Service, General Technical Report INT-220, Intermountain Research Station.

Cole, D.N. 1988. "Disturbance and Recovery of Trampled Montane Grassland and Forests in Montana," research paper INT-389, Ogden, Utah. USDA Forest Service, Intermountain Forest and Range Experiment Station.

Cole, D.N. 1989a. "Low Impact Recreational Practices for Wilderness and Backcountry," general technical report INT-265, Ogden, Utah. USDA Forest Service, Intermountain Forest and Range Experiment Station.

Cole, D.N. 1989b. "Wilderness Campsite Monitoring Methods: A Sourcebook," general technical report INT-259, Ogden, Utah, USDA Forest Service, Intermountain Forest Experiment Station.

Cole, D.N. 1990. "Ecological Impacts of Wilderness Recreation and Their Management," *Wilderness Management*, North American Press, Golden, Colorado, pp. 425-466.

Cole, D.N. 1993. "Trampling Effects on Mountain Vegetation in Washington, Colorado, New Hampshire and North Carolina," research paper INT-464, Ogden, Utah. USDA Forest Service, Intermountain Forest Experiment Station.

Cole, D.N. 1995a. "Disturbance of Natural Vegetation by Camping: Experimental Applications of Low Level Stress," *Environmental Management*, vol. 19, no. 3, pp. 405-416.

Cole, D.N. 1995b. "Experimental Trampling of Vegetation: Relationship Between Trampling Intensity and Vegetation Response," *Journal of Applied Ecology*, vol. 32, pp. 203-214.

Cole, D.N., M.E. Petersen, R.C. Lucas. 1987. "Managing Wilderness Recreation Use: Common Problems and Potential Solutions," general technical report INT-230, Ogden, Utah. USDA Forest Service, Intermountain Forest Experiment Station.

Doucette, J.E., D.N Cole. 1993. "Wilderness Visitor Education: Information About Alternative Techniques," general technical report INT-295, Ogden, Utah. USDA Forest Service, Intermountain Forest Experiment Station.

Edington, J.M., M.A. Edington. 1986. *Ecology, Recreation and Tourism*, Cambridge University Press, New York, New York.

Farrell, B.H., D. Runyan. 1991. "Ecology and Tourism," *Annals of Tourism Research*, vol. 18, pp. 41-56.

Fishbein, M., I. Ajzen. 1975. *Belief, Attitude, Intention and Behavior: An Introduction to Theory and Research*, Addison-Wesley Publishing Company, Reading, Massachusetts.

Gakahu, C.G. 1992. *Tourist Attitudes and Use Impacts in Maasai Mara National Reserve*, Wildlife Conservation International, Nairobi, Kenya.

Garland, G.G. 1987. "Rates of Soil Loss From Mountain Footpaths: An Experimental Study in the Drakensberg Mountains," *Applied Geography*, vol. 7, pp. 41-54.

Giongo, F., J. Bosco-Nizeye, G. Wallace. 1994. *A Study of Visitor Management in the World's National Parks and Protected Areas*, College of Natural Resources, Colorado State University, Fort Collins, Colorado.

Gramann, J.H. 1982. "Toward a Behavioral Theory of Crowding in Outdoor Recreation: An Evaluation and Synthesis of Research," *Leisure Sciences*, vol. 5, no. 2, pp. 109-126.

Gramann, J.H., R.J. Burdge. 1984. "Crowding Perception Determinants at Intensively Used Developed Outdoor Recreation Sites," *Leisure Sciences*, vol. 6, pp. 167-186.

Hammitt, W.E., D.N. Cole. 1987. *Wildland Recreation: Ecology and Management*, John Wiley and Sons Inc., New York, New York.

Hampton, B., D.N. Cole. 1995. *Soft Paths: How to Enjoy the Wilderness Without Harming It*, Stackpole Books, Mechanicsburg, Pennsylvania.

Harroun, L.A., E.A. Boo. 1995. "The Search for Visitor Carrying Capacity: A Review of Tourism's Impact Management Methodologies and their Use in Protected Areas," draft, World Wildlife Fund, Washington, D.C.

Hawkins, J.P., C.M. Roberts. 1993. "Effects of Fecreational Scuba Diving on Coral Reefs: Trampling on Reef Flat Communities," *Journal of Applied Ecology*, vol. 30, pp. 25-30.

Haysmith, L., J.D. Hunt. 1995. "Nature Tourism," *Wildlife and Recreationists: Coexistence Through Management and Research*, Island Press, Washington, D.C.

Heberlein, T.A. and B. Shelby. 1977. "Carrying Capacity, Values and the Satisfaction Model: A Reply to Greist," *Journal of Leisure Research*, vol. 9, pp. 142-148.

Hendee, J.C., G.H. Stankey, R.C. Lucas. 1990. *Wilderness Management*, North American Press, Golden, Colorado.

Hollenhorst, S., L. Gardner. 1994. "The Indicator Performance Estimate Approach to Determine Acceptable Wilderness Conditions," *Environmental Management*, vol. 18, pp. 901-906.

Jacob, G.R., R. Schreyer. 1980. "Conflict in Outdoor Recreation: A Theoretical Perspective," *Journal of Leisure Research*, vol. 12, no. 4., pp. 369-380.

Kenchington, R. 1991. "Tourism Development in the Great Barrier Reef Marine Park," *Ocean and Shoreline Management*, vol. 15, pp. 57-78.

Knight, R.L., D.N. Cole. 1991. "Effects of Recreational Activity on Wildlife in Wildlands," transactions of the North American Wildlife and Natural Resources Conference, vol. 56, pp. 238-247.

Knight, R.L., D.N. Cole. 1995a. "Factors That Influence Wildlife Responses to Recreationists," *Wildlife and Recreationists: Coexistence Through Management and Research*, Island Press, Washington, D.C.

Knight, R.L., D.N. Cole. 1995b. "Wildlife Responses to Recreationists," *Wildlife and Recreationists: Coexistence Through Management and Research*, Island Press, Washington, D.C.

Knight, R.L., K.J. Gutzwiller. 1995. *Wildlife and Recreationists: Coexistence Through Management and Research*, Island Press, Washington, D.C.

Knight, R.L., S.A. Temple. 1995. "Wildlife and Recreationists: Coexistence Through Management," *Wildlife and Recreationists: Coexistence Through Management and Research*, Island Press, Washington, D.C.

Kuss, F.R., A.R. Graefe and J. J. Vaske. 1990. *Visitor Impact Management: A Review of Research*, vol. 1, National Parks and Conservation Association, Washington, D.C.

Larson, R.A. 1995. Balancing Wildlife Viewing With Wildlife Impacts: A Case Study," *Wildlife and Recreationists: Coexistence Through Management and Research*, Island Press, Washington, D.C.

Lawrence, T.B., D. Wickins. 1997. "Managing Legitimacy in Ecotourism," *Tourism Management*, vol. 18, no. 5, pp. 307-316.

Leung, Y.F., J.L. Marion. 1996. "Trail Degradation as Influenced by Environmental Factors: A State of the Knowledge Review," *Journal of Soil and Water Conservation*, vol. 51, no. 2, pp. 130-136.

Liddle, M.J. 1991. "Recreational Ecology: Effects of Trampling on Plants and Coral," *Trends in Ecology and Evolution*, vol. 6, no. 1, pp. 13-17.

Liddle, M.J. 1997. *Recreation and the Environment, The Ecological Impact of Outdoor Recreation and Ecotourism*, Chapman and Hall, London.

Liddle, M.J., L.D. Chitty. 1981. "The Nutrient Budget of Horse Tracks on an English Lowland Heath," *Journal of Applied Ecology*, vol. 18, pp. 841-848.

Liddle, M.J., A.M. Kay. 1987. "Resistance, Survival and Recovery of Trampled Coral on the Great Barrier Reef," *Biological Conservation*, vol. 42, pp. 1-18.

Liddle, M.J., H.R.A. Scorgie. 1980. "The Effects of Recreation on Freshwater Plants and Animals: A Review," *Biological Conservation*, vol. 17, no. 2, pp. 183-206.

Lucas, R.C. 1979. "Perceptions of Non-motorized Recreational Impacts: A Review of Research Findings," *Recreational Impact on Wildlands*, Ogden, Utah. USDA Forest Service, Intermountain Forest and Range Experiment Station.

Lucas, R.C. 1990. "Wilderness Recreation Management: A General Overview," *Wilderness Management*, North American Press, Golden, Colorado.

MacFarland, C., M. Cifuentes. 1995. "Case Study: Biodiversity Conservation and Human Population Impacts in the Galápagos Islands, Ecuador," proceedings of the Human Population, Biodiversity and Protected Areas, American Association for the Advancement of Science.

Machlis, G., D.L. Tichnell. 1985. *The State of the World's Parks: An International Assessment of Resource Management, Policy, and Research*, Westview Press, Inc.

Manning, R.E. 1979. "Impacts of Recreation on Riparian Soils and Vegetation," *Water Resources Bulletin*, vol. 15, no. 1, pp. 343.

Manning, R.E. 1985. "Crowding Norms in Backcountry Settings: A Review and Synthesis," *Journal of Leisure Research*, vol. 17, no. 2, pp. 75-89.

Marion, J.L. 1991. *Developing a Natural Resource Inventory and Monitoring Program for Visitor Impacts on Recreation Sites: A Procedural Manual*, natural resource report, NPS/NRVT/NRR91/06, U.S. Department of the Interior, National Park Service, Washington, D.C.

Marion, J.L. 1994. "An Assessment of Trail Conditions in Great Smoky Mountains National Park," research/resources management report, 152, U.S. Department of the Interior, National Park Service, Southeast Region, Atlanta, Georgia.

Marion, J.L. 1995. "Environmental Auditing: Capabilities and Management Utility of Recreation Impact Monitoring Programs," *Environmental Management*, vol. 19, no. 5, pp. 763-771.

Marion, J.L., D.N. Cole. 1996. "Spatial and Temporal Variation in Soil and Vegetation Impacts on Campsites: Delaware Water Gap National Recreation Area," *Ecological Applications*, vol. 6, no. 2, pp. 520-530.

Marion, J.L., Y.F. Leung. 1997. "An Assessment of Campsite Conditions in Great Smoky Mountains National Park," research/resources management report, U.S. Department of the Interior, National Park Service, Great Smoky Mountains National Park, Gatlinburg, Tennessee.

Marion, J.L., L.C. Merriam. 1985a. "Predictability of Recreational Impact on Soils," *Soil Science Society of America Journal*, vol. 49, no. 3, pp. 751-753.

Marion, J.L., L.C. Merriam. 1985b. "Recreational Impacts on Well Established Campsites in the Boundary Waters Canoe Area Wilderness," Station Technical Bulletin ADSB2502, Agricultural Experiment Station, University of Minnesota, St Paul, Minnesota.

Marion, J.L., C.S. Rogers. 1994. "The Applicability of Terrestrial Visitor Impact Management Strategies to the Protection of Coral Reefs," *Ocean and Coastal Management*, vol. 22, pp. 153-163.

Marion, J.L., J.W. Roggenbuck, R.E. Manning. 1993. "Problems and Practices in Backcountry Recreation Management: A Survey of National Park Service Managers," natural resources report NPS/NRVT/NRR93/12, U.S. Department of the Interior, National Park Service, Washington, D.C.

Mieczkowski, Z. 1995. "Environmental Issues of Tourism and Recreation," University Press of America, Inc., New York, New York.

Monti, P., E.E. Mackintosh. 1979. "Effect of Camping on Surface Soil Properties in the Boreal Forest Region of Northwestern Ontario, Canada," *Soil Science Society of America Journal*, vol. 43, pp. 104-112.

Norris, R. 1994. "Ecotourism in the National Parks of Latin America," *National Parks*, vol. 68, no. 12, pp. 33-37.

Pritchett, W.L. 1979. *Properties and Management of Forest Soils*, John Wiley and Sons, New York, New York.

Roggenbuck, J.W., D.R. Williams, A.E. Watson. 1993. "Defining Acceptable Conditions in Wilderness," *Environmental Management*, vol. 17, no. 2, pp. 187-197.

Salm, R.V. 1986. "Coral Reef and Tourist Carrying Capacity: The Indian Ocean Experience," *UNEP Industry and the Environment*, vol. 9, no. 1, pp. 11-13.

Shelby, B. 1980. "Crowding Models for Backcountry Recreation," *Land Economics*, vol. 56, pp. 43-55.

Stankey, G.H., D.N. Cole, R.C. Lucas, M.E. Petersen, S.S. Frissell. 1985. "The Limits of Acceptable Change (LAC) System for Wilderness Planning," general technical report INT-176, Ogden, Utah. USDA Forest Service, Intermountain Forest Experiment Station.

Stankey, G.H., S.F. McCool, G.L. Stokes. 1990. "Managing for Appropriate Wilderness Conditions: The Carrying Capacity Issue," *Wilderness Management*, North American Press, Golden, Colorado.

Stankey, G.H., R. Schreyer. 1987. "Attitudes Toward Wilderness and Factors Affecting Visitor Behavior: A State of Knowledge Review," proceedings at the National Wilderness Research Conference, July 23-26, Fort Collins, Colorado, U.S. Forest Service, General Technical Report INT-220, Ogden, Utah. USDA Forest Service, Intermountain Research Station.

Sun, D., M.J. Liddle. 1993. "A Survey of Trampling Effects on Vegetation and Soil in Eight Tropical and Subtropical Sites," *Environmental Management*, vol. 17, no. 4, pp. 497-510.

United States Department of the Interior, National Park Service. 1991. "Natural Resources Management Guideline," Government Printing Office, NPS-77, Washington, D.C.

United States Department of the Interior, National Park Service. 1997a. "A Summary of the Visitor Experience and Resource Protection (VERP) Framework," Denver Service Center, Publication NPS D-1214, Denver, Colorado.

United States Department of the Interior, National Park Service. 1997b. "The Visitor Experience and Resource Protection (VERP) Framework: A Handbook for Planners and Managers," Publication NPS D-1215, Denver Service Center, Denver, Colorado.

Vaske, J.J., M.P. Donnelly, B. Shelby. 1993. "Establishing Management Standards: Selected Examples of the Normative Approach," *Environmental Management*, vol. 17, no. 5, pp. 629-643.

Wagar, J.A. 1964. "The Carrying Capacity of Wild Lands for Recreation," The Society of American Foresters, Forest Science Monograph 7, Washington D.C.

Wallace, G.N. 1993. "Wildlands and Ecotourism in Latin America: Investing in Protected Areas," *Journal of Forestry*, vol. 91, no. 2, pp. 37-40.

Weaver, T., D. Dale. 1978. "Trampling Effects of Hikers, Motorcycles and Horses in Meadows and Forests," *Journal of Applied Ecology*, vol. 15, no. 2, pp. 451-457.

Whittaker, D., B. Shelby. 1988. "Types of Norms for Recreation Impacts: Extending the Social Norms Concept," *Journal of Leisure Research*, vol. 20, no. 4, pp. 261-273.

Wilson, J.P., J.P. Seney. 1994. "Erosional Impact of Hikers, Horses, Motorcycles, and Off Road Bicycles on Mountain Trails in Montana," *Mountain Research and Development*, vol. 14, no.1, pp. 77-88.

CHAPTER 8

Taking Ecotourism
to the Next Level
A Look at Private Sector Involvement With Local Communities

Costas Christ

"Small is beautiful," said the philosopher and writer E.F. Schumacher. When it comes to private-sector tourism development involving local communities, that is just the type of success there has been—small scale. As ecotourism has evolved in recent years, one finds that throughout Africa (as discussed in this chapter), and much of the rest of the world, a growing number of small entrepreneurs, including individual lodge owners and nature tour operators, are successfully involving local communities in their operations. These developments are consistent with the two most fundamental principles of ecotourism—bringing direct economic benefits to local people and contributing to the conservation of nature.

AUTHOR'S NOTE: *This chapter focuses on private sector-driven involvement with local communities in ecotourism development. It presents several case studies—all from Africa—for easy comparison. The examples illustrate local communities that had traditional leadership structures in place and where the private sector was willing to carry out successful "capacity building" within those communities when financial management skills, organizational structures and business knowledge were lacking. This chapter does not examine the larger issues of community-based tourism where enterprises are initiated, owned and operated by the communities themselves. However, the issues raised here, and many of the conclusions reached, are relevant across the entire spectrum of local community involvement with nature-based tourism.*

The case studies of Oliver's Camp Limited and Dorobo Tours and Safaris are based on firsthand research, including on-site visits in Tanzania, interviews with the owners and managers, and a review of company documentation including newsletters and brochures. Additional secondary sources were sought out, as noted in the references. In regards to Conservation Corporation Africa, I served as their Program Director from 1996-1997, and was responsible for ecotourism monitoring and project development. During this time, I gained an in-depth understanding of Conservation Corporation Africa's ecotourism practices, both in the field and in corporate decision making. The Conservation Corporation Africa case study is based on extensive firsthand knowledge of the company's field projects, properties and operational procedures. It includes a review of public documents and other secondary resources as cited in the references at the end of this chapter.

The achievement of community involvement with small-scale private-sector tourism development has not come about easily. It has been the result of trial and error, and of learning from the mistakes of early ecotourism entrepreneurs who struggled to give true meaning to the idea of responsible travel to natural areas that conserves the environment and sustains the well-being of local people. But why should community involvement in tourism even matter to the private sector? Is it just a philanthropic activity? What's in it for the businessman/investor? When it comes to nature-based tourism, one does not have to look far to find the answers. Statistics continue to show that nature-based tourism remains one of the fastest growing segments of the industry, with more and more nature-based tourism activities taking place outside of designated national parks or reserves on village or community lands where people and wildlife, in addition to other natural resources, live in close relationship to each other. If this relationship is one of hostility, it may destroy the business environment on which tourism growth depends. When villagers in the Prachuab Khiri Khan region of Thailand poisoned an elephant watering hole in May 1997, killing a family herd of rare Asian elephants, they were retaliating for not receiving benefits from nature-based tourism development in the area. Instead, the elephants were causing damage to their subsistence crops. The villagers' actions against the animals seriously undermined the tourism market for the region.

Sadly, there are numerous examples worldwide of similar situations. Local communities have clashed with nature-based tourism projects or enterprises, their people having been left out of the economic benefits equation. In these circumstances, it has been learned again and again that community involvement with private-sector tourism development makes sound business sense. But how does it work? What are the problems and promises of private-sector community involvement in nature-based tourism? The following case studies provide some examples.

OLIVER'S CAMP LIMITED
ECOTOURISM OUTSIDE TARANGIRE NATIONAL PARK IN NORTHERN TANZANIA

One example of a small-scale, successful ecotourism operation involving local communities can be found at Oliver's Camp in Tanzania. Founded in 1992, Oliver's Camp, Ltd., is a self-financed commercial tourism enterprise that actively promotes community-based conservation. The goal of Oliver's Camp is to develop a commercially successful tourism product in the northern safari circuit of Tanzania, while providing positive conservation results and tangible economic benefits from tourism for the local Maasai in the Loboir Soit and Emboreet villages along the eastern wildlife dispersal area of Tarangire National Park (known as the Lokisale Game Controlled Area). Oliver's Camp presented a proposal to the two local villages and to the Tanzanian government's wildlife department, recommending a core wildlife conservation area of 20 square kilometers within the Emboreet village area on which to base the camp. A larger "activity area" of 320 square kilometers (an ideal wilderness setting), on which Loboir Soit village was located, would also be conserved for longer walking safaris. In essence, Oliver's Camp was seeking a long-term lease agreement with the villages. In return, the camp proposed a per-tourist per-day "wildlife conservation fee" of $12 to be divided between the two villages. This figure was felt to be reasonable both in terms of cost to the client and level of benefit to the communities and was agreed to by the villagers. In addition, Oliver's Camp requested the following from the villagers (Dorobo Tours and Safaris Ltd. and Oliver's Camp, 1995):

- that domestic livestock not be allowed to graze in the wilderness conservation area (except in times of real need);
- that the wilderness conservation area and the larger activity area not be farmed or burned, and trees not be cut for charcoal production; and
- that village members discourage the harassment of all wildlife, while retaining all grazing and water rights in the larger activity area.

The government's wildlife department supported the lease agreement by encouraging the village councils to proceed. This official backing was critical, as all wildlife is cared for by the state in Tanzania, and this project was perceived as a non-consumptive wildlife utilization scheme. An initial, short-term (six month) agreement was reached allowing operations to begin, while more detailed discussions for a proposed long term (99-year) lease on the wildlife conservation area took place with the village councils. Oliver's Camp financed all costs for a series of meetings and trips for more than a year to bring together the village councils for further discussions. They continued to pay the $12 per-person, per-night levy throughout this time, despite having no signed lease agreement beyond the initial six-month period. A considerable amount of time and money was put into an endeavor to educate the local villagers about the tourism operation itself, the potential economic benefits to the community, and the long-term conservation benefits for their community-owned land. The village was concerned about how the "wilderness conservation fees" would be paid. Part of the agreement with Oliver's Camp was to open a village bank account with several members of the village council (elected by the villagers themselves) who signed on behalf of the community (Dorobo Tours and Safaris Ltd., and Oliver's Camp, 1995).

Finally, a 99-year lease agreement was made and signed with Emboreet village, followed by a similar agreement with Loboir Soit village. Between 1993 and 1997, more than $40,000 was generated in tourist fees paid directly to the two villages, according to the lease agreements (Oliver, 1997). These funds have since been spent on maintaining a village borehole and water pump, expanding the village school, and purchasing food for villagers during a period of drought, among other village projects and needs identified by the villagers themselves. The example of Oliver's Camp serves to show two points: that successful ecotourism is taking place at the small-scale level, and, that effective cooperation (e.g., leasing arrangements) between local communities and the private sector can be achieved with a commitment on the part of the entrepreneur to bear the financial costs and risks of capacity building (education and training) in the community. Costs associated with this commitment involve organizing meetings to keep the process moving forward, as well as making initial investments in the project, often before a long-term lease or concession agreement is reached. Another type of cost incurred involves time, as local communities do not always respond according to the deadlines set by business investors for a given project. Patience to see the process through is essential if an agreement that is beneficial to all is to be achieved.

Perhaps the largest risk of investing in a tourism venture with a lease agreement signed by a village council involves the fact that the community may or may not have actual rights to the land in question. As the Oliver's Camp owner explains (Oliver, 1997):

Land that village communities consider their own may or may not be recognized by higher authorities within the government. Any title deeds or land documents held by such a village must be researched and understood and fully checked at the regional land office. Also, traditional village boundaries are often vague. For example, one village discussed a site for our permanent camp, signed a lease agreement with us and received income from our activities with full knowledge that the site was, in fact, another village's land area. It became very clear to us early on that we were going to be the driving force in identifying village boundaries.

DOROBO TOURS AND SAFARIS
PROMOTING COMMUNITY-BASED CONSERVATION
WITHIN THE NGORONGORO-SERENGETI ECOSYSTEM

Dorobo Tours and Safaris, also in Tanzania, has initiated far-reaching and successful community-based tourism ventures, and serves as a further example of how the private sector is succeeding with ecotourism at the small-scale level. Unlike Oliver's Camp, which is primarily a permanent camp facility, Dorobo is a tour operator with no permanent lodge or camp. Instead, it operates mobile camps and walking safaris in the heart of Maasailand, in Tanzania. This area is rich in both wildlife and local culture, and the land is owned and occupied by the Maasai people, which is the way Dorobo wants to see it remain (T. Peterson, 1997).

As a private business setting out to make a profit through nature-based tourism, Dorobo was also guided, from its inception, by clear ecotourism goals: 1) to promote sustainable natural resource management by communities directly dependent on land resources, 2) to support indigenous cultures as they interface with the modern world, and 3) to promote the conservation of wilderness, primarily as a resource option for local peoples, and also for its inherent worth (D. Peterson, 1997).

Three brothers own and manage Dorobo Tours and Safaris. As one of them notes (T. Peterson, 1997):

> *Our belief is that wildlife and wilderness need to be an economic option for local communities living on the land. This is especially true among the Maasai in Africa. Otherwise, these wildlands simply will not be able to compete with the pressures of expanding agriculture. We're doing this as a business to earn money, but we also have a commitment to a larger conservation ethic.*

Like Oliver's, Dorobo signed lease agreements with several local communities that included exclusivity clauses (the right of Dorobo Safaris only to bring tourists into a certain wilderness area inhabited by the Maasai). However, driven by a strong sense of ecotourism mission, Dorobo sought only five-year use agreements, "in order to avoid alienating villagers from their own land through long-term leases" (T. Peterson, 1997). In the first five years, Dorobo has paid the four villages with which they have established ecotourism partnership projects $50,000 through a combination of annual concession fees ($500 per year) and bed-night levies, amounting to $10-$20 per person, per night, depending on the area visited (T. Peterson, 1997). With nearly ten years of hands-on ecotourism fieldwork behind them, Dorobo has identified several issues that have dominated their private-sector experience and its challenges with local community involvement (T. Peterson, 1997):

- Extensive time and commitment are needed on the part of the entrepreneur in meeting with the communities involved and working out an effective concession or lease agreement that meets each party's concerns and needs.
- There is still no real official policy, framework or support from government agencies involved, particularly in developing nations for how a private-sector entrepreneur can carry out effective community involvement with tourism. There is nothing that says, "Here is what you can do, here is how to proceed, and this is what you must avoid." In this regard, especially at the official level, ecotourism still has a long way to go.
- Capacity building within villages and communities stills falls largely on the private sector, and they are often the least able to meet this need.

According to Dorobo, "capacity building within communities, and lack of careful government policy framework is what scares off many private investors from engaging in local community involvement" (T. Peterson, 1997). To help meet this challenge, Dorobo is now raising funds to support full-time capacity building in several villages where they have land-use agreements in order to strengthen transparent and democratic ways of handling revenue from the tourism project, and to foster greater input and coordination between Dorobo and the villages (D. Peterson, 1997). Dorobo is also documenting their private-sector experience with community involvement and making it available to relevant government agencies to help establish a better understanding of the process for other private-sector investors seeking to operate according to ecotourism principles.

Oliver's Camp and Dorobo Safaris are not unique in their private-sector experience with launching a tourism project with community planning and involvement, nor in their success at keeping the projects going. Tortilis Camp in Kenya, Lizauli Traditional Village in Namibia, and Bishangari Tented Camp in Ethiopia are among numerous other examples of development projects on the African continent (see Appendix for contact details). Elsewhere, the Kapawi Ecological Lodge in Ecuador, the Ulu Ai village-based tourism project in Sarawak, and the Lisu Lodge in Thailand are among many small-scale ecotourism projects worldwide that have met similar challenges and have achieved notable successes in implementing community involvement.

These successes in small-scale ecotourism development between the private sector and local communities raise a critical question: Is community planning and involvement with private-sector ecotourism development destined to remain in the realm of the small nature-based tour operator, the single lodge owner, or the individual tented camp concession? Small may be beautiful, but is ecotourism confined to tiny enclaves, islands of small-scale private-sector successes in a sea of massive commercial nature-based tourism growth and expansion?

That, perhaps, is the greatest challenge facing ecotourism today. Can the principles of ecotourism be put into practice successfully, not only at the small-scale private-sector level (with business revenues totaling $1-$2 million per year or less), but also at the large-scale corporate level, where assets and revenues exceed $50 million annually? Can large, private-sector corporations involved in tourism make the commitment in time and resources necessary to achieve successful community planning and involvement?

CONSERVATION CORPORATION AFRICA
AN ETHIC OF CARING

The results achieved by Conservation Corporation Africa, one of the world's largest nature-based ecotourism companies, may help to answer the question posed above. Founded in 1990, Conservation Corporation is committed to adhering to the principles of ecotourism, as illustrated in its mission statement: "Care of the land, wildlife and people" (Conservation Corporation Africa, 1997). Conservation Corporation set out to develop the large-scale potential of the ecotourism industry—beginning on the African continent—by building a commercially successful portfolio of up-market lodges and camps in remote wilderness areas. The company believes that by embracing the principles of ecotourism it will ensure that the wilderness areas in which it operates remain both economically viable as conservation sites and ecologically sustainable in the long term. The company calls this approach to ecotourism "conservation development" (Varty, 1996).

Using an integrated approach, commercial nature-based tourism development, nature conservation and rural venture capital investment are combined to achieve the important ecotourism goals of protecting ecologically fragile environments and promoting direct economic benefits for local communities. Conservation Corporation does not seek to own wilderness land (nor does it consider it appropriate for private-sector corporations to do so); rather, it endeavors to create partnerships with national and regional governments and, most importantly, with the local communities intimately associated with that land. Security of tenure is sought via long-term use agreements, with the resulting rental, lease and traversing fees flowing directly to the local communities.

From the start, Conservation Corporation has aimed big, with assets and revenues exceeding $60 million and a corporate goal of establishing 60-100 of the world's finest luxury lodges and camps, each located in a remarkable, pristine wilderness area. In 1990, Conservation Corporation had one ecolodge, Londolozi Camp, on the western border of Kruger National Park in South Africa. As of April 1998 the company had within its ecotourism portfolio, four private sanctuaries (two owned, two leased) and more than 20 lodges and camps located across the African continent.

In the early stages, and to assure that its business growth and expansion remained consistent with the principles of ecotourism, Conservation Corporation created its own Rural Investment Fund (RIF) as a direct program and department within the company. The aims of the RIF were to: ensure that ecotourism activities were discussed and endorsed by the local communities, to raise funds and support local economic benefits through community development projects, and to illustrate how the private sector can address sustainable development in rural economies through carefully conceived and implemented nature-based tourism enterprises. In order to set up viable economic and social development projects, the RIF operated much like a traditional community development agency within the corporate structure of the company, investing time and utilizing its infrastructure, resources and capital to work with local communities in and around Conservation Corporation lodges and camps. Project funding was secured from national and international sources, (from both private individuals and donor agencies), but not from Conservation Corporation itself. However, the $100,000+ in annual costs to run the RIF was derived directly out of the profits generated by Conservation Corporation's tourism operations (Christ, 1997). Project staff at the RIF included a director, a development manager (whose primary role was to write proposals and secure funding), a regional manager, a community liaison officer and three field workers.

Between 1991 and 1997, Conservation Corporation leveraged more than $1 million through the RIF to fund development projects within communities existing next to Conservation Corporation lodges, camps and private reserves, primarily in South Africa. These projects have included everything from building classrooms in village areas to constructing a residential health clinic serving 30,000 people in an area where only limited medical facilities previously existed. The purpose and focus of these efforts has been to involve communities directly in the economic benefits of tourism by actively seeking a way for local peoples to coexist in a beneficial relationship with nature-based tourism (Christ, 1996a).

While Conservation Corporation also strives to adhere to the principles of environmentally sustainable design in the building of its lodges and camps, and environmentally friendly management in its operations, it apparently remains the only large-scale private-sector tourism corporation of its size attempting to carry out effective local community planning and involvement as part of its operating mission. Other large, private-sector corporations operating in the tourism industry have shown interest in, and taken action on, the "environmentally sensitive" side of the ecotourism equation. For example, InterContinental Hotels and Resorts has taken steps to promote sound environmental management within the international hotel sector worldwide (Intercontinental Hotels and Resorts, 1995), Dusit Hotels and Resorts has established an excellent environmental awareness program at their properties (Dusit Hotels and Resorts, 1995), and Serena Lodges and Hotels has set a precedent for African hotel groups by establishing an ethic for environmentally sensitive operations (Serena Lodges and Hotels, 1997). However, these corporations have basically avoided community planning and involvement for the simple reason that such initiatives take time, money and special expertise in order to work. As the Oliver's Camp, Dorobo and Conservation Corporation examples help to illustrate, only those who have shown a genuine commitment to the principles of ecotourism have been willing to go the long haul in making community planning and involvement in private-sector ecotourism development a reality.

In its own defense, the private sector is quick to point out that many rural communities living adjacent to, or on, remote wilderness land have had little experience with either commercial business or the tourism industry. Furthermore, communities may or may not have uniformly recognized village councils or committees for decision making. A private-sector investor interested in community planning and involvement must invest time and money in supporting capacity building within these communities. Such capacity building includes but is not limited to:

- basic education in understanding legal documents, such as title deeds, occupancy rights, land use rights and lease agreements;
- financial management training, including understanding fee structures, banking procedures, accounting and transparency;
- strengthening of decision making structures, including village councils and project oversight committees; and
- tourism enterprise development training, including community-managed craft centers, cultural centers, and guiding opportunities.

At the most basic level, the local community must have the ability to engage in an educational discussion on technical issues such as lease agreements and project impacts/benefits, thereby allowing for informed decisions to be made. Suspicions on both parts must be overcome for trust to be established.

Ecotourism experience has thus far shown that in most instances, the costs involved in this capacity building, including meetings, education, business training, drafting legal documents and bringing in local or regional government representatives to further discussions, are borne by the private investor. Where conventional business decisions often need to be made quickly or according to investor timetables, village and community decision making moves slowly, at best. Furthermore, the process is often delayed by local or internal power struggles within the communities themselves. As the owner of Oliver's Camp states (Oliver, 1997):

> It may take years of meetings and enormous amounts of time...As {our} meetings developed, the issues presented gained more support or objection, and village attendance at such meetings varied tremendously. Many meetings were called off, some seemed to be forgotten, while some were vibrant displays of community concern, attended by large numbers of villagers.

In the areas where Conservation Corporation has established its projects and engaged in the task of community planning and involvement, the reality has been much the same. Time, patience and money are very real costs sustained by the private-sector investor in such circumstances. It is the challenge of providing capacity building to the community involved that prevents many large-scale entrepreneurs from taking on true community planning and development in a rural tourism enterprise. The costs and benefits of community involvement to the small-scale private-sector developer and the large-scale company attempting to abide by the principles of ecotourism can be very different. A small company with one camp, or only one or two lease agreements, goes through the community planning and involvement operation initially, and then works to maintain a relationship with that community to ensure a successful ongoing project. On the other hand, a large corporation with numerous lodges and camps in many different countries and involving a wide range of communities must repeat the same challenging and often costly process over and over. One benefit for Conservation Corporation, however, is that each new experience in private-sector tourism development with local community planning and involvement brings with it a more profound understanding of "how to do it better" the next time.

The successful model of community involvement at Conservation Corporation's Phinda Resource Reserve in South Africa (established in 1992, and involving the communities of Mduku, Mngobokazi and Nibela), laid the foundation for community planning and involvement efforts at other Conservation Corporation properties. Kichwa Tembo, located on a Maasai group ranch in Southern Kenya, Mnemba Island off the northeast coast of Zanzibar, and Klein's Camp bordering Serengeti National Park in Tanzania, all established dialogues with the local communities regarding their interests and concerns (Christ, 1996b; Conservation Corporation Africa, 1996).

As seen in previous examples, ample research and models exist to illustrate the success of small-scale, private-sector involvement with local communities. To date, Conservation Corporation Africa stands alone as a pioneer private-sector ecotourism company willing to tackle the challenge of community planning and involvement in the arena of "large-scale" commercial tourism development. To that end, the experience of Conservation Corporation Africa may very well prove that it can succeed at that level, or show why it does not. So far, the positive continues to outweigh the negative in this large corporate ecotourism operation. This is evidenced by Conservation Corporation's continuing success in achieving ecotourism goals. In 1997, a Conservation Corporation property, Phinda, was awarded the coveted British Airways Tourism for Tomorrow Award for achieving an outstanding example of ecotourism principles put into action. It was the second time in five years that the award has gone to a Conservation Corporation project.

However, problems associated with Conservation Corporation's rapid expansion in recent years have also served to undermine some of its more glowing ecotourism accomplishments. For example, in its rush to open two new luxury ecolodges on the banks of the Zambezi River near Zimbabwe's Victoria Falls, the construction crews used by Conservation Corporation clear cut as many as 65,000 trees, some as old as 300 years, to quickly install electrical power lines to the lodges. Local environmentalists were outraged and took the company to task for a gross violation of its own ecotourism standards. Conservation Corporation itself apparently was caught off-guard by the tree felling, and was not even aware that it had taken place (Tweedie, 1996). The company became a victim of its own massive expansion and the resulting lack of careful planning that had been its founding trademark.

A similar incident occurred in Tanzania when builders at the newly opened Conservation Corporation Ngorongoro Crater Lodge accidentally extended two room units beyond the concession boundary and into the neighboring protected conservation area. The local conservation area authorities threatened to have them taken down, but in the end they were left standing, as the resultant damage, although limited, had already been done. Despite these setbacks and a revenue shortfall in 1997 that resulted in the reorganization of the company, including the downsizing of the RIF community initiatives (putting them under the direct leadership of lodge managers), Conservation Corporation is still setting the industry standard for ecotourism success at the large-scale commercial level.

Final conclusions on whether ecotourism is commercially viable at the large corporate level cannot yet be drawn. Initial results are showing that not only is community planning and involvement possible on this scale, but it is a vital contributor to the sustainability of the nature tourism industry itself.

In conclusion, the challenges inherent to the private sector in pursuing community planning and involvement remain the same for both small-scale and large-scale tourism companies. Governments and non-governmental agencies can help to lessen private investors' time and monetary cost burdens through support programs geared to promote projects involving the private sector and local communities. For example, governments can support private investment that promotes implementation of ecotourism principles by giving tax breaks and reducing licensing fees for those private investors who engage in community. In Kenya, the Kenya Wildlife Service's *Community Wildlife Service* and *Wildlife for Development and Benefit Sharing* programs are aimed at strengthening the relationship potential between the private sector and local communities cooperating together in nature tourism enterprises by providing tourism investors with guidelines and support in working with local communities. Likewise, among NGO groups, the Namibia Community Based Tourism Association, initiated in Namibia in 1995 with the support of donor funds, acts to assist with capacity building within communities in order to enable successful joint ventures with the private sector to take place. However, because such governmental, and even non-governmental, support remains limited at best, there is a great need for this kind of outside support to encourage more private-sector involvement with local communities within the nature-based tourism industry.

Finally, if ecotourism is an experiment—and it still is—there are now enough positive results to take it very seriously. The days are gone when one wondered whether adopting the principles of ecotourism could make tourism become a catalyst for nature conservation and community development. There is, finally, ample evidence that this is true. To date, however, successful examples are almost exclusively at the small-scale level. Ecotourism is now at a crossroads. In order to move ecotourism successfully forward in the years ahead, we must try to apply the same criteria which have shown results at the small-scale level, to the large-scale commercial nature-based tourism sector. This will encourage a growing number of private-sector, nature-based tourism companies, who have shown a willingness to become more sensitive to ecotourism issues, to get involved not only with ecologically friendly operations but to extend their commitment into the most challenging arena of ecotourism practice today—successful community involvement.

References

Christ, C. 1996a. "Conservation Corporation: Ecotourism through Rural Investment," unpublished report, November, Conservation Corporation Africa, Nairobi, Kenya.

Christ, C. 1996b. "CCA Summary of East Africa Lodges and Camps," unpublished report, Conservation Corporation Africa, Nairobi, Kenya.

Christ, C. 1997. March. "Ecotourism and Its Role in Africa Tourism Promotion," International Tourism Exchange: Africa Forum, Messe Berlin Gmbh., Berlin, Germany.

Conservation Corporation Africa. 1996. January. "10 Facts to Know About RIF," Rural Investment Fund Programme: An Overview, unpublished document, Conservation Corporation Africa, Johannesburg, South Africa.

Conservation Corporation Africa. 1996. "Phinda Resource Reserve: Rural Investment Fund Developments," unpublished document, Conservation Corporation Africa, Johannesburg, South Africa.

Conservation Corporation Africa. 1997. "Company Brochure: Edition I," Conservation Corporation Africa, Johannesburg, South Africa.

Dorobo Tours and Safaris Ltd., Oliver's Camp. 1995. "Potential Models for Community-Based Conservation among Pastoral Communities Adjacent to Protected Areas in Northern Tanzania," *Community-Based Conservation in Northern Tanzania*, Department of Wildlife, Dar es Salaam, Tanzania.

Dusit Hotels and Resorts. 1995. "Environmental Management for Hotels," Dusit Hotels and Resorts, Bangkok, Thailand.

InterContinental Hotels and Resorts. 1995. "InterContinental Hotels and Resorts Environmental Review," InterContinental Hotels and Resorts, London, England.

Oliver, P. 1997. May 15. Personal communication, owner, Oliver's Camp.

Peterson, D. 1997. May. Draft newsletter, unpublished document, Dorobo Tours and Safaris Ltd., Arusha, Tanzania.

Peterson, T. 1997. June 14. Personal communication, co-owner, Dorobo Tours and Safaris Ltd.

Serena Lodges and Hotels. 1997. "Serena's Commitment to the Environment," unpublished presentation, Serena Lodges and Hotels, Arusha, Tanzania.

Tweedie, K. 1996. December. Draft news article on Conservation Corporation Africa Zimbabwe lodges, unpublished document, Conservation Corporation Africa, Johannesburg, South Africa.

Varty, D. 1996. August. Personal communication, chairman, Conservation Corporation Africa.

ADDITIONAL READINGS

Christ, C. 1995. April. "Report of the Community-based Tourism Enterprise Workshop," World Wildlife Fund, Windhoek, Namibia.

Conservation Corporation Africa. Undated. "An Integrated Approach to Ecotourism," unpublished document, Conservation Corporation Africa, Johannesburg, South Africa.

Hammer, J. 1996. March 4. "Shifting the Balance between Man and Beast," *Newsweek*.

Oliver, P., D. Peterson. "Ecotourism Outside Tarangire National Park in Northern Tanzania," unpublished document, Arusha, Tanzania.

PRIVATE SECTOR LODGE CONTACTS

Tortilis Camp Ltd.
(Amboseli, Kenya)
c/o Stefano Cheli
P.O. Box 39806
Nairobi, Kenya

Lizauli Traditional Village
(East Caprivi, Namibia)
c/o Maxi Louis
Manager, NACOBTA—Life Programme
Private Box 9681
Windhoek, Namibia

Bishangari Tented Camp
(Lake Langano, Ethiopia)
c/o Project Manager
Farm-Africa
P.O. Box 5746
Addis Ababa, Ethiopia

Kapawi Ecological Lodge
c/o Daniel Koupermann
Canodros S.A.
Luis Urdaneta
14-18 y Ave Ejercito
Guayaquil, Ecuador

Ulu Ai Village Community-based Tourism Project
c/o Borneo Adventures Sdn Bhd
55 Main Bazaar
93000 Kuching
Sarawak, Malaysia

Lisu Lodge
c/o Vincent Tabutear, Managing Director
East West Siam, Building One, 11th Floor
99 Wireless Road
10330 Bangkok, Thailand

New Approaches to Community-based Ecotourism Management
Learning From Ecuador

Andy Drumm

INTRODUCTION

Local communities see ecotourism as an accessible development alternative which can enable them to improve standards of health and education, and their general quality of life, without having to sell off their natural resources or compromise their culture. In the absence of other sustainable alternatives, their participation in ecotourism is often perceived as the best option for achieving their aspiration of sustainable development. In the author's experience, active local community participation in the planning process and in operation management is essential in order to achieve the conservation and sustainable-development goals of ecotourism. For example, one of the most common complaints of nature tour operators who employ or rent lands from local people in their operations is that in spite of prior agreements, the locals continue to hunt or fell trees along routes designated as tourism areas. In cases where the community is actively involved in tourism planning and management, as is the case with the Cofan of Zabalo (see Case Study 3, later this chapter), this complaint does not arise.

The author differentiates between ecotourism (which implies conservation, education, responsibility and active community participation) and nature tourism

AUTHOR'S NOTE: *This essay is based largely on my eight years of field observations while working as a consultant, advisor and ecotourism operator with indigenous communities in the Amazon region of Ecuador and also with campesino communities in the Andes, on environmental and sustainable development issues, principally ecotourism development.*

(which, in common with ecotourism, takes place in natural areas, but does not imply all of the elements). From the beginning, nature tourism has used attractions on land belonging to local and indigenous communities (who often do not possess legal title despite traditional occupation of the area). However, the benefits have typically remained in private-sector hands and bank accounts a long way from the rainforests, rivers, key wildlife species' habitats and people who actually live there.

Community-based ecotourism management refers to ecotourism programs which take place under the control and with the active participation of the local people who inhabit or own a natural attraction. Wesche (1996) presents a very useful account of the development of this phenomenon among Ecuadorean Amazon indigenous communities.

The participation of local communities in the planning and management of tourism activities has traditionally been the weak link in the process of evolution from nature tourism to ecotourism. Local and indigenous communities have been incorporated in nature tourism, if at all, as a source of cheap labor, or as a colorful object of interest in the itineraries of private-sector operated tours. These communities often receive insignificant economic benefits and little or no role in the planning or management of the operation of which they were part. Under these conditions, tourism provides few incentives for communities to conserve their natural resources and does not reinforce cultural values. Nature tourism, like most forms of tourism—and other resource exploitation activities such as oil, mining, cattle ranching and plantations—has typically tended to perpetuate exploitative relationships between private companies and local communities, and has generated negative environmental impacts.

THE EXPERIENCE

In recent years, Ecuador has witnessed the emergence of indigenous and campesino political organizations which has led to greater participation in political activity at the national level. Among other benefits, this has resulted in advances in the recognition of land rights. Growing political autonomy at the grassroots level has contributed to making the country a world leader in the diversity and growth of community ecotourism enterprises.

With legalized jurisdiction over enormous extensions of Amazon rainforest and thus greater scope for self-determination, local people can now get a grip on the tourism (and other resource-based) activities taking place in their often ecologically spectacular backyards. This has left more than one nature tour operator pining for the good old days of free access to natural and cultural attractions. This evolution in relations between communities and private enterprises has led to a wave of new-found commitment to sustainability among some tourism operators, who have turned to criticizing communities' insufficient conservation achievements as an argument for resisting the change in traditional power relations.

Ecuador, especially in the Amazon region, is witnessing an unprecedented boom in the start-up of community-based tourism enterprises. However, due to a lack of access to the market most are functioning well below capacity, even though community-based operations do have the advantage of being able to operate at lower levels of occupancy than their private-sector colleagues.

This explosion in community tourism enterprises has not followed any particular model of management, but rather has given birth to a number of different strategies and organizational patterns whose degree of success or failure is still to be evaluated. The case studies in this chapter will illustrate some leading examples.

The organizational model followed by a particular community when developing an ecotourism project relates to the initial motivation for the project. It may be internally inspired as a community project to achieve development goals, or by individuals or families within a community who have developed experience with the activity and contacts elsewhere. Alternatively, it may develop externally, through a tour operator with an eye for a new product, or via a non-governmental organization which sees community ecotourism development as a means to conserve a valuable natural resource, or as a pathway to rural development.

Typically, tourism projects with community participation are initiated by NGOs or private-sector companies from outside the destination. The communities in or around the visited areas tend to be marginalized in the planning process and in the management of the operation. This stems from a top-down, or paternalist, approach sometimes adopted by outside managers. The lack of access to planning and management decisions undermines the goal of environmental conservation by limiting the involvement of community members to employee or quasi-employee status, which, in turn, limits the necessary "shareholder" effect that enhances the development of community commitment to natural resource protection.

WHEN AND WHY COMMUNITIES
SET UP THEIR OWN OPERATION

Although the very concept of tourism is alien as an activity to some rural and indigenous communities, it is not a completely new idea for most. For years many have had tourism experience as workers in lodge and infrastructure construction on or near their territory, as low-level employees in the kitchens and in cleaning roles at lodges, as canoe drivers, and, occasionally, as guides and suppliers of handicrafts. Indigenous people have also been involved as attractions in the itineraries of tour operators and guides from outside their area. In such instances they have received visitors and provided "cultural presentations" such as blow gun demonstrations or dressing up in pseudo-traditional garb to play music and dance. Additionally, they may have witnessed economic benefits and other impacts accruing to neighboring communities involved in the activity.

COMMUNITIES AND TOUR OPERATORS

It is often a degree of discontent with the existing relationship between the community and the tourism industry, represented by guides or operators, which leads host communities to reject tourism in the area altogether, to seek more beneficial terms with the outside operator, or to manage tourism themselves.

The Quichua communities of Añangu and Pañacocha, for example, felled trees across streams providing access to lakes on their territory to prevent tour operators from entering. Tourism operators bring in cooks, outboard motor drivers and guides from outside the community, significantly reducing the income and training opportunities for local inhabitants. This also results in a missed opportunity to strengthen the link between tourism benefits and conservation.

Operators choose to hire staff from the outside the destination for several reasons. They often have greater confidence in the work quality and reliability of city-based staff. They also wish to avoid the expense of training indigenous people. Lastly, operators believe they have greater potential for control over staff and of the operation in general if they bring in their own workers to fill the tourism roles rather than having indigenous people fill these roles as fellow participants.

Rejection of this practice may force local communities to terminate relations with the "outside" operator or to modify them to suit community aspirations. Communities tend to aspire to greater economic returns for facilitating the use of their ecotourism attractions (wildlife, forests, fields, lakes and rivers) by outside operators and for their labor and handicrafts.

The typical tour operator/community relationship does not generate community stability; rather, it leaves the community vulnerable to the imposition of economic returns decided externally, to changes in itineraries, and ultimately to abandonment if the relationship ceases to provide the returns the operator requires. It is in response to these two situations—low economic benefits and instability in relation to tourism—that many community ecotourism projects are initiated. This has been the case with the Quichua community of Playas de Cuyabeno, which, while continuing to be a source of employees for a large outside operator as they have done for six years, has built its own accommodation and has begun to receive tourists in its own right. These were also significant motivations for the Quichua of Capirona, the Sionas and Siecoyas of Laguna Grande in Cuyabeno, and the Huaorani.

COMMUNITIES AND NGOs

More recently, conservation non-governmental organizations (NGOs), as part of their strategies, have become involved in the development of community-based ecotourism projects as a means for stimulating sustainable development in ecologically important areas. In such cases, the NGO often replaces the tour operator as intermediary with the market, providing funds to communities for infrastructure, promotion and training programs. This is the case with the Fundación Maquipucuna, owner of a 4,500-hectare reserve in the Andean cloud forest. This NGO has produced ecotourism development plans and organized guide training courses for local communities as well as financed tourism infrastructure (Drumm, 1997a). Without the same economic pressures and priorities as a private company, an NGO has no need to cut the corners of adequate planning; instead, it focuses on ecotourism-generating benefits directly and principally to the local community.

Frequently, programs developed with the help of NGOs operate through the existing infrastructure of the organization and are not subject to the same government controls and tax regimes as tour operators. Consequently, they are often perceived by private-sector tourism companies as presenting unfair competition. However, NGO support is usually the only way a community-based operation can develop an ecotourism operation with a chance of success.

At the same time, NGOs often fail to appreciate the significance of their inexperience in the field of tourism development, leading them to create unrealistic expectations within the community as to the speed and scale of future benefits. Sometimes, this has resulted in the building of tourism infrastructure "white elephants" which lowers community confidence in outside support. The case of a large, U.S. Agency for International Development (USAID)-funded project known as SUBIR is a good example. The Cofan community of Sinangue on the upper Aguarico was one of several indigenous communities funded by SUBIR to develop ecotourism. Then, without adequate orientation or training of the community, SUBIR built accommodation infrastructure in the community, equipped it, raised community expectations, and then pulled out abruptly, due to internal organizational problems.

COMMUNITY/TOURISM RELATIONSHIPS

Clearly, not all communities wish to be involved in tourism activities (a fact that should be respected by outside agencies). However, those that do may choose from a range of relationships of greater or lesser involvement. Options include the following:

- renting land to an operator to develop while simply monitoring impacts;
- working as occasional, part- or full-time staff for outside operators;
- providing selected services such as food preparation, guiding, transport or accommodations (or a combination of several or all of these) to operators;
- forming joint-ventures with outside operators with a division of labor, which allows the community to provide most services, while the operator takes care of marketing; and
- operating fully independent community tourism programs.

In each case, full community involvement in all stages of planning and management is essential to ensure healthy development. Preferably before initiating the operation, it is necessary to identify social and cultural, as well as economic and environmental indicators in order to facilitate the monitoring of tourism impacts. Such monitoring is almost always absent or inadequately informal. Monthly meetings are often most practical, whereby a community-designated ecotourism coordinator reports on developments, the state of defined indicators (and income and spending), and concerns to be answered, and then modifies programs accordingly. Elected community leaders then make decisions on distribution of income, investments and so on.

It is important for community operations to be developed in coordination with their neighbors in order to avoid conflicts and competition. This is usually best achieved through the involvement in the project of the organization or federation to which the community will typically belong. The organization should also benefit from the activity and have the capacity to ensure that it develops in the best interest of all its members. Tourism income through, for example, a per-visitor fee paid by the tourist to the organization, can help build the necessary capacity.

The consistency of the quality of the ecotourism services provided by the community and, therefore, the economic viability of the operation, is related to the degree of community involvement in the planning and management of the ecotourism operation.

CHALLENGES TO COMMUNITY-BASED MANAGEMENT
TRAINING

In order for communities to assume full roles as players in ecotourism development, adequate and comprehensive training opportunities are necessary in all spheres of ecotourism management, including guiding, languages, food preparation, accountancy and administration. Ecotourism can, and should, supplement more traditional economic activity in communities. Therefore, as community operations may often run at low occupancy levels, training should not be seen as a process of deculturization or as disruptive to traditional social patterns; rather, it should be viewed as the provision of additional new skills to be used as, and when, required by all members of the community with an interest in participating. There is ample scope here for women to participate in the same training opportunities as men, thereby increasing their access to direct economic benefits. Often, it is the younger members of the community, either because of their better language skills or greater enthusiasm, who occupy the roles in direct contact with the visitor. This has sometimes exposed them to a more intense process of acculturation through the adoption of foreign clothes, habits and expectations. It is essential that community elders (both men and women) be contracted as instructors in ecotourism training courses so that the context in which ecotourism will develop is clearly defined as being within community and culturally established boundaries. Although NGOs have often played a constructive role in education and training by contracting experts, more coordination is needed with tour operators to identify priorities. Government institutions, often slow in grasping the concept of ecotourism and community-level dynamics, should be more active in this area as well. However, it is the private sector that has the clearest interest. Yet, perhaps remarkably, the private sector, for reasons cited earlier, rarely invests in the necessary training.

Some companies which work with communities have indeed invested in training, organizing local workshops, field trips for community members to ecotourism operations in other regions, and on-the-job training programs. In these cases, a greater feeling of well-being, confidence and control in the community is generated. This is reflected in greater tourist satisfaction, which stems from tourists receiving better quality service and sensing they are welcome in a community that is benefiting from the enterprise.

Community-based guides are limited by their lack of fluency in English, German and other languages, and it is unlikely, in the medium term, that this will change. For this reason ecotourism operators who require a high quality of interpretation will continue to send bilingual naturalists to accompany their groups and to work alongside local guides in the communities. Such outside or city-based naturalist guides could benefit immensely if they could take part in training courses led by indigenous and local people. Outside naturalist guides often lack the necessary social and cultural dimension because community participation in imparting local knowledge is generally not valued. Using the expertise of the indigenous and local people as trainers and instructors would be extremely valuable both to enhance the skills of outside naturalist guides and to empower men and women whose skills and knowledge have been generally overlooked.

ACCESS TO THE MARKET

Connecting the product to the potential visitor is the Achilles heel of community ecotourism enterprises. Their very nature is rural and remote, without access to the tools of tourism communication—telephone, fax and e-mail. This means that unless at least one member of the community moves to town to set up office (itself a major challenge) tourist arrivals will be a hit and miss affair, slow to increase at best.

While NGOs can provide some assistance in this regard, the organized and well-connected private operator is best suited to assist with marketing. This provides interested parties with an excellent opportunity to establish mutually beneficial relationships with community-based operations, rather than to fear them as potential competitors. Many communities have established verbal agreements with one or more city-based tour operators to provide the link with the market in exchange for low net prices to which the operators add a mark-up. However, these agreements usually lack explicit guidelines on anything other than price arrangements and itineraries.

It may be possible to collate contact information for community operations in a guide or brochure (see Wesche and Drumm, 1998), which could be made available in capital cities or even in foreign embassies, though state support for such a project may run into the sort of political problems outlined below. Additionally, the lack of communications with communities from capital cities makes reservations difficult, so that there may often be an element of risk for a visitor in showing up at a community unexpectedly. The Ecuadorean Ecotourism Association is recommending that the Ministry of Tourism establish a national register of community-based ecotourism programs with the aim of facilitating both better ecotourism planning as well as promotion (Asociación Ecuatoriana de Ecoturismo, 1998).

PARTICIPATION IN PLANNING AND MANAGEMENT

Though effective planning and management is crucial to the proper functioning of ecotourism, it continues to be largely absent. Effective control over tourism development through participation in planning and management requires structural change at the national level. First, it must be recognized that ecotourism is a planned activity. The strategic tourism planning, normally carried out by the tourism ministry, or equivalent government body, including the zoning of appropriate land uses, the designation of "ecotourism use zones" and the elaboration of a code of ecotourism ethics, requires multi-sectorial participation, including that of community level representatives. Zones designated for ecotourism development require management plans, and community participation in the development of these plans is essential.

Developments that propose accommodation with more than 20 beds or destinations that anticipate more than 500 visitors a year should require an environmental and socio-cultural impact assessment. Ecotourism associations and government departments should encourage and assist each of the sectors involved in ecotourism, including communities, to develop and implement guidelines to ensure sustainability. But additionally, when communities enter into tourism management agreements with private companies or NGOs, these should be approved by the elected community authority, include explicit financial and operational arrangements that constitute a legally binding document. Finally, it should be a basic tenet of ecotourism operations located in community-owned natural areas that all groups be accompanied by a local guide, though not necessarily exclusively. All of the above recommendations were made via multi-sectorial consensus in the National Forum on Community Participation in Ecotourism held in Quito in 1997 (Asociación Ecuatoriana de Ecoturismo, 1998).

POLITICS AND LEGALITY

The social and political context of the communities involved in ecotourism has to be recognized by the outside players. A community will usually belong to a federation or association of communities, which should also be involved in the process so as to avoid the creation of social and political conflicts and divisions between neighboring communities, and to facilitate the wider distribution of benefits. Typically, governments, with the encouragement of the mainstream nature tourism private sector, fail to recognize the special needs (and sustainable economic development potential) of remote rural and indigenous communities operating in tourism. The remoteness, lack of mobility and near non-existent economic resources of most communities make it virtually impossible for them to travel to distant capital cities to confront the expensive and often monolithic and labyrinthine bureaucratic procedures required to form a standard tour operator company. Even if they could easily do so, the conversion of a community operation into a company may cause unnecessary internal social and cultural conflicts within the community. The Capirona and RICANCIE case study below illustrates these problems, which undermine any benefits generated by ecotourism as well as the very rationale for the activity within the community.

CASE STUDIES

A series of case studies from Ecuador illustrates the diversity of community–based ecotourism management experiences.

THE HUAORANI OF QUEHUERI'ONO

The Huaorani are an Amazon indigenous group who live within and around Yasuni National Park, a UNESCO Biosphere Reserve, in Ecuador. They are still in a very early stage of acculturation, having first been been contacted by evangelist missionaries in 1956. Consequently, they are very vulnerable to outside influences, such as oil companies, missionaries and tourism. Tourism in this region is mostly of the low-budget backpacker variety. Visitors typically hire guides and tour companies in frontier gateway towns for three- to eight-day camping tours along rivers in the Huaorani's rainforest territory. The tours typically stop in one or more small riverside communities to take photos of the Indians and perhaps purchase handicrafts at low prices.

The guides have little or no formal training, usually speak only Spanish, and often carry shotguns for bravado and to reduce their costs by hunting for food that can be served to the tourists (Drumm, 1991). The Huaorani, sometimes success-fully, ask for a fee for the passage of the tourists through their village or territory.

This fee may range from $50 to $100, depending on the community and on the individual who encounters the tourists, as well as what the outside guide is prepared to pay. In other instances, guides may make deals with one individual within a community, paying him directly for access. These private negotiations cause divisions and internal problems within the community. Often the guides underpay or promise to "pay next time." This has led to occasional hostility towards tourists and guides and even confiscation of outboard motors and cameras. The Organization of the Huaorani People (ONHAE) has attempted to exert some control over tourism fees and behavior but has met with little success, due largely to the resistance of guides and tour companies, and the lack of personnel and finance to follow up.

One community of approximately 100 people on the Río Shiripuno, Quehueri'ono, was concerned about the negative impacts tourism was having, but conscious of the need to find an alternative source of income to abandoning their homes to work as laborers for oil companies. In 1995, the village opted to establish a new kind of relationship with an ecotourism operator, TROPIC Ecological Adventures, which was committed to helping them protect their natural and cultural resources. A relationship between the owner of the company and the community had been previously established in the course of a collaboration to bring the community's problems with an oil company to international public attention. In conjunction with TROPIC, a Quito-based operator owned by the author, the community has built a cabin in the traditional Huaorani style to receive up to eight guests once a month for stays of two-to-six days duration. This reflects an estimated limit of acceptable change calculated by TROPIC, discussed with and accepted by the community. The two parties felt that, in this case, the potential change in social organization and traditional culture, such as the concentration of income in one family or the creation of consumer habits like cigarette smoking and the use of sunglasses, represents a more immediate limit than does the deterioration of the natural environment due to visitor pressure. However, the risk of negative social and cultural change is one of the most difficult to appreciate in a community unaccustomed to the long-term impacts of tourism.

A series of planning and orientation meetings with the whole community over a period of nine months covered a wide range of issues, including the concepts of ecotourism and conservation, potential environmental and cultural impacts, management, income levels and distribution, training and others. The decision to locate the guest cabin in the forest outside the community (a 45-minute walk) was one of the suggestions offered by TROPIC and was aimed at avoiding unnecessary disruption of daily life in an infrequently visited community. The agreement between Quehueri'ono and TROPIC requires a Huaorani guide always to accompany the visitors, and a bilingual naturalist to complement and translate the local guide's interpretation. Additionally, Huaorani canoe drivers and canoes must be employed. For an initial period, TROPIC has brought a cook from outside the community to train Huaorani cooks in food preparation; the Huaorani cooks will eventually take over the job. To avoid increasing pressure on wildlife, food hunted by the indigenous group is not given to visitors; instead, most food is brought in from outside. However, locally abundant crops such as papaya, manioc and bananas are purchased by TROPIC in the community.

Salaries for the various jobs are calculated by doubling what a person would earn as a laborer for an oil company. Additionally, the community receives a per-person, per-night fee, significantly higher than what other operations are usually paying. This fee is presented to the president of the community during the community meeting, which is held upon the arrival of each group. As of 1997, the money was distributed evenly among all the families; plans exist to establish a community savings account as has been done successfully by Capirona. The community meetings also serve to open communication between the Huaorani and the visitors.

The visitors are interviewed as to their country of origin, their motivation for coming and other such information. The community then presents to the visitors their issues of concern and evaluates the development of tourism in the community. In this way a real dialogue and cultural exchange takes place between visitor and host. To help create the tourism management capacity at organizational level, a further fee (in 1997, the equivalent of $5) is paid per visitor to ONHAE. Visitors to Quehueri'ono spend more to visit Huaorani territory than those entering other villages with other operations. Numerous comments from guests indicate that they do so gladly, because in return they receive a quality interpretative experience as well as the satisfaction of knowing that real benefits are being generated by their visit. Both TROPIC and the Huaorani intend that the initial visit will simply be the beginning of a longer-term relationship between the tourists and their hosts. An important element of TROPIC's programs is the aim to inspire and motivate the visitors so that on returning to their own country, they work to raise funds and consciousness on behalf of the people and places that they have visited. In this way TROPIC has created a constituency of foreign-based supporters for Ecuador's Amazon peoples and rainforests. This has generated letter writing; cash donations to finance training workshops, HF radios, and solar panels; and helped facilitate the establishment of a non-profit foundation—Acción Amazonía—which focuses, full time, on generating political and economic support for those Amazon communities seeking help to defend their environmental and cultural integrity.

The Huaorani organization, ONHAE, sees the Quehueri'ono experience as a pilot program which may come to represent the model tourism operation for the territory. Because of its success, this model could eventually be implemented in other Huaorani communities. This might then displace the current operation types (usually based in Amazon frontier towns like Baños and Coca, as well as Quito), which focus on the low-budget and backpacker travelers who put low cost above environmental and cultural considerations. These operations have widespread negative impacts: the hunting of wildlife, the dynamiting of rivers to catch fish, low or no income generation, disrespect for culture, and so on.

However, working with such a remote community does present certain challenges. For example, it is necessary to limit expectations with regard to income, constantly emphasizing and encouraging complementary activities in order to avoid over-dependence on ecotourism. Moreover, it is necessary to monitor limits of acceptable change while encouraging enough tourists to make the program worthwhile to the community. In this case cultural limits are exceeded before environmental damage occurs. The threat of unpredictable cultural impacts is always present and something that the conscientious operator is often more sensitive to than the tourist-keen community. It is very important to establish a range of indicators in conjunction with the community to facilitate the monitoring of social and cultural change.

CAPIRONA AND RICANCIE*

The Napo Runa are probably the most acculturated of the Amazon indigenous groups who have lived in the foothills of the Andes for thousands of years. Successive governments have considered Amazonia to be an "empty space," useful for resolving the social and economic problems in the rest of the country as a migration pole, as well as for an internal colony for the extraction of natural resources. This form of insertion into the national economy has created a local economy dependent on external conditions, based on the irrational use of natural resources and contributing to the gradual deterioration of the local peoples' quality of life, especially that of the indigenous people. More recently in the region, the sort of tourism which presented the indigenous people as one more "tourism attraction" was promoted by foreign and national operators without generating local economic benefits. Consequently, many problems have been created in indigenous communities, including internal divisions as many families moved out of the community to work for low wages; the weakening of traditional forms of social organization such as communal work parties; and, above all, an accelerated acculturation, especially among the young.

In 1990, Capirona, a Napo Runa community, decided direct involvement in tourism was a source of income which would not involve the destruction of their natural resources. Since that time, the experiment has matured, and has overcome diverse limitations and problems. It now constitutes a model that combines promoting visits to natural attractions and cultural exchange with the protection

*This section is adapted from the writings of T. Tapuy, Coordinator of RICANCIE, 1997.

of natural resources and the development needs of the indigenous people. The success of the Capirona experience led to considerable interest from other Napo Runa communities; today a network (RICANCIE) of 12 communities exists. With a small amount of financial assistance from the community development NGO Ayuda en Acción, RICANCIE has developed a tourism infrastructure that includes guest cabins featuring traditional designs, materials and techniques, as well as trails and food preparation in the jungle. In addition, RICANCIE has trained community guides and created tourism packages that include hikes in the forest, canoe trips, the practice of traditional sports, knowledge of oral tradition, and the opportunity to share community daily activities—all within a perspective of co-habitation and cultural exchange. In order to control possible socio-cultural impacts, a list of regulations (see Capirona Guidelines) has been devised by which tourists, guides and the community are expected to abide.

The creation of the network has permitted the rationalization and control of the flow of tourists to the communities, especially in high season. The network currently has a physical capacity of 200 beds. In 1997, 800 people visited, down from 1,200 in 1996. The flow of visitors is not the result of a concentrated promotional campaign but rather a campaign restricted to friends in foreign universities, research NGOs with whom RICANCIE has worked closely, and a small number of travel agencies with whom RICANCIE has begun to work. Most tourists are students, researchers and friends of nature and come from the U.S. and Europe. The reinvestment of tourism revenues at the community level is permitting the development of other sustainable economic activities, such as handicrafts development, small animal raising, aquaculture, agroforestry and so forth. Additionally, it is resolving social problems and providing new services as evidenced in the creation of a radio communication system, motorized canoe transport (which not only helps tourism, but also helps get products to market), and a fund for emergencies. There has also been a re-valuation of cultural values and knowledge, not for sale as a commodity to tourists, but as fundamental elements in community identity.

The success of RICANCIE has reinvigorated the role of elders as transmitters of culture and women as repositories of traditional knowledge. Ecotourism appears to be an important economic activity, and above all a motivation to find other sustainable alternatives, though this has proven to be a difficult task. At the moment RICANCIE's main efforts are focused on the consolidation of their community programs through a continuous process of technical and socio-organizational training, the aim of which is to establish efficient tourism management while respecting socio-cultural conditions. The fact that indigenous people want to insert themselves in the market does not mean they disappear as peoples.

One of the greatest limitations to the development of RICANCIE's plans is the existing tourism law which does not contemplate community-managed tourism, but demands that communities convert themselves into companies. For the most part, these companies are based on individualism with a priority on economic profit. This demand contradicts the traditional form of community organization, and threatens to leave RICANCIE without the capacity to control a possible outbreak of mini-companies, which would then generate internal competition and cause social and cultural conflicts. Given this situation, RICANCIE has seen it necessary

---

CAPIRONA GUIDELINES

1. Donations or exchanges of clothing and other personal articles with the community members are prohibited.

2. Help us maintain our community way of life by not giving individual tips.

3. If you would like to make a donation to the whole community, please direct it to the community leaders or the program directors.

4. Place all garbage in its place and please take with you what you brought to the community, especially plastic products.

5. Photographs are permitted providing permission is asked and granted. Nature is full of beautiful and diverse landscapes and curiosities for taking pictures.

6. People enjoy the sounds of the jungle; if you decide to bring a radio please use headphones and keep the volume low.

7. Collection of plants, insects or animals is prohibited without prior authorization.

8. Please do not enter a house without being invited.

9. Don't make promises that are difficult or that you can not keep, such as sending photos.

10. The consumption of drugs and excessive use of alcohol is prohibited.

11. Please wear clothing appropriate for your protection (from insects, the sun, etc...); this will also demonstrate your respect for others.

12. Given that we desire to protect the integrity of our community and way of life, we do not allow visitors to stay in the tourist facilities or community for longer than the agreed period.

13. Please maintain the appropriate distance that should exist between guides/community members and tourists. This will help to maintain the co-living arrangement of the program. Please avoid intimate contact, which could disturb ethical and moral traditions of the community.

to fight for the law to recognize ecotourism management from a community perspective. This demand has not been well received by many sectors that manage tourism in Ecuador due to a mistaken interpretation of the community organization's intentions. By no means is RICANCIE asking for preferential or paternalist treatment before the law; instead, it has asked that the law recognize a different way of operating in tourism, without affecting other types of operation recognized by the law. Official recognition of RICANCIE's activities would permit its adequate regulation, establishing the necessary controls for it to be efficiently run. It was hoped that eventually, RICANCIE's efforts would be rewarded with legal recognition for the community enterprise by the Ministry of Tourism. RICANCIE believes that the acknowledgement that Ecuadorean society is pluricultural in character should not be limited to simple declarations; rather, it should be made real in the judicial framework of the state. (In November 1997, RICANCIE, unable to access needed credits and limited by its "illegality," which inhibited promotion of the product, decided to constitute itself as a corporation.)

THE COFAN OF ZABALO

Another of Ecuador's indigenous Amazon people, the Cofan, have more experience with community ecotourism management than other villagers. The Cofan began to receive tourists as long ago as 1979. It was then that Randy Borman, the Ecuadorean-born son of North American missionaries who lives as a Cofan, started guiding groups sent by a U.S.-based outbound operator into the rainforest near the community of Doreno on the upper Aguarico River. In 1984, Borman and several other Cofan families migrated downstream, deeper into the forest, away from invading settlers and Texaco's toxic waste dumping, to found the community of Zabalo (Borman, 1995). Later, the nearby Cuyabeno Wildlife Reserve was extended to include the area around the community. Borman formed a "company" composed of those heads of families prepared to invest labor in building guest cabins and trail infrastructure. However, those who did not wish to bear the risk have not lost out. Other community members benefit from occasional employment as assistants, maintenance and construction workers, canoe drivers, and so forth. Additionally, handicraft sales, which frequently exceed company earnings (Wunder, 1996), are a source of income for all community members, including women and children, and even for relatives visiting from Doreno and other Cofan communities who come to sell their wares.

Over the years the program has evolved with the incorporation of a number of Cofan guides. These guides have gained experience from twice-weekly visits to their territory, escorting up to four groups of 12 tourists from a large Ecuadorean operator, which moved into the region in 1991. The community has also developed programs with other city-based, inbound operators. Some community members have even gained the confidence to try their hand as independent operators, building their own guest cabins in other parts of the 10,000-hectare territory. Unfortunately, the Cofan's inspirational example has encouraged other communities in the area to develop operations that offer cheaper access to similar natural attractions without the same conservation commitment. As most private tour operators still tend to give greater priority to low prices than to environmental responsibility, some have preferred these communities, contributing to a drop-off in tourist arrivals in Zabalo.

The National Forum on Community Participation in Ecotourism (Asociación Ecuatoriana de Ecoturismo, 1998), which included participation from all sectors—including community, private, governmental and non-governmental—recommended a series of measures to instill greater responsibility in tourism development in natural areas. These included a requirement, inspired by the Zabalo experience, for communities to zone their territories and develop ecotourism management plans for approval by a multi-sectorial National Ecotourism Commission in order to obtain operating permits. Although the difficulty in direct communications and access to the market continue to be a source of frustration for Zabalo, the community remains a leader in the sector in terms of linking practical conservation to ecotourism benefits. They have zoned their territory into hunting and non-hunting/ecotourism areas. Animals freely migrate from the ecotourism area, which serves as a reservoir, into the hunting zone where they may be utilized for food. Furthermore, a self-imposed control system levies fines on community members taking ecotourism-valued species such as toucans and parrots and for exceeding rational-use quotas in the hunting zone.

CONCLUSION

These three case studies illustrate a range of community-based management models. In the medium term, because of the lack of direct participation, difficulties in communication, access to the market, language limitations and inadequate training opportunities, it appears unlikely that more than a handful of communities will develop the capacity to be completely self-sustaining. Thus, there is a clear opportunity, which a few ecotourism operators and NGOs are beginning to realize, to establish positive relationships with the owners of ecotourism attractions with a view to long-term stability for ecotourism operations and the natural and cultural resources on which they depend. However, governmental recognition of the different physical, social and cultural circumstances experienced by communities is long overdue. Private-sector tourism companies would do well to overcome their nervousness of what they perceive as new competition and encourage governments to create the necessary legal frameworks which will allow communities to assume their full role in ecotourism development and resource conservation.

REFERENCES

Asociación Ecuatoriana de Ecoturismo. 1998. "Politicas y Estrategias Para la Participacíon Comunitaria en el Ecoturismo," Asociación Ecuatoriana de Ecoturismo, Quito.

Borman, R. 1995. "Torista Semamba – Una Experiencia Indígena con el Ecoturismo," *Ecoturismo en el Ecuador—Trayectorias y Desafíos*, DDA, Intercooperation, UICN, Quito.

Drumm, A.F. 1991. "An Integrated Impact Assessment of Nature Tourism in Ecuador's Amazon Region," report prepared for FEPROTUR-Naturaleza, Quito. (available from the author).

Drumm, A.F. 1997a. "Evaluación de la Potencial Ecoturístico de la Comunidad de Yunguilla," unpublished report, Fundación Maquipucuna, Quito.

Drumm, A.F. 1997b. "Informe Final, Foro Nacional de Participación Comunitaria en el Ecoturismo," *Taller Regionál Amazonía*, tena 5, al 7, de junio, 1997, unpublished report. Asociación Ecuatoriana de Ecoturismo, Quito.

Tapuy, T. 1997. "Estrategias Para la Gestian Turistica de Comunidades Indigena: La Red Indigena del Alto Napo Para la Convivencia Intercultural y el Ecoturismo," (RICANCIE), unpublished report, Ricancie, Tena.

Wesche, R. 1996. "Developed Country Environmentalism and Indigenous Community Controlled Ecotourism in the Ecuadorean Amazon," *Geographische Zeitschrift*, 84 Jahrgang, 1996, heft 3 and 4, pp. 157-168.

Wesche, R., A.F. Drumm. 1998. *Defending Our Rainforest—A Guide to Community-based Ecotourism in the Ecuadorean Amazon*. In press.

Wunder, S. 1996. "Ecoturismo, Ingresos Locales y Conservación," *El Caso de Cuyabeno*, UICN, Ecuador.

Guidelines for Community-based Ecotourism Programs

Lessons From Indonesia

Keith W. Sproule and Ary S. Suhandi

OVERVIEW

There are various terms in use designed to link tourism development with conservation of natural and cultural resources, including ecotourism, nature-based travel, adventure travel, sustainable tourism and alternative tourism. For the purposes of this chapter, the fine distinctions between each of these terms will not be pursued. Worthy of concern, however, is that no broadly accepted criteria for what constitutes any of these concepts has emerged. Many writers and practitioners have begun to assert that tourism should satisfy conservation and development objectives in order to be considered sustainable (Lindberg et al., 1996). Although significant resources have been devoted to developing this type of tourism on the assumption that these objectives can be achieved, lessons from the field have begun to highlight that without proper planning and integration, individual projects tend to operate in isolation, failing to significantly influence either conservation or development, or the policy support necessary to bring their potential to fruition.

Still, the hope that ecotourism can indeed achieve both conservation and development objectives remains an enduring one. This hope is made all the more tantalizing because it is a goal that is not too difficult to conceptualize.

WHAT IS COMMUNITY-BASED ECOTOURISM?

At its most basic, community-based ecotourism refers to ecotourism enterprises that are owned and managed by the community. Furthermore, community-based ecotourism implies that a community is caring for its natural resources in order to gain income through tourism, and is using that income to better the lives of its people. It involves conservation, business enterprises, and community development.

In any community-based ecotourism enterprise there will be direct and indirect participants and beneficiaries. It is important that a sizable percentage of the community has some level of involvement and some level of benefit. One model for managing community-based ventures involves creating a management committee to oversee the ventures. In such a model, the direct participants would be the managing committee and the actual workers involved with producing products or services for sale. In some instances those who are the primary users of a resource might be involved as participants in the project as well. Indirect participants would be the members of the broader community who select the management committee of a project and who do not directly use the natural resources involved in such an enterprise.

Direct beneficiaries would be employees, craft producers, guides, porters and so on. Indirect beneficiaries would be community members as a whole as recipients who receive the benefits of development projects, educational projects, training and other programs funded by tourism revenues. How issues of participation and identification of beneficiaries are determined has a lot to do with how "community" is defined.

WHEN WE SAY "COMMUNITY," WHO ARE WE TALKING ABOUT?

A community is a group of people, often living in the same geographic area, who identify themselves as belonging to the same group. The people in a community are often related by blood or marriage, and may all belong to the same religious or political group, class or caste.

Although communities can have many things in common, they are still very complex and should not be thought of as one homogenous group. Communities are comprised of specific groups, such as tenants and landowners, the wealthy and the poor, and old and new residents. Different interest groups within the community are likely to be affected variably by the changes associated with tourism. How these groups respond to such changes is influenced by kinship, religion, politics and the strong bonds which have developed between community members over generations. Depending on the issue, a community may be united or divided in thought and action (United Nations Food and Agriculture Organization, 1990).

ISSUES TO BE AWARE OF WHEN DEVELOPING COMMUNITY-BASED ECOTOURISM

The "community base" for community enterprises is rarely, if ever, all encompassing. Community members with some initial disadvantages—such as poor housing, insufficient land or income—tend to be among those excluded from participation in ecotourism enterprise development. And, depending on how the ecotourism enterprise is designed, they may be excluded from the benefits of ecotourism development as well.

THE ISSUE OF PARTICIPATION

Though there is increasing recognition of the need to involve communities in participation in general, there is much less agreement about exactly who should participate and to what extent. How a community chooses to define participation will be important for determining what level of participation will satisfy the ecotourism project goals. It is a very tricky subject. For even where attempts at all-inclusive community involvement are well thought out, participation has sometimes been decided on the basis of political affiliation, land ownership, kinship or gender. For instance, there are a growing number of examples of ecotourism enterprises that include overnight stays in villagers' homes, lodging often referred to as "homestays." However, some homestay projects exclude those who are not well-connected, or whose homes are too small, or perceived to be inadequate for lodging outside guests. Level of education, English language ability and even age have also been used to limit participation.

GENDER AS AN ISSUE

The role of women has proven a challenge for many community groups pursuing ecotourism enterprises. In some instances, gender issues have been dealt with overtly, such as in those communities that have decided ecotourism enterprises are strictly young men's ventures. In other instances, decisions based on gender have not passed community scrutiny. Many communities and cultures have unspoken restrictions on what roles would be appropriate for women within such ventures. While ecotourism may be welcomed as a new source of income by women in rural areas, quite often women are restricted from the most lucrative aspects of the enterprise, often working as cooks or cleaners.

Still, there are significant opportunities not to be overlooked. Though many communities may find it inappropriate for women to work as forest guides, for example, it may in other cases be quite possible for women to assume responsibility for leading village tours. As women are often responsible for meal preparation, structures can be established whereby they receive the payments for food. And in many locations the sale of crafts stands out as an extremely promising approach for nurturing women's participation.

Equality should be the guiding principle for community-based projects, although it is rarely, if ever, possible to fully achieve. As with any venture, individual abilities, such as energy, willingness to take risk, or willingness to make a time commitment are deciding factors. Overall, it is important to recognize that when designing a community-based venture, failure to allow for open and equitable access to participation at the outset can limit the success of a project or program later on.

ECOTOURISM CAN BE DIVISIVE

An additional concern among community groups pursuing ecotourism is that the introduction of such ventures can reinforce existing divisions in their communities and/or create new ones. This situation is in no way confined to tourism, but may be more acute than with other community projects in that the activity involves highly visible contact with outsiders so that returns may be perceived to be high. Issues of fairness, as well as jealousies and exclusions, have confronted many community-based ecotourism ventures.

One approach being tried in several areas is the maintenance of a community bulletin board on which all decisions and actions are posted. This has proven particularly helpful where money is concerned. Posting the agreed-to prices being charged for products and services sold (e.g., guide services or stays at the community guest house) will inform everyone as to how much money is actually involved. Consciously reinforcing decisions by making public statements, and/or by reading them aloud, can help ensure that all members of a community, including illiterate or semi-literate members, are aware of what has been agreed to.

Being open about how much money is involved with an ecotourism enterprise is often described as being "transparent." Many groups have found that keeping their record books transparent has helped reduce accusations of financial fraud or corruption—one of the most divisive issues that can arise with any community project.

DECISION MAKING

A community may be defined as local people residing in a particular area, and although it is in the community's best interest for everyone to be involved in decision making processes affecting the community, it is not always possible for all residents to come together simultaneously. Therefore, direct participants (sometimes collectively called a Management Committee) are selected to represent the larger population, or indirect participants. Regarding tourism, these recognized representatives make decisions such as: what tourism enterprises should be undertaken, who will manage them, what the benefits to the community will be, and how the benefits will be distributed. These management positions can be challenging, since divisiveness is not uncommon, but, are also very sought after, since control of expenditures is often a requirement of participation.

PLANNING PROCESSES

It is quite likely that introducing a new ecotourism enterprise into a community will raise questions about participation and distribution of benefits. One way of addressing these difficult issues is for project proponents to discuss questions, such as those found below, ahead of time. Planning to address the twin issues of participation and distribution of benefits can help resolve many potential problems early on. Remember that these are only some of the questions that should be asked during the planning process. No doubt there will be others that are specific to the community and to the ecotourism enterprise envisioned.

DEFINING "COMMUNITY"—How will community be defined? Will it be defined based on geography (e.g., everyone who lives within one area), or, will it be based on some other factor, such as family or clan? However it it defined, will it be acceptable to everyone who is likely to be affected? Although the number of community participants in the project might be small, the number of community residents likely to be impacted may be quite large.

PARTICIPATION—Who will be a part of the community-based ecotourism enterprise? Who will provide the time and effort required to develop such an enterprise (e.g., who will help construct the new trails or build the guest house)? How will the work be divided? Will participation depend upon the ability to perform physical labor, or will there be other methods of participation, such as cash payments or in-kind contributions? Will men and women participate equally? Will there be opportunities for both young and old? Rich and poor? Those with schooling and those without? Will efforts be made to train those without skills so that they may participate equally?

DECIDING WHO DECIDES—Who will be involved with actual decision making? Will everyone decide everything? Or, will a smaller number of people be given responsibility to decide on behalf of the rest? Will there be a governing committee? How will members of such a committee be determined? Will they be elected or appointed? How many people will participate? How many is too many? How many is too few? What will their job titles be? What duties will they perform? Will there be compensation for serving on such a committee? Will there be ways for committee members to be held accountable for their actions?

BENEFITS—How will prices for goods and services be determined? Who will collect the money? How will the money be divided (e.g., how much will the provider of the service or creator of the craft receive)? Will any percentage go into a general fund? How will accounts be maintained? Is anyone trained to keep a record book?

FINANCIAL INVESTMENT—What level of financial investment is necessary to establish the enterprise? From where will the funding come? If the government or an outside agency (donor or international NGO) is involved, is the financing to be based on a grant or loan? When is the enterprise projected to be fully financially sustained? Are these projections realistic? How will non-financial investments, mainly village level labor or time commitments, be compensated?

PARTNERS IN THE PROCESS

When developing new ecotourism enterprises, many communities have found it important to work in partnership with other organizations. There are several important "partners" in the process of developing community-based ecotourism enterprises:

- the government tourism bureau and natural resource management agencies, especially the park/forest service;
- non-government organizations (NGOs), especially those involved with environmental issues, small-business management and traditional community development;
- the established tourism industry, particularly tour operators;
- universities and other research organizations;
- other communities, including those with a history of tourism and those just beginning; and
- additional partners in the process, which may include other international organizations, public and private funding institutions, national cultural committees, and many others.

The following section will give a brief overview of why and how two of these partners, governments and NGOs, can help a community to develop successful ecotourism enterprises.

GOVERNMENT PARTNERS

Government officials have a critical role to play in formulating policies for ecotourism. For instance, the government park service generally has responsibility for managing protected land areas, which can include national parks, reserves, forests and/or sanctuaries. The park service may also have responsibility for managing tourism to protected areas as part of its overall management obligations. For the majority of protected lands, rules and regulations are legislated at the national level. Government officials can decide, for example, to create a law requiring entrance fee systems for some or all of the parks, and to ensure that a portion of the collected money returns to the park.

Although most ecotourism activities happen at the local level, these activities also need to fit into systems designated at the national level. The degree of intervention such integration requires will naturally vary. Government officials are also responsible for many of the structures and services outside the protected area that greatly affect tourism, including airports, roads, and even things such as health clinics.

Government officials and their policies can easily advance or hinder ecotourism development; therefore, government can be an important partner in developing an ecotourism enterprise, especially if the community is located near a protected area. Specific ways government can help a community develop ecotourism enterprises include:

- providing coordination between a project and other related projects in the region;
- providing technical assistance through established government departments, such as the department of the environment, social services or cooperatives;
- providing market research and promotional assistance for projects through the tourism bureau;
- providing financial support for community-based ecotourism enterprises in some instances;
- reducing, deferring or exempting tax payments from the community; and
- developing and implementing policies that allow for the flexible development of community-based ecotourism enterprises.

The following are three specific issue areas in which government can work as a partner with communities striving to develop ecotourism enterprises.

CONCESSIONS

Concessions are contracts with the government that give the holder of the contract (the concessionaire), the "right" to provide services to tourists visiting protected areas. Often the criteria for selecting a concessionaire are either ill-defined or too stringent for communities to satisfactorily meet. Constraints may include capital requirements, mandatory attendance at meetings conducted in the capital city, or basic issues of literacy in dealing with the application forms. Without concession rights, it can be virtually impossible for communities to develop ecotourism enterprises that legally operate inside protected areas. If it is necessary to establish a concession in order to develop tourism facilities at the nearby protected area, surrounding communities should plan to partner with both the park service and an NGO familiar with small business development practices.

GUIDE LICENSING / REGISTRATION REQUIREMENTS

Tourism bureaus' requirements for guide licensing and registration are often difficult for community groups to satisfy. For example, a seemingly simple requirement, such as a written test or driver's license, can create a severe constraint for communities with low literacy levels or income levels that keep the possibility of vehicle ownership out of reach. Tourism bureaus might offer to provide the necessary training or establish less stringent criteria for community applicants in order to assist them in meeting regulatory requirements.

PROMOTIONAL MATERIALS

Most government tourism bureaus include the promotion of national tourism destinations as part of their mandate. These bodies can help community-based ecotourism enterprises "get the message out" about their projects. Some methods for promoting projects include leaflets, maps highlighting their locations, and inclusion in larger, more comprehensive national tourism brochures.

The process of preparing such material can be a catalyst for serious discussion in a community setting. Asking a community group to decide just how it would like its hamlet described to visitors, or how to describe a particular attraction such as a waterfall, can help to organize and prioritize ideas behind a community initiative. Likewise, mapping activities, especially those requiring discussions of distance and time, can be quite fruitful if only for the discussion such topics can generate.

Examples of promotional efforts elsewhere include: the preparation of a community-based tourism guidebook, which provides information to visitors about a country-wide trail of community-based ventures (prepared by the Belize Ministry of Tourism and the Environment in collaboration with a local NGO); the production of videos highlighting the ventures (Belize Tourist Board); and familiarity "fam" tours designed to educate travel agents and tour operators about community initiatives (conducted by Conservation International in support of the Scarlet Macaw Trail project, Peten, Guatemala). Many ventures have sought to have their information listed in international guidebooks such as Lonely Planet. This strategy requires extensive letter writing efforts, but the importance of being listed for the lower-end, backpacker tourists cannot be overstated. A U.S. Agency for International Development (USAID) funded project in the Maya Forest of Guatemala, Mexico and Belize paid for the production of a handbook to, "provide practical information for promoting community ecotourism attractions" (Pedersen, 1995).

NGO PARTNERS

Local non-government organizations (NGOs) can be valuable partners in the process of developing community-based ecotourism enterprises in almost any area.

They can be sources for training, technical assistance, advocacy at the national level, and in some instances, can also provide financial assistance. In addition, these organizations often have members or constituencies that want information and guidance on ecotourism issues, so they can also influence the consumers of ecotourism—the ecotourists.

Many communities already work with local NGOs in such areas as health, agriculture, small-business development or conservation programs. Some examples of NGOs that assist community groups in developing ecotourism enterprises can be found in the case study of Bina Swadaya Tours (page 224).

INDONESIA COUNTRY OVERVIEW

Indonesia covers only 1.3% of the earth's surface, yet harbors 10% of all flowering plants, 12% of the world's mammals, 16% of the world's reptiles and amphibians, 17% of all birds, and more than a quarter of known marine and freshwater fish species. Overall, it is one of the richest countries in terms of biological diversity. The many islands of the archipelago support a wide range and variety of habitats, from lowland rainforests, mangroves, savannah grasslands, swamp forests and limestone hills, to mountain forests, alpine meadows and snow-capped mountains near the equator. About 59% of Indonesia's land area is covered with forest, representing almost 10% of the world's remaining tropical forest. About 110 million hectares are classified as protected forest, and 18.7 million hectares have been declared conservation areas—divided into 8.1 million hectares of nature sanctuary (suaka alam) and 10.6 million hectares of nature conservation area (kawasan pelestarian alam). The nature conservation area is divided again into 10 million hectares of national parks (taman nasional), 223,000 hectares of forest recreation park (tahura), and 381,000 hectares of nature recreation park (taman wisata alam) (KLH, 1995).

ECOTOURISM IN INDONESIA: CONCEPT AND PRINCIPLE

Ecotourism in Indonesia is still in a very early stage of development. In the Indonesian language, the term "ecotourism" is still ambiguous. It is translated into several terms: "ekowisata" (ecotourism), "wisata lingkungan" (nature tourism), and "wisata eko" or "wisata ekologis" (ecological tourism). The Indonesian Ecotourism Network (Indecon) uses the term "ekowisata," while representatives from the Ministry of Environment prefer to use "wisata ekologis."

The Indonesia Ecotourism Network (Indecon) conducted a symposium to address emerging ecotourism issues in the country, including an acceptable definition. Based on the results of that symposium, Indecon defines ecotourism as "responsible travel to protected natural areas, as well as to unprotected natural areas, which conserves the environment (natural and cultural) and improves

BINA SWADAYA TOURS
A UNIQUE HYBRID

Bina Swadaya is the largest non-government organization in Indonesia. It has a 30-year history of assisting community development projects throughout the Indonesian archipelago. In 1988, Bina Swadaya began advertising tours to several of its most prominent development projects. These tours were organized in response to requests from international visitors who were interested to learn more about grassroots activities in the country. From these non-traditional beginnings, Bina Swadaya Tours (BST) began.

BST has the unique position of being a for-profit business that has emerged from a development NGO. BST maintains the Bina Swadaya Development Agency mission of helping to alleviate poverty and protect Indonesia's environment and heritage while operating as a for-profit business. BST pursues its mission through the content of the tours it arranges. Typical destinations of a BST tour include remote areas and villages, national parks and protected areas, and Bina Swadaya development projects. BST includes donations to each of these projects in the cost of each tour.

BST also works to help educate tourists on how to travel responsibly and to help them understand the issues of development from its unique perspective as an outgrowth of a community development organization. Every BST tour member receives a pre-trip educational packet containing BST's code of ethics for responsible travel. In the past several years, with the increasing growth of tourism to rural areas, BST has been called upon to conduct training programs which help villages and community groups establish ecotourism enterprises of their own. Drawing upon its unique experience in the development sector and its business knowledge of the tourism industry, BST has become a leading advocate for sustainable community-based ecotourism development in Indonesia. As the director of BST is quick to point out, assisting new communities in developing ecotourism enterprises is good business for BST; it increases the number and diversity of the destinations it is able to offer to its clients.

When asked to describe a typical BST tour client, the director responds:

The type of tour BST runs attracts an alternative type of tourist. People interested in understanding life in rural areas, how people live, how they get by. Most of our tours utilize small-scale enterprises, which can sometimes mean no hot water showers, etc. Of course we can arrange any type of tour, including one with deluxe accommodations, but our "average client" is seeking small-scale, which is what we provide (Sumarwoto, 1997).

the welfare of local people" (Indecon, 1996). This definition is intentionally similar in wording and intent to the international definition used by The Ecotourism Society (TES).

As part of the UNCED Agenda 21 process, the Ministry of Environment prepared a country report for Indonesia. Based on Global Agenda 21 and the General Guidelines of National Development (GBHN), Agenda 21-Indonesia makes the link between economic development and social development, protection of natural resources and the environment; and provides a new paradigm to attain sustainable development in Indonesia. Ecotourism is viewed by the Ministry as an approach to sustainable development, consistent with the principles of Agenda 21-Indonesia.

In keeping with the framework of Agenda 21-Indonesia, Indecon promotes five principles for ecotourism development in the country.

1: RESPONSIBILITY, CONCERN AND COMMITMENT TO CONSERVATION

- Take the "carrying capacity" of ecotourism destinations into consideration during the planning and design phases.
- Manage the overall number of tourists, the tourism infrastructure and facilities in accordance with the destination's carrying capacity.
- Enhance/increase the host communities' and visitors' environmental awareness.
- Employ local resources sustainably.
- Minimize the negative impact of ecotourism development.

2: CONSULTATION WITH, AND CONSENT FOR, ECOTOURISM DEVELOPMENT BY THE LOCAL COMMUNITY

- Develop partnerships with the local community throughout the process of ecotourism project planning and development.
- Clearly and truthfully inform the local community about the development's purpose and intent in the area.
- Give the local community the free choice of accepting or refusing ecotourism developments in its area.

3: BENEFITS TO THE LOCAL COMMUNITY

- Open opportunities for local community residents to participate actively, as well as passively, in ecotourism development.
- Empower the local community to increase its socio-economic welfare.
- Improve the local community's expertise and skill.

4: SENSITIVITY AND RESPECT FOR LOCAL CULTURE AND RELIGIOUS TRADITIONS

- ~◆ Introduce a code of ethics for tourists and tour operators.
- ~◆ Work with the local community to compose a local code of ethics for tourists and tour operators in accordance with the community's socio-cultural values and religious traditions.

5: OBSERVATION OF GOVERNMENT REGULATIONS AND LAWS

- ~◆ Observe laws on environmental management.
- ~◆ Observe laws for conservation of natural resources and their ecosystems.
- ~◆ Observe laws for spatial planning.
- ~◆ Observe laws for protected area management.
- ~◆ Observe laws for tourism and other government regulations.

ECOTOURISM IN PRACTICE

Cochrane (1996) found many practical difficulties to developing ecotourism in Indonesian protected areas, due to the areas' often remote locations—far from large population centers and reachable only by long, time-consuming journeys which many tourists are reluctant to endure. Once arriving at a park, tourists aspire to see the wealth of Indonesian wildlife and are often frustrated by the characteristics of the animals, which are shy, solitary, arboreal and nocturnal. This phenomenon is prevalent at many national parks and areas formally declared as tourism destinations. The problems of accessibility will, in time, be eased by continuing improvements in the infrastructure, particularly road, boat and flight links. However, appreciation of parks and other places of interest will not change for the better if there is no integrated program for protected area management.

An additional constraint is the lack of positive promotion, which is tied to the currently limited number of visitors. There is a need for cooperation between the parks and the Dinas Pariwisata (tourism board) in publishing promotional packages. Leaflets and brochures created by the Dinas are usually not very informative about natural attractions. At the same time, parks themselves publish brochures and guides that tend to focus almost exclusively on inventories of species, biological research and the ecological function of the protected area. Information from each sector could potentially create an interesting tourism leaflet if combined (Sammeng, 1995).

The following case study of ecotourism enterprise development at Gunung Halimun National Park, Java, Indonesia, is an effort to address the constraints identified above. It is also an effort to operationalize mechanisms for community involvement in ecotourism developments currently being undertaken in Indonesia, with the goal of achieving both conservation and development objectives. As with many similar projects in other parts of the developing world, this particular project was underwritten by a grant from the U.S. Agency for International Development (USAID), and as such, has a focus not just on project design and implementation, but also on monitoring and evaluation. These latter points are only briefly touched upon, as the goal is to highlight how mechanisms for community involvement have been designed and implemented. It is also too early in the project's life cycle to be able to evaluate with any insight the degree to which the conservation and development objectives have or have not been achieved, though as with many projects in mid-stream, the project's supporters believe that things look good.

ECOTOURISM ENTERPRISE DEVELOPMENT AT GUNUNG HALIMUN NATIONAL PARK

PROJECT OVERVIEW

Established in 1992, Gunung Halimun (Misty Mountain) National Park, contains the largest tract of remaining primary lowland forest in Java and is home to 23 mammal species, at least two of which (the Javan gibbon and the grizzled langur) are endemic and endangered. The park also supports more than 200 bird species, of which 18 are endemic, and over 500 plant species. Indigenous Kasepuhan and other Sudanese communities live in and around the park and depend heavily on its natural resources. The park protects an important watershed for Java. However, GHNP's resources are threatened by small-holder and plantation agriculture, infrastructure development, small-scale gold mining, and unsustainable fuel wood and non-timber forest product harvesting.

In contrast to the conservation threats mentioned above, an unprecedented set of positive circumstances for sustainable ecotourism development exists as follows:

- sustained Indonesian economic growth of 6.6% in 1993, 6.9% in 1994 and 7.2% in 1995;
- a middle class bigger than any in Indonesia's history, and one that is eager for recreational and nature-based travel opportunities;
- the creation of a two-day weekend as of April 1995, giving the middle class more leisure time;
- the 1992 designation of Gunung Halimun (the "Misty Mountain"), as a National Park, a short three-hour drive from Jakarta; and
- no competition for Gunung Halimun (the last remaining continuous forest area in western Java) as a source of natural solitude for Jakartans: the only nearby alternative park, Gunung Gede Pangrango, is known to be jammed with over 10,000 people on a typical weekend.

To counter the threats to the area, and to take advantage of an unprecedented set of positive circumstances, a unique consortium of organizations came together for the purpose of working with local communities to develop an ecotourism enterprise and conservation awareness program geared to attracting more domestic and international visitors from nearby Jakarta. Thus was born the Gunung Halimun Consortium in 1995.

WHY INCLUDE LOCAL COMMUNITIES?

As discussed earlier, one of the functions of local participation is that people have a sense of ownership in projects and programs that affect them. Establishing mechanisms for people to be actively involved as owners and managers of ecotourism enterprises has been a priority of the Gunung Halimun Ecotourism Enterprise Development Project. Therefore, priority areas of project implementation have specifically addressed issues of distributional equity and sought the participation of different sectors of society in decision making, revenue sharing and job creation.

WHAT EXACTLY IS BEING DONE?

Each of the three participating villages has built a guest house complex, constructed trails with appropriate signage, developed marketable handicrafts, trained local naturalist guides, and undergone intensive food and beverage preparation training.

GUEST HOUSE CONSTRUCTION—Guest house accommodations sleep eight to ten clients, have been built by community members on community-donated land, and have been constructed in accordance with traditional designs and materials. They also feature modern conveniences: flush toilets (the first for two of the villages), washrooms, septic tanks, water collection and storage systems, handmade dressers, and beds with new factory mattresses. Next to each of the guest houses is a communal dining area, complete with kitchen, dining tables, traditional porch/rest areas and handmade matting. The gardens around each of the guest house complexes have been planted with native vegetation.

TRAIL CONSTRUCTION AND INTERPRETATIVE SIGNS—Each of the villages has constructed trails to nearby natural destinations, such as waterfalls or mountaintops. In many cases, this involved upgrading existing trails traditionally used by village residents for hunting, forest product gathering or cutting bamboo. Signs indicating direction and providing a certain level of interpretation have been posted in both Indonesian and English.

HANDICRAFT PRODUCTION—Residents in each of the villages have undergone intensive training in the production of handicrafts for local use and sale to visitors. These training sessions have built on native design and construction techniques, highlighting and expanding upon traditionally manufactured products in each area. Significantly, handicraft training has opened a window of participation for older residents to benefit from ecotourism developments in their area.

LOCAL NATURALIST GUIDE TRAINING—Up to ten residents in each community have undergone intensive guide training to improve their ability to guide visitors through the labyrinth of trails and natural wonders in the area. Training sessions have included: identification of native flora and fauna; understanding and addressing visitor expectations; learning the importance of time and distance; rating difficulty of destinations; first aid; and language training (to the extent possible). Guides taking visitors inside the park area are now working in cooperation with the national park management authority.

FOOD AND BEVERAGE PREPARATION—Groups from each of the participating villages have undergone intensive food and beverage preparation training, with a special emphasis on hygiene. Trainees spend week-long sessions at a small hotel in a nearby city studying food preparation.

Who are the Consortium Members?

The GHNP Consortium evolved from the recognition that a diversity of skills and organizations was vital to enable both the tourism development and conservation goals to succeed. Each of the consortium partners brings a unique set of qualifications to the project. Consortium members include:

- Biological Sciences Club
- Wildlife Preservation Trust International, USA
- National Park Management Authority
- University of Indonesia
- McDonald's Corporation, Indonesia

BIOLOGICAL SCIENCES CLUB (BScC)—The Biological Sciences Club has been working in GHNP for two decades. Although primarily focused on issues of biological diversity within the park, BScC believes that community concerns about development opportunities must be addressed hand-in-hand with conservation concerns. As the primary project implementer, BScC has field managers working within the three project communities. They are working to strengthen local community capacity to meet the project objectives in enterprise development. This is being done through extensive training and follow-up support to ensure that new ideas, concepts and practices are understood and implemented.

WILDLIFE PRESERVATION TRUST INTERNATIONAL (WPTI)—As an international conservation organization, WPTI brings regional and global perspective on critical conservation issues to the consortium. WPTI's Indonesia program, for example, focuses on viable economic solutions to critical issues of biodiversity conservation, providing technical and managerial support to the project through its Indonesia program coordinator.

NATIONAL PARK MANAGEMENT AUTHORITY: THE DIRECTORATE GENERAL OF FOREST PROTECTION AND NATURE CONSERVATION (PHPA), GOVERNMENT OF INDONESIA—The Directorate General of Forest Protection and Nature Conservation (PHPA) is the government agency responsible for overseeing protected areas throughout the country of Indonesia. PHPA works with the consortium on the legal and policy implications of allowable access and use of resources in protected areas. In addition, PHPA and BScC each collaborate on the design and construction of trails and appropriate signage in and around the project communities.

UNIVERSITY OF INDONESIA CENTER FOR BIODIVERSITY CONSERVATION—The Center for Biodiversity Conservation (CBC) at the University of Indonesia (UI), assists with monitoring the environmental, social and economic impacts of the project on participating communities. For instance, communities around Halimun have historically produced handicrafts made chiefly from rattan and bamboo, such as baskets, hats, handbags and traditional household tools. A monitoring plan has been prepared to assure that any increase in handicraft production for sale to tourists does not lead to the unsustainable use of those resources.

McDONALD'S CORPORATION—McDonald's Corporation demonstrates a unique level of involvement by the private sector in supporting conservation efforts in Indonesia. They have done an outstanding job of focusing marketing efforts and linking promotional materials to their restaurant clientele. For much of 1997, posters portraying Gunung Halimun's endangered species and describing ecotourism opportunities provided by participating communities, could be found hanging in McDonald's throughout the Jakarta metropolitan area.

GHNP Ecotourism Enterprises: Target Marketing

Market analysis conducted during the project planning phase concluded that, in comparison with other Indonesian national parks, Gunung Halimun was of minimum appeal to foreign tourists traveling with limited vacation time. The appropriate target markets for Gunung Halimun, in order of priority were determined to be:

~~ middle-class Indonesians living in Jakarta and surrounding districts;
~~ expatriates living in Jakarta and surrounding districts;
~~ university and high school students; and
~~ foreign tourists.

To date, information on visitor origin would seem to justify the appropriateness of these target markets, although marketing efforts to that end may be fulfilling the prophecy. Marketing efforts to "introduce" the guest houses to representatives of the media and the established tourism industry have included familiarization "fam" tours, slide presentations and the mass mailing of project brochures and publications.

MONITORING OF THE ECOTOURISM ENTERPRISES

The GHNP Consortium has been monitoring the social, biological and economic impact of project developments since the opening of guest houses in early 1997.

SOCIAL MONITORING ACTIVITIES—Community participation in the project and community welfare (defined broadly) are the two primary indicators being monitored. Data on actual community involvement in enterprise activities is collected according to the number of active members, gender, age, profession and ethnic group. Methods for data collection include log books (maintained by the field manager in each village), participatory rural appraisal (PRA) and interviews.

BIOLOGICAL MONITORING ACTIVITIES—Baseline monitoring data on water quality, extraction of materials for handicraft production (principally bamboo and rattan), and primate and bird populations, is gathered prior to the start of project activities and continues on a quarterly basis. Residents of each community have received training in the process of this data gathering and now conduct a significant part of the monitoring taking place.

ECONOMIC MONITORING ACTIVITIES—Community members, especially those involved with the actual operations of the enterprises, began receiving cash payments for services including guiding, portering, food preparation, transportation (usually by motorbike), handicraft sales and maintenance, soon after the opening of each of the guest houses.

Table 10.1 indicates baseline figures (compiled for the year March 1997 through February 1998), for East Halimun, North Halimun and South Halimun guest houses combined. Due to the relative proximity to Jakarta, East Halimun guest house receives the most visitors, followed by North Halimun and then South Halimun. Monetary figures are given in rupiah, and no exchange is provided since rates varied widely during this period. The source for this data is the Gunung

Halimun project office (contact information is provided following the reference list at the end of this chapter).

Table 10.2 indicates guest house revenue distribution and explains each item in detail for a clearer understanding of expenditures.

The system for distribution of revenue was devised by the enterprise participants in each village, with the support of project staff. The actual division of revenue is done by a selected representative from each village who oversees maintenance of the registration book and makes payments. Accumulations and payments for each

TABLE 10.1
GUEST HOUSE BASELINE FIGURES
(IN RUPIAH)

Number of tourist arrivals 845
Average length of stay..1.4 days
Nationality
  Indonesian 672 (80%)
  Foreign 173 (20%)

Purpose of visit
  Relaxation..45%
  Exploration of the Forest 21%
  Research 2%
  Other 323%

Total tourist expenditures ....Rp 43,851,835
Average expenditure per person..Rp 51,900

Breakdown of expenditures
  Rooms 40.1%
  Food and Beverages 35.8%
  Guides and porters..6.7%
  Handicrafts 8.0%
  Donations..1.9%
  Other..7.5%

Cost of ecotourism services ....Rp 21,588,125
Net revenue to enterprises ....Rp 22,263,710
Direct benefit to enterprise participants (cash) ....Rp 13,358,220
Average per participant per year ....Rp 178,110
Average household income ....Rp 1,563,984
Percent of household income..11%

category are discussed on a regular basis at project meetings. Each village has opened a bank account to manage the accumulation of project funds in the various categories. Signatories to the account include the chairperson, as well as the project liaison for each village. Training in record keeping was a necessary first step in order for this system to become operational.

TABLE 10.2
GUEST HOUSE REVENUE DISTRIBUTION SYSTEM AT GHNP

ITEM	NORTH HALIMUN	SOUTH HALIMUN	EAST HALIMUN
Government Tax	5%	5%	5%
Salary	30%	30%	30%
Maintenance	15%	15%	15%
Community Fund	13.3%	15%	10%
Conservation	10%	15%	10%
Education	10%	10%	7.5%
Land Tenure	6.7%	—	12.5%
Petty Cash	10%	10%	10%

DESCRIPTION OF ITEMS (ABOVE)

Government Tax	Paid to local government authorities.
Salary	Salaries paid to daily workers at each guest house for cleaning, registration, maintenance, etc.
Maintenance	For facilities maintenance at each guest house, including repairs, fixtures, new mats, replacement utensils, etc.
Community Fund	Used for community-related projects decided upon by enterprise participants and community leaders (for example, funds were used to improve bathing facilities at the community mosque).
Conservation	Principally for guide training, sign construction and purchase of maps for hanging in guest houses.
Education	For funding training programs (including language instruction and management training), and to offset transportation costs associated with attending such programs.
Land Tenure	Paid in those villages where the land used for the guest houses came from a private source.
Petty Cash	Held for small purchases.

What Issues Have Emerged in the Process of Implementation Thus Far?

Nothing is ever as it appears, which is particularly true with projects that involve a multitude of players, including international donors, NGOs, governments and communities. The priorities of these different bodies do not always fully coincide in their objectives or desired outcomes, despite extensive consultation and planning during the design phase. Issue areas at the midway point in the Gunung Halimun Ecotourism Enterprise Development Project can best be discussed by looking at those on the community level and at the consortium level.

On the community level, issues of participation and compensation arose early on. As the land for two of the guest houses was "donated" through various means in each of the participating communities, agreements about compensation, and distribution of compensation, needed to be addressed. This was particularly true for one village where the land was given by the village youth who, several years earlier, had begun to level the area as a ball field. Agreement was made all the more difficult because of the informal nature of this group.

Another very difficult issue arose toward the end of the first year of implementation, when rumors that the project intended to "Christianize" the population began to spread. The tender nature of relations between religious groups in Indonesia made this rumor an immediate priority for everyone involved. Project staff, most of whom happen to be Muslim, quickly arranged village meetings to re-state and re-affirm the project goals with village residents. The origin of the rumor is impossible to pinpoint, though it certainly seems to have stemmed more from a lack of understanding about the project than from any specific incident or exchange between project staff or visitors. This situation serves to underscore a central tenet in the conduct of any work at the community level—there can almost never be too much communication. And, though certainly a challenge, it is necessary to extend the lines of communication beyond the active participants and "regular" meeting attendees.

On the consortium level, an interesting issue has been the role of McDonald's Corporation. The original Memorandum of Understanding between the participating institutions cites "technical support" being received from McDonald's as their in-kind contribution to project implementation. To date, that technical support has come in the form of market strategy development. The value of this support is hard to quantify, but it is safe to say that their marketing assistance has been pivotal for publicity in the target market of Jakarta. In fact, McDonald's has effectively done everything they said they would do. The issue for some of the other consortium members has been that McDonald's has also benefited by broadcasting their participation with this conservation effort.

Another issue is the hesitancy of the park management authority staff to become involved in community development activities. This may in part be due to their traditional policing role as well as their lack of expertise and training in community liaison and tourism. Issues pertaining to inter-agency cooperation and coordination loom on the horizon as various plans for development in and around the park continue to be raised in various arenas.

CONCLUSION

The premise of this chapter is that successful community-based ecotourism development—that is, ventures that satisfy both conservation and development objectives—is supported by partnerships between local communities, government agencies, NGOs and the private sector. Such partnerships are recognized to emerge from areas of mutual benefit to each of the sectors involved. Policies, then, are seen as formal mechanisms for achieving the goals of mutual benefit through collaboration and are an overt manifestation of the need for collaboration and cooperation in achieving conservation and development objectives.

Partnerships, then, should be viewed as an integral part of the design and development of community-based ecotourism ventures and deemed indispensable for achieving a positive policy and planning framework for the development of such ventures.

REFERENCES

Cochrane, J. 1996. "The Sustainability of Ecotourism in Indonesia: Fact and Fiction," *Environmental Change in South-East Asia: People, Politics, and Sustainable Development*, Routledge, London.

Indecon (Indonesia Ecotourism Network). 1996. *Newsletter #2*, Jakarta, Indonesia.

KLH. 1996. "Draft of National Strategy on Ecotourism Development", Jakarta, Indonesia.

Lindberg, K., J. Enriquez, K. Sproule. 1996. "Ecotourism Questioned: Case Studies from Belize," *Annals of Tourism Research*, vol. 23, no. 3, pp. 543-562.

Pedersen, A. 1995. *Promotion of Community-based Ecotourism in the Maya Forest*, Management Systems International, Washington, D.C.

Sammeng. 1995. "Kebijaksanaan dan Langkahlangkah Strategis Pengembangan Ekotourisme," unpublished paper presented at the National Workshop on Ecotourism Development in Indonesia, Bogor, Indonesia.

Sumarwoto. 1997. Personal communication, director, Bina Swadaya Tours.

United Nations Food and Agriculture Organization (FAO). 1990. "The Community's Tool Box," FAO, Rome.

CONTACT INFORMATION FOR THE GUNUNG HALIMUN PROJECT

GHNP Community-based Ecotourism Enterprise Project

Kantor Konsorsium Pengembangan Ekoturisme
Taman Nasional Gunung Halimun Jawa Barat
Jl. Samiaji Raya, No. 33, Bumi Indraprasta
Bantarjati, Bogor 16153
Indonesia
Tel/fax (62-0251) 336886
e-mail: bcn-ni16@indo.net.id

EDITORS

Kreg Lindberg is an independent consultant and researcher, and serves as an adjunct research associate with The Ecotourism Society (TES). His research interests include various aspects of ecotourism, as well as the economic and social impacts of tourism generally. He is published in various professional journals, including *Annals of Tourism Research*, and is on the editorial boards of *Journal of Sustainable Tourism* and *Pacific Tourism Review*. He has consulted and conducted research in Australia, the United States, Denmark, China, Indonesia, Sweden and Belize for organizations such as the Australian Commonwealth Department of Tourism, the U.S. National Park Service, New South Wales (Australia) National Parks and Wildlife Service, the World Wildlife Fund (WWF-US), the World Resources Institute, the FAO, and the World Bank. He received his Ph.D. in forest social science and a minor in economics from Oregon State University. *His address is: c/o The Ecotourism Society; P.O. Box 755, North Bennington, VT 05257; Phone: 802 447 2121; Fax: 802 447 2122; e-mail: ecomail@ecotourism.org; Web: www.ecotourism.org.*

Megan Epler Wood is President of The Ecotourism Society (TES). Since 1990, she has worked with board members, advisors and members from around the world to shape an organization that defines ecotourism as a tool to conserve natural resources and provide sustainable development opportunities worldwide. She has acted as spokesperson and lecturer on these issues for TES and as an instructor of training workshops for countries including Trinidad, Fiji, Costa Rica, Kenya and Brazil. She teaches an annual international workshop on Ecotourism Planning and Management for The George Washington University and has led two international Ecolodge Forums in Costa Rica and the U.S. Virgin Islands. Epler Wood is a strong proponent of guidelines and evaluation programs for the ecotourism industry, and was the editor of the first international *Ecotourism Guidelines for Nature Tour Operators* and co-coordinator of the first Green Evaluations Program for nature tour operators in Ecuador. She has researched how community participation in ecotourism can be improved, and has published an analytical report on this issue for the Latin America Division of The Nature Conservancy. Epler Wood has authored, co-authored and edited newsletters, articles and books for The Ecotourism Society since 1993, and was the founder of The Ecotourism Society publication division. She holds an MS in Wildlife Biology, was the recipient of a Fulbright Scholarship, and has been inducted into Who's Who for Executives for the years 1999/2000. She is also a producer of films and videos on the natural world which have been broadcast by both The National Audubon Society and The National Geographic Society. *She can be contacted at: The Ecotourism Society; P.O. Box 755, North Bennington, VT 05257; Phone: 802 447 2121; Fax: 802 447 2122; e-mail:ecomail@ecotourism.org; Web: www.ecotourism.org.*

David Engeldrum is a writer and editor for HVS Eco Services, an environmental consulting firm dedicated exclusively to the hospitality industry. He is a graduate of the State University of New York at Stony Brook and frequently writes on environmental issues. He has also covered a variety of topics as a newspaper reporter and as a sportswriter for United Press International. A former chef, he has had numerous recipes published in Long Island Chefs Magazine. *His address is: HVS Eco Services; 372 Willis Ave., Mineola, NY 11501; Phone: 516 248 8828, ext. 235; Fax: 516 742 3059; e-mail: dce@hvs-intl.com.*

CONTRIBUTORS

Alison Allcock was a co-author of Australia's National Ecotourism Strategy and is currently Manager of Analysis and Forecasting at the Bureau of Tourism Research at Australia's Department of Industry, Science and Tourism. *She can be reached at: the Bureau of Tourism Research; CPO Box 1545, Canberra, ACT 2601, Australia; Phone: 61 2 6213 6935; Fax: 61 2 6213 6983; e-mail: aallcock@dist.gov.au.*

Dr. William (Bill) T. Borrie is Assistant Professor of Outdoor Recreation Management at The University of Montana School of Forestry. His research is focused on the visitor experience in wilderness areas and National Parks, and the threats (technological, management, etc.) to those recreational experiences. Other interests include the perceived notion of wilderness, and the behavior of protected-area visitors. He teaches classes in wildland recreation management and wilderness management. He has held appointments at the University of Melbourne and Bendigo College, and has worked in protected areas in Australia, Germany and the U.S. He is Book Review Editor for the international *Journal of Leisure Sciences*. He received his Ph.D. from the Virginia Tech Department of Forestry. *His address is: School of Forestry, University of Montana; Missoula, MT 59812; Phone: 406 243 4286; Fax: 406 243 6656; e-mail: borrie@forestry.umt.edu; Web: http://www.forestry.umt.edu/people/borrie.*

Héctor Ceballos-Lascuráin is a Mexican architect and environmentalist. He is currently Director General of the Program of International Consultancy on Ecotourism, Special Advisor on Ecotourism to IUCN (The World Conservation Union) and Advisor to both The Ecotourism Society and the World Tourism Organization. He is credited with coining the term "ecotourism" and its preliminary definition, in 1983. Mr. Ceballos-Lascuráin has performed research and provided consultations in 63 countries worldwide, on all aspects of ecotourism planning and development, including the architectural design of ecolodges and other environmentally friendly facilities. He has authored or co-authored more than 80 books, reports and articles, and is presently implementing Yemen's National Ecotourism Strategy. *He can be contacted at: Program of International Consultancy on Ecotourism; Camino Real A1, Ajusco 551,*

Col Xolalpa (Tepepan) Tlalpan, Mexico City D.F. 14649, Mexico; Phone: 52 5 676 8734; Fax: 52 5 676 5285; e-mail: ceballos@laneta.apc.org.

Costas Christ is the Director of the U.S. Peace Corps in Uganda. He is the co-owner of Tamu Safaris, a private tour operator focusing on ecotourism in Africa. He served as the Program Director of Conservation Corporation Africa, one of the world's largest ecotourism organizations, from 1996 to 1997, and was the Regional Coordinator for the The Ecotourism Society for six years before being appointed to the Board of Directors, on which he continues to serve. Between 1987 and 1995, he served as the Regional Director for Africa and Asia Programs at the School for International Training. In the U.S., Costas' articles and essays on travel and foreign affairs have appeared in *The New York Times*, the *International Herald Tribune*, the *London Sunday Times* and *Boston Globe*, among others. He holds an M.A. in International Studies from the University of Oregon and recently completed work on his first book, *Always Face the Lion: An Unexpected Journey through Africa*. *His address is: Tamu Safaris; P.O. Box 247, West Chesterfield, NH 03466; Phone: 1 800 766 9199.*

Andy Drumm is an environmentalist who has spent time as a naturalist guide and divemaster in the Galápagos Islands and the Amazon. He works as Ecotourism Specialist for The Nature Conservancy and is currently President of TROPIC Ecological Adventures, an Ecuadorean-based ecotourism operator, which he founded in 1993. He is president of the Amazon Commission of the Ecuadorean Ecotourism Association and of the non-profit organization Acción Amazonía, which promotes the defense of environmental and cultural integrity in collaboration with indigenous organizations and communities in the Amazon. *He can be reached at: TROPIC Ecological Adventures; Avenida República, 307 y Almagro, Edificio Taurus, Apto. #1A, Quito, Ecuador; Phone: 593 2 225 907 or 93 2 234 594; Fax: 593 2 560 756; e-mail: tropic@uio.satnet.net; Web: www.tropiceco.com.*

Paul F. J. Eagles is a Professor of Environmental Planning at the University of Waterloo Department of Recreation and Leisure Studies and is cross-appointed to the School of Urban and Regional Planning and the Department of Biology. He has a B.S. in Biology from the University of Waterloo, an M.S. in Resource Development from the University of Guelph and a Ph.D. in Planning from the University of Waterloo. He has published over 200 papers during his 25-year academic career on a variety of subjects within the broad field of environmental and recreation planning. He has a special interest in the planning and management of parks and protected areas, and is presently the Chair of the Task Force on Tourism and Protected Areas, which reports to the World Commission on Protected Areas of the World Conservation Union (IUCN). *He can be contacted at: Department of Recreation and Leisure Studies, University of Waterloo; Waterloo, Ontario, N2L 3G1, Canada;*

Phone: 519 888 4567, ext. 2716; Fax: 519 746 6776; e-mail: eagles@healthy.uwaterloo.ca; Web: http://www.ahs.uwaterloo.ca/rec/taskfce.html#Task.

Tracy A. Farrell is a doctoral student in the Virginia Tech Department of Forestry, Natural Resource Recreation program. She received her M.S. degree in Forest Resources Management—Recreation and Tourism from the SUNY College of Environmental Science and Forestry. Her dissertation research includes the monitoring of trails and campsites at a Patagonian park, and a comparative case study of Central American parks, to identify the impact of recreation, tourism and ecotourism visitation and to develop decision making frameworks that are capable of reducing undesirable environmental effects. *Her address is: Virginia Tech Department of Forestry; 310 Cheatham Hall, Blacksburg, VA 24061-0324; Phone: 540 231 6958; e-mail: tfarrell@vt.edu.*

Jill Grant was co-author of Australia's National Ecotourism Strategy and managed the National Ecotourism Program for two years. She is currently Assistant Manager of Environmental and Indigenous Tourism in the Office of National Tourism, Department of Industry, Science and Tourism, Australia. *You can reach her at: Office of National Tourism; CPO Box 9839, Canberra ACT 2601, Australia; Phone: 61 2 6213 7037; Fax: 61 2 6213 7098; e-mail: jillgrant@dist.gov.au.*

Bryan R. Higgins is a Professor of Geography, Coordinator of the Planning Program, and Director of Educational Travel at Plattsburgh—State University of New York. He received a B.S. in Biology cum laude and an M.A. and Ph.D. in Geography from the University of Minnesota. He has been awarded over 30 research grants from a diverse spectrum of federal, state and local agencies within the United States, including a 1988 Fulbright Research Grant. His research has addressed a wide variety of topics in geography and planning including the human dimensions of ecotourism, environmental planning, economic development, American Indians, and urban and regional planning. *You may reach him at: Department of Geography and Planning, Plattsburgh—State University of New York; 101 Broad Street, Plattsburgh, NY 12901; Phone: 518 564 2406; e-mail: higginbr@splava.cc.plattsburgh.edu.*

Jeffrey L. Marion serves as Unit Leader of the Cooperative Park Studies Unit affiliated with Virginia Tech in Blacksburg, Virginia. He reports to the Patuxent Wildlife Research Unit of the U.S. Geological Survey. His research specialty is recreation ecology, a discipline that seeks to describe the types, amounts and rates of ecological changes resulting from visitation to protected areas, including relationships with influential environmental, use-related and managerial factors. He has conducted research and monitoring studies in numerous U.S. National Parks and Wilderness areas and is initiating similar work in Central and South American protected areas. He received his M.S. and Ph.D. degrees in Park and

Recreation Resource Management from the University of Minnesota. *You can contact him at: Virginia Tech Department of Forestry; 304 Cheatham Hall (0324), Blacksburg, VA 24061; Phone: 540 231 6603; e-mail: cpsu@vt.edu.*

Simon McArthur has ten years experience in nature-based tourism and visitor management, and is widely published on various aspects of these fields. He has international experience in cultural tourism and ecotourism, and has reviewed and developed plans in these fields for various tourism operations in Mexico, and Central and South America. Simon recently assisted with the development of an international tourism policy and strategy framework for the World Wide Fund for Nature. Simon spent several years working in the field of interpretation with the Tasmanian Parks and Wildlife Service, and several more with Forestry Tasmania, developing a range of visitor monitoring and research programs, visitor management strategies and tourism policy. During the past few years as a consultant, he has planned and assisted with the establishment of many tourism and ecotourism developments, working, for example, in Australia and overseas with a number of international adventure tourism operations. Some of his recent projects in this field have included Australia's National Ecotourism Accreditation Program, a Nature-based Tourism Strategy for the Protected Areas of New South Wales, several Visitor Impact Management Models, a Tourism Optimisation Management Model for Kangaroo Island (South Australia), the redevelopment of Sydney's Quarrantine Station, and an environmental management plan for the operation of Australia's first green hotel at the site of the 2000 Olympics. Simon has been Vice President of the Interpretation Australia Association for many years and is Secretary of the Ecotourism Association of Australia. *You can reach him at: Manidis Roberts Consultants; Level 4, 88-90 Foveaux St., Surry Hills, NSW 2010, Australia; Phone: 61 2 9281 5199; Fax: 61 2 9281 9406; e-mail: simonm@mrc.aust.com.*

Dr. Stephen (Steve) **F. McCool** is Professor and Coordinator of Recreation Management at the The University of Montana School of Forestry. Dr. McCool is currently involved in a number of research and application projects concerning relationships between people and their natural environments, in particular, the appropriateness of various conceptual approaches to natural resource planning, dimensions of public participation in planning processes, and a variety of issues associated with protected-area planning and management. He has held faculty positions at Utah State University and the University of Wisconsin at River Falls. He holds a Ph.D. from the University of Minnesota. From 1987 to 1993, he served as the Director of the Institute for Tourism and Recreation Research at the University of Montana, and from 1993 to 1995, worked as co-leader of the Social Sciences staff of the Interior Columbia Basin Ecosystem Management Project. He is a member of the World Commission on Protected Areas and currently serves on the IUCN Task Force on Tourism and National Parks. *His address is: School of Forestry, University of Montana; Missoula, MT 59812; Phone: 406 243 5406; Fax: 406 243 6656; e-mail: smccool@forestry.umt.edu.*

Keith W. Sproule has worked on ecotourism-related projects in Latin America, Southeast Asia and the Caribbean for the Asian Development Bank, USAID, World Wildlife Fund, EarthKind International, PACT, The Ecotourism Society and the private-sector tourism industry. He served as technical assistant to the Belize Ministry of Tourism and the Environment from 1992 to 1994, where he helped draft national policies and legislation addressing ecotourism development. He was Associate Director for Programs at Wildlife Preservation Trust International (WPTI) for three years, which operates conservation projects throughout the tropics. He holds an M.A. in International Affairs from the Johns Hopkins University School for Advanced International Studies and a B.S. in Environmental Studies from the University of Vermont. *You can contact him at: 240 Echo Place; Boulder, CO 80302; Phone: 303 448 1812; e-mail: kwsproule@aol.com.*

George H. Stankey is a Research Social Scientist with the People and Natural Resources Program at the USDA Forest Service Pacific Northwest Research Station in Corvallis, Oregon. He has spent nearly 30 years involved in research, policy analysis, and training, related to the management of protected areas. He has written numerous papers dealing with the role of ecotourism in protected areas and, with co-author Stephen F. McCool, conducted a number of workshops on using the Limits of Acceptable Change (LAC) framework in managing tourism impacts and experiences. He holds a Ph.D. in geography from Michigan State University. *You can reach him at: Department of Forest Resources, Oregon State University; Corvallis, OR 97331; Phone: 541 737 1496; Fax: 541 737 3049; e-mail: stankeyg@ccmail.orst.edu.*

Ary S. Suhandi is the Conservation Enterprise Coordinator for Conservation International, Indonesia. He has worked on ecotourism development projects throughout Indonesia for both the public and private sector. He has served as a consultant to the Asian Development Bank, Government of Indonesia and many private-sector firms. He has a B.A. in Conservation Biology from Indonesia's National University. *You can contact him at: e-mail: arys@cbn.net.id*

LOCATIONS

SITES